Rethinking Economics

Rethinking Economics

Markets, Technology and Economic Evolution

Edited by
Geoffrey M. Hodgson and Ernesto Screpanti

Edward Elgar

Published by
Edward Elgar Publishing Limited
Gower House
Croft Road
Aldershot
Hants GU11 3HR
England

Edward Elgar Publishing Limited
Distributed in the United States by
Ashgate Publishing Company
Old Post Road
Brookfield
Vermont 05036
USA

A CIP catalogue record for this book
is available from the British Library

A CIP catalogue record for this book
is available from the US Library of Congress

ISBN 1 85278 416 4

Printed in Great Britain by
Billing & Sons Ltd, Worcester

STP

Contents

List of Tables

List of Contributors

Mary K. Farmer, School of Social Sciences, University of Sussex, Brighton, United Kingdom.

Dominique Foray, École Centrale Paris CNRS, Paris, France.

Frederick C. v. N. Fourie, Department of Economics, University of the Orange Free State, Bloemfontein, South Africa.

Pierre Garrouste, MRASH, Université Lumière Lyon 2, Lyon, France.

Richard M. Goodwin, Institute of Economics, University of Siena, Italy.

Geoffrey M. Hodgson, Department of Economics and Government, Newcastle Polytechnic, United Kingdom.

Maureen McKelvey, Department of Technology and Social Change, University of Linköping, Sweden.

Mark L. Matthews, Science Policy Research Unit, University of Sussex, Brighton, United Kingdom.

Mario Morroni, Department of Economics, University of Bergamo, Italy.

Ernesto Screpanti, Department of Economics, University of Trieste, Italy.

Marc R. Tool, Department of Economics, California State University, Sacramento, United States of America.

Ulrich Witt, Faculty of Economics, University of Freiburg, Germany.

Preface

In 1988, at an historic meeting at Mansion House in Grim's Dyke (North London) between American institutionalists and heterodox European economists of different persuasions, a decision was made to launch a new European association which could amass a sustained and influential alternative to the analyses and policy prescriptions of the neoclassical orthodoxy. This is how the European Association of Evolutionary Political Economy (EAEPE) was born. Today, the Association has over 350 members in different European countries and the US. The membership of economists from the East European countries, searching for an alternative to both the centrally planned and the market economy, has also grown rapidly since 1989.

This volume is one of two of the first publications of EAEPE, based on the second Annual Conference of the Association, which was held in Florence in November 1990. The conference, with its ambitious title 'Rethinking Economics: Theory and Policy for Europe in the 21st Century', was a great success, eliciting, as it did, a wide range of papers and active discussion on questions of economic theory and on patterns of restructuring in Europe (the subject matter of the companion volume).

To the pleasure of the organizers, the conference produced a surprisingly high level of consensus over the issues discussed; a consensus rooted in a political economy drawing upon the work of such antecedents as Marx, Keynes, Polanyi, Veblen, Commons, Myrdal and Kaldor. It was widely felt that this, at the very least, would secure the longevity of the Association and, with it, prospects of a broad heterodox alternative to neoclassical economics. The building blocks of such an approach are evident both in this volume and in the accompanying volume on the dynamics of structural and institutional change in Europe, *Towards a New Europe?*

1.   Introduction

Geoffrey M. Hodgson and Ernesto Screpanti[1]

> Ask us not the formula to open up worlds for you,
> but a crooked syllable like a withered briar.
> Only this we are able to say anew,
> what we are *not*, and for what we do *not* aspire.
>
> Eugenio Montale, 'Don't Ask Us the Word'[2]

CHAOS IN ECONOMICS AND THE ECONOMICS OF CHAOS

For about 30 years after the end of the Second World War, during the decades of political stability and economic boom, there was a prevailing consensus in economic theory. Neoclassical microeconomics combined with a bowdlerized Keynesianism in the textbooks, and leading theorists proclaimed that their understanding of economic phenomena and systems was virtually complete. All was seen to be well, and little work remained but to gather more data, estimate a few more functions for forecasting purposes, and solve some residual puzzles.

Today, in contrast, economics is in chaos. The proclamation of a 'Crisis in Economic Theory' by Daniel Bell and Irving Kristol in 1981, in a celebrated collection of essays, now seems almost an understatement. The crisis has reached chaotic proportions for several reasons and is illuminated by many examples. First, theoretical work in game theory and elsewhere has raised questions about the very meaning of 'hard core' notions such as rationality. As Robert Sugden (1990, p. 89) argues, 'game theory may rest on a concept of rationality that is ultimately little more than a convention'. Consequently, the very definition of what is termed 'neoclassical economics' has become unclear, and orthodoxy is beginning to lose the ability to police its own boundaries.

Secondly, the door having been bolted for decades, mainstream theorists now, albeit in a limited fashion, admit discussion of problems of imperfect or asymmetric information and even 'bounded rationality'. Whilst these are

1

welcome developments they have created havoc with orthodox presuppositions. For instance, as Joseph Stiglitz (1987) has elaborated, even standard
demand analysis is now called into question.

Thirdly, the intrusion of chaos theory into economics has put paid to the
general idea that economics can proceed simply on the criterion of 'correct
predictions'. With non-linear models outcomes are over-sensitive to initial
conditions and thereby reliable predictions are impossible to make in regard
to any extended time period. In particular, chaos theory has confounded the
rational expectations theorists by showing that even if most agents knew the
basic structure of the economic model, in general they cannot derive reliable
predictions of outcomes and thereby form any meaningful 'rational expectations' of the future (Grandmont, 1987).

Fourthly, the development of general equilibrium theory has now reached
a serious impasse. Quite early on it was realized that the potential diversity
amongst individuals threatened the feasibility of the project. Consequently,
many types of interaction between the individuals have to be ignored. Even
with the restrictive psychological assumptions of rational behaviour, severe
difficulties are faced when the behaviours of a number of actors are brought
together. As Kenneth Arrow (1986, p. S388) has been led to declare: 'In the
aggregate, the hypothesis of rational behavior has in general no implications.'
Consequently, it is widely assumed that all individuals have the same utility
function. Amongst other things this denies the possibility of 'gains from
trade arising from individual differences' (Arrow, 1986, p. S390). Thus,
despite the traditional celebrations of individualism and competition, and
despite decades of formal development, the hard-core theory of orthodox
economics can handle no more than a grey uniformity amongst actors.

Fifthly, recent research into the problems of the uniqueness and stability
of a general equilibrium have shown that it may be indeterminate and unstable unless very strong assumptions are made, such as that society as a whole
behaves as if it were a single individual. Addressing such problems Alan
Kirman (1989, p. 138) thus concludes: 'If we are to progress further we may
well be forced to theorise in terms of groups who have collectively coherent
behaviour. ... The idea that we should start at the level of the isolated
individual is one which we may well have to abandon.'

The theoretical implications of the uniqueness and stability results discussed by Kirman are dramatic, and they go well beyond the traditional
criticisms of general equilibrium analysis. A fundamental consequence is the
breakdown of the individualistic or atomistic type of economic analysis
typically associated with a few fundamental assertions: that the rationality of
self-interested and autonomous individuals is sufficient to produce and
maintain equilibrium and social order; that such an equilibrium is efficient;
and that social institutions like the state can interfere only to disrupt the

equilibrium conditions. Clearly, this type of socio-economic reasoning has had a long string of liberal followers since it was promoted by Bernard Mandeville in the *Fable of the Bees* (1714). The general presumption is that from private vices, public virtues spring. The indeterminacy and instability results produced by contemporary theory lead to the conclusion that an economy made up of atomistic agents has not structure enough to survive, as its equilibria may be evanescent states from which the system tends to depart (Ingrao and Israel, 1985; Kirman, 1989).

There are many other problems, from capital theory to monetary analysis, from the theory of the firm to the economics of welfare. For the moment we have confined ourselves to some special cases only. These conspire to undermine the very ontological and methodological foundations of orthodoxy. In sum, '*homo rationalis insatiabilis*', so beloved by economists, this pale simulacrum of *homo sapiens*, is a fake. A society simply made up of such molecules of desire is an impossibility.

Of course, there are those who will continue to bury their heads in the sand. Many, faced with the prospect of introducing their students to such mayhem, and armed with the naïve belief that economics is a more-or-less complete and established box of tools, will continue to reel out the textbook verbiage as before. At the same time, many textbook authors go on stuffing their volumes with an increasing amount of largely empty formalizations. Students are taught less to think, more to assimilate dogma and to perform tricks of technique. But blinkered insularity cannot calm the cacophony and confusion in the subject at large.

It must be stressed, however, that not all economists brought up in the neoclassical tradition are exposed to the foregoing criticisms. On the contrary, one of the promising aspects of the current process of creative destruction in economic theory is the tendency for even mainstream economics to lose its limpidity, while, as we have suggested, the boundaries between orthodoxy and heterodoxy are becoming increasingly blurred. Consider the diverse wealth of insights now coming from research fields such as game theory, public economics, social choice theory, the theory of justice, industrial organization studies, property rights theory and ecological economics.

STRANGE ATTRACTORS

Neither have the heterodox traditions in economic theory been free from problems. For example, after a rapid rise in scholarship and interest in the late 1960s and early 1970s, Marxian economics has reached an impasse. There are many reasons for this, both external and internal. We may note in passing the theoretical and empirical weaknesses of some 'laws' associated with Marxism, such as the laws of the falling rate of profit or of the immiserization of the proletariat. Further, Marxism has been scarred by penetrating criticisms of some of its fundamental concepts and ideas, concerning, for instance, the theory of the state and of social classes. A variety of approaches and schools have spawned within Marxism. The creativity of several of these is undeniable, but many have become ossified and they are often disengaged from crucial debates in modern economic theory.

During the 1970s, Marxist economists had become polarized into the 'fundamentalists', who were less willing to amend Marx, on the one hand, and various kinds of neo-Marxists, including Sraffians, on the other. Throughout this decade much time and energy was taken up by internal debates, neglecting the vital and critical dialogue with other streams of thought. Even today the fundamentalists are still searching for the 'correct' definition of 'value' and refining the latest solution to the 'transformation problem'. Strangely, after it had led the clarion calls for 'relevance' in the 1960s and 1970s, Marxism itself now seems less capable of addressing the concrete structures and processes of contemporary capitalism.

Here too, the most serious débâcle is ontological and methodological. With hindsight, the tedious debates on value theory gave a clue. The century-long controversy over the 'transformation problem' ended with the simple result: the sole correct solution to the problem is nothing but its dissolution. But this clue leads to more revelations. Today, many economists sympathetic to Marxism are prepared to accept that the labour theory of value is a residue of 'Ricardian naturalism': a 'substance theory of value' of doubtful meaning and validity (Lippi, 1979; Mirowski, 1989). Thus *homo faber* too – the supposed creator of value through the power of abstract nerve and muscle – is a fake. Value at best is a social phenomenon, not a substance at all.[3] It is through such an escape route that the more creative Marxist economists have reached the real world.

We cannot delve into all the historico-philosophical considerations involved in the above discussion of different streams of economic theory. But it is hard to resist the temptation to observe a common reason at the roots of the débâcle of economic value theory. It is indeed impressive that two major theoretical schools of thought have come to a point of breakdown over the same kind of underlying issue, and in the same period of time. They both have subsided at their methodological and ontological foundations. The cracks widened visibly in the 1980s, but the problems were there long before.

Today, of course, the dismal science has much more on offer than merely neoclassicism and Marxism. We cannot but celebrate the proliferation of 'neo', 'new', 'post' and other sundry theoretical approaches now on the market. There are neo-Keynesians, Post Keynesians, new Keynesians, new classicals, post-classicals, Austrians, neo-Austrians, Schumpeterians, neo-Schumpeterians, behaviouralists, neo-Ricardians, new institutionalists, neo-institutionalists, plain institutionalists and more: an orgy of delights heralding an exhaustion of meaning.

Amongst this culture of epigones consider a single further case. It is well known that the various Post Keynesian approaches are united more by their common dislike of 'neoclassical' theory and less by any coherence or agreement upon fundamentals (Harcourt, 1982). But whilst embracing the legacy of Keynes, and despite the recent instructive scholarship on Keynes's deeper vision (Carabelli, 1988; Fitzgibbons, 1988; O'Donnell, 1989), the Post Keynesians have generally evaded the more fundamental ontological and methodological matters. Of course, there are a few exceptions, such as Sheila Dow (1985), but the main Post Keynesian effort has been to concentrate instead on alternative approaches to formal economic modelling. This situation has led to some disenchantment with this school, with attempts to redefine the 'Post Keynesian' label, or to formulate an underlying methodology. We welcome such efforts, but in our view the fruit is not yet on the vine.

This is not, nor is it meant to be, an exhaustive survey of 'neoclassical' theory and its rivals.[4] What is asserted here, however, is that chaos has infected all the main schools and branches of theoretical economics. Consequently, any degree of complacency or self-assuredness amongst representatives of either mainstream or heterodox approaches is likely to indicate insularity rather than adequacy.

ORDER OUT OF CHAOS

It is partly for reasons discussed above that we are resisting the temptation to present the ideas and approaches collected here as a well-defined alternative, appropriately packaged and labelled, to current orthodoxy. In recent years a number of books have appeared with bold claims to present an 'alternative' to 'neoclassical' theory. The editors do not believe that a well-developed and viable alternative yet exists, other than in the form of a few tentative signposts through the current mire. Thus we are not making the claim to present a full alternative theoretical system here, neither does the current collection encompass all the topics of our concern. It is simply a pertinent selection of views: helpful explorations in the attempt to find a route through the chaos.

At some future stage such ideas might develop into a more clearly formed alternative to orthodoxy. If so, it is bound to become labelled by its friends or by its foes, and indeed it will have to be so marketed if it is to survive and prosper. To accept a label at the outset, however, is to take on a great deal of dubious theoretical baggage and many associated misconceptions. Consequently, we are asking the reader to follow our example, to refrain from the labelling habit, and to assess the ideas themselves for their intrinsic worth.

Nevertheless, and unfortunately, new ideas do not fall from the sky, and a few remarks on the circumstances which led to this collection of essays are in order. All the papers here gathered were presented at a conference on 'Rethinking Economics: Theory and Policy for Europe in the Twenty-First Century' in Florence, Italy, in November 1990. The conference was organized by the European Association for Evolutionary Political Economy, a body founded in 1988. A companion volume, edited by Ash Amin and Michael Dietrich, addresses the European dimension of the conference proceedings.

Although leading representatives of the Veblen-Commons tradition of American institutionalism could claim paternity, and were present at the birth of this Association, the founders were aware of the lack of a corresponding tradition of 'institutionalism' in Europe. This deficiency is both an asset and a disadvantage. Whilst the consequent lack of tradition meant an absence of consensus and self-identification, the inherent fluidity and openness encouraged both the innovation and absorption of other ideas.[5]

As a result, a variety of European trends and schools of thought have found a place within the Association and at its conferences. For some, the influence of Marxism still remains strong. For others the mentor may be Kaldor, Kalecki or Keynes. In addition there has been a welcome for the theoretical stimulation provided by the Austrian School. The influence of all these can be detected here, along with that of other prominent thinkers such as Nicholas Georgescu-Roegen, Gunnar Myrdal, Karl Polanyi, Joseph Schumpeter and Thorstein Veblen.

However, eclecticism, whilst initially necessary, is not a solution. A road through chaos has to be built with something more durable. On the one hand, the existence of such initial variety provides greater evolutionary potential for the subject. The critical evaluation and 'evolutionary selection' of ideas and theories can be most fruitful if the degree of variety and diversity is sufficient for creative intercourse. On the other hand, diversity should not be cultivated to the point that division and discord are the result.

It is in this context and spirit that the following essays are presented. We shall now move on to discuss some prominent theoretical themes, as well as some aspects of divergence, that run through the collection.

WHAT IS ECONOMICS?

One of the most obvious common features of the essays collected here is their interdisciplinary character. As well as orthodox and heterodox economics, insights are drawn from sociology, philosophy, political science, history, biology and systems theory, in addition to other disciplines. However, what is involved here is not the dubious *mélange* of much interdisciplinary work. It is not a question simply of seasoning economics with insights from sociology, philosophy and elsewhere. The problem, in part, is with the basic ingredients.

Furthermore, there is a belief to be found amongst the editors and authors that not only 'economics' but the very definition of 'the economy' is problematic. Consider first the question of 'economics'. A science is normally defined as the study of a particular aspect of objective reality: physics is about the nature and properties of matter and energy, biology about living things, psychology about the psyche, and so on. But amongst economists, the prevailing practice for many years has been to regard this subject as being defined not principally as a study of a real object – the economy – but primarily by a method or type of analysis. This provides a convenient means for dealing with dissidents. Anyone who does not accept these assumptions, methods and theories is then regarded as simply not an economist. It is not a question whether they are right or wrong; those who disagree are simply sent into exile, into the sociology department or elsewhere.

Also, such a definition of economics rebuts criticism and potential change at its hard core. If the subject is defined by its basic methods and theories, then its fundamentals thereby become inert. If the other sciences had followed such an example then it would still be taught at universities that the earth was at the centre of the universe and that the material world consisted simply of the four elements of earth, water, air and fire.

Apart from being a recipe for intolerance, the aforementioned definition of economics elevates formalism and axiomatics to unwarranted heights. At the outset, the assumptions are taken as given and unquestionable. Agents must maximize because economists assume they do, and so on. For the theoretical economist the game becomes one of simply drawing logical conclusions from pre-ordained assumptions, in combination with secondary assumptions which may be more malleable. Attempts to address the real world, or to evaluate basic assumptions on the basis of engaging conceptualizations of such a reality, are downgraded. The situation has become so absurd that one is likely to find out very little about real economies by asking some of even the most influential theoretical economists. As the man put it: they simply do not know.

Fortunately, however, there are signs of change afoot. Especially in areas of applied economics, an increasing number of economists, even some brought up in the mainstream tradition, have been concerned to address the complexities of the real world. Consider, for example, the very real and productive efforts since the early 1970s, even by orthodox industrial economists, to open up the 'black box' of the firm and to understand its inner workings. This implicit search for realism should be made explicit in the definition of economics itself.

The editors take the view that economics should not be constituted by fixed methods or assumptions. Fortunately, the current anguish over hard-core notions such as rationality is likely to undermine the idea that economics is defined in such a manner. Before we wait for this to happen, however, we would like to define economics as the study of the processes and social relations governing the production, distribution and exchange of wealth and income. Economics is thus an attempt to address aspects of the real world; it is defined by its orientation towards a real object. Hence economics does have to embrace a single methodology or set of hard-core assumptions; it can encompass diversity and debate at the level of fundamentals. Economics should prosper with more competition between, rather than the existing near-monopoly of, such basic ideas.

In connection with the above grievances about the discipline, some writers have proposed a terminological counterrevolution. Long ago Jevons and Marshall abandoned the term 'political economy' in favour of 'economics'. The former's motivation was that economics sounded much more like 'mathematics, ethics, aesthetics' (Jevons, 1879, p. 48). The latter's was that political economy seemed to soil the science with the world of politics and the interests of political parties (Marshall and Marshall, 1879, p. 2). Economics, on the contrary, seemed to connote 'a science pure and applied, rather than a science and an art' (Marshall, 1920, p. 36). To us, however, these are all good reasons to prefer the old and glorious name. Political economy is thereby less reducible to a branch of applied mathematics, does not shrink from the sordid world of 'political bodies', and knows that no social science can be entirely free of judgements of value.

Ultimately, it may be necessary to join this counterrevolution, but we hesitate to concede the ground covered by 'economics' to those more satisfied by the existing state of affairs in our discipline.[6] The ontological, methodological and other theoretical problems discussed briefly above do not justify such an abandonment. At best, we can use 'political economy' to connote the wider and more pluralistic approach that we favour.[7]

CONCEPTIONS OF THE ECONOMY

Whatever the chosen title of the science, the definition of the 'economy' still remains problematic. A particular type of approach to this question is represented here, and evidenced to some extent in the majority of the essays (Tool, Fourie, Morroni, Farmer and Matthews, McKelvey, and Hodgson). It involves the assertion that economic reality is necessarily embedded within broader social relations, culture and institutions.

An entity such as 'the market', for instance, cannot be represented simply as the arena in which individual agents collide (Fourie). The market is itself a social institution, and is reflective of a particular kind of social culture. A modern theory of pricing should not disregard the corporate structures and institutions through which prices are initially formulated (Tool).

Such general points are thematic in this volume. However, the interactions between individuals, institutions and culture are highly complex. No single type of response is evidenced here, rather a diversity of views addressing some crucial, common, but controversial themes.

ACTION AND STRUCTURE

Whilst the stress on the cultural and institutional integument of all 'economic' life is essential, it creates substantial problems. Orthodox theory has ignored these by its treatment of individuals as both atomistic and pre-existent to their cultural and institutional environment. The farewell to orthodoxy made here puts the thorny old matter of the relation between agent and structure at the centre of the theoretical stage.

Some of the essays address this issue directly (Farmer and Matthews, Witt) others more obliquely (Fourie, Hodgson, McKelvey). Nevertheless, the questions raised are highly complex and there is not complete agreement, either between the contributors or even the two editors. Quite often the disagreement arises from different definitions and utilizations of terms such as subjectivism, individualism, and methodological individualism. More importantly, it sometimes relates to questions of substance.

In its treatment of the individual, textbook microeconomic theory is substantially deficient. At first, the sanctity of the individual is glorified by treating tastes and preferences as given, and by regarding the economy as reducible to such pre-given and consequently atomistic units. But the individual is then degraded by the treatment of actions as mechanical responses to given preference functions, by the neglect of the unique manner in which the individual appraises sense data and the uniqueness of individual knowledge, and by the failure to recognize and encompass real spontaneity and the true novelty of choice.

We think it is necessary to avoid any excessive emphasis on subjectivity and individuality. Such a stress would underestimate the cultural and institutional context, or regard it simply as an albeit unintended consequence of individual actions, and thereby reducible to them.

Nevertheless, the other extreme offers no salvation. If the individual is regarded simply as determined by the social integument, then one type of reductionism is simply traded for another. Instead of a type of 'methodological individualism' we flip to the obverse error of 'methodological holism'. Neither is satisfactory. The problem is to articulate the relationship between agency and structure in a manner which preserves both the structured nature of action and the reality of choice and action itself.

PRODUCTION VERSUS ALLOCATION

Traditional economics proclaims itself as the 'science of choice' but makes choice unreal by rendering it predetermined. Yet this elevation of a fictional choice serves to concentrate the analysis on the allocation of given resources. Economics thus shies away from the sphere of production, the processes of creation of wealth. In so far as production is considered, it is itself reduced to a problem of allocation: the dilemmas of 'unlimited ends with scarce means'. Exchange, not production, becomes the epitome of all economic life.

The first consequence of this is that the analysis of the processes of production is ignored. Indeed, for over 100 years there was very little to rival, let alone surpass, Adam Smith's analysis of the division of labour in the *Wealth of Nations*, or Marx's analysis of production in the first volume of *Capital*. Fortunately, however, the labour process debates of the 1970s and 1980s put the issue back on the agenda, and there are more recent examples of more rigorous and conclusive scholarship in the area (Morroni).

A second consequence is the neglect of technological change. Symmetrical with its treatment of tastes and preferences as exogenous, traditional economic theory typically takes technology as given. At best, there are switches of apparently known and blueprint-defined technology. This deficiency is not rectified simply by invoking the name of Joseph Schumpeter and tacking a few innovative waves on to orthodox theory. As recent scholarship makes clear (Arthur, 1989; Clark and Juma, 1987; Dosi *et al.*, 1988; Freeman, 1990), much deeper issues are at stake, concerning the very nature of technological knowledge and the appropriate theoretical paradigm for processes of this type.

A third consequence is the neglect of the antithetical and inevitable concomitant of production, that is, destruction. Production cannot occur without the conversion of some energy and raw materials into an unavailable form, and thereby the destruction to some extent of the natural environment. Smith and Marx paid little heed to this, and here the greatest insights come from Nicholas Georgescu-Roegen and his invocation of the entropy law in the economic process (Georgescu-Roegen, 1971; Dragan and Demetrescu, 1986). He argues that production by humans, like evolution and life in general, is a local and temporary opposition to this entropy law, by importing matter from the environment and organizing it into a usable form. It would be better if economics addressed such crucial and relevant ideas, rather than imitating entropy through its own internal manifestations of theoretical chaos.

STRUCTURAL DEVELOPMENT VERSUS ADDITIVE GROWTH

During the 1950s and 1960s the advanced capitalist economies experienced a golden age of prosperity. Many contemporary economists thus came to conceive of growth as a smooth and harmonious process, and to elaborate theories which ignored the structural and developmental features of any substantial economic transformation. The disruptive and discontinuous aspects of growth, involving technological change, social relations, institutions and policy regimes, were either trivialized or taken as exogenous. However, the dislocations of the 1970s dispensed a summary justice for those edifying parables. Today, quite independently of the internal problems of growth models of the Solow-Swan type, such instruments of explanation have fallen into disfavour. Even Robert Solow (1985) has now taken a pledge that history should not be so despised.

More recently, the theory of economic growth has again become one of the more exciting fields of research. There are at least four major new themes that characterize contemporary work on economic change, and all of them are represented to some degree in the essays gathered here.

The first theme concerns the accommodation of parametric change. If technical progress is not 'manna from heaven', and is embodied in capital goods and human skills, then it is not reasonable to account for its occurrence in terms of a parameter in the production function. The real problem is to explain the rhythm and direction, the quantity and quality, the breadth and diversity, of technological evolution and economic growth. Similar propositions apply to social relations and institutions. For instance, if growth and technological change are affected by industrial relations or entrepreneurial dynamism or government policy choices, then it is necessary to account for these 'variables' too.

These dimensions of economic change are results of the decisions and interactions of many economic agents acting within and alongside social institutions and aggregates. Consequently, an attempt has to be made to endogenize not only technical but also social and institutional transformations. This is the second theme dominating contemporary research in economic change: the interconnection of the economic, the social and the political dimensions of growth.

The third theme has to do with the nature of structural change. Clearly, merely parametric alterations cannot encompass this. Here, it is the qualitative and structural aspects that matter. Economics should be able to draw key insights from modern mathematics (differential topology, catastrophe theory, bifurcation theory, chaos theory and so on) which are related to notions of structural stability and instability. A central idea here is that the occurrence of smooth economic growth over a long period is no guarantee that such a felicitous trajectory will continue. There is always the possibility of abrupt morphogenetic change. Interestingly, such structural disruptions do not need to be exogenous events. Working latently during the periods of peaceful development, built-in mechanism can prepare for eventual catastrophic change. Alternatively, the hidden mechanisms can give rise to long wave phenomena alongside much shorter cycles (Goodwin).

A fourth theme is path dependence. Although the problem was recognized long ago,[8] many economic theorists have now accepted that the future development of an economic system is affected by the path it has traced out in the past. This contrasts with the preceding view that, within limits, from whatever starting point, the system will eventually gravitate to the same equilibrium, and thus real time and history could be safely ignored.

Modern mathematics, especially the study of non-linear dynamic models, has put path dependency back on the agenda. There are at least two mathematical arguments which convey the basic idea. First, whenever a dynamic system has more than one stable critical point, the particular equilibrium towards which the system gravitates will depend upon the path taken out of equilibrium, the initial conditions and the external shocks. Secondly, in chaotic models the dynamic path is extremely sensitive to initial conditions in such a way that the outcome can change dramatically with a small change in the latter. Further, as each present instant embodies a set of 'initial conditions' for the future development of the system, the 'initial conditions' change at every moment of time.

MICROFOUNDATIONS AND MACROSIMPLICITY

Because of some of the fundamental problems with general equilibrium theory described above, the entire project of placing macroeconomics on microeconomic foundations is now facing intractable difficulties. The move away from the bowdlerized Keynesianism of the postwar decades was in pursuit of the dream that macroeconomics could be placed on the 'firm microfoundations' of functions describing individual, maximizing behaviour.

Although some reduction to elemental parts is inevitable in any science, the obsession with the particular unit of the maximizing, self-contained individual should be called into question. Alternative approaches are emerging from the present wave of heterodox enquiry, and some are discussed in this book. Studies in industrial economics, for instance, raise the question of the appropriate level of analysis (Foray and Garrouste) as well as the particular relationship with innovation and growth in the national dimension (Hodgson, McKelvey).

Taking stock of these developments, at present it is still difficult to trace out with any precision the new methodology that may emerge, or the shape of the new economics of the future. Nevertheless, some of the common basic features and elementary principles can be discerned.

A first principle is that human behaviour cannot be reduced to the choices and decisions of isolated individuals alone. Circumstances are in part a consequence of individual actions, but also individuals are moulded by circumstances including their interactions with others. For example, consumer behaviour cannot be studied without any consideration of the social moods and fashions which help mould individual preferences.

A second principle is that the factors sustaining human behaviour cannot be reduced to any *a priori*, abstract, general and ahistorical hypotheses. No fictitious psychology can remove the need for well-founded knowledge of actual human behaviour in its cultural and institutional context.

In sum, macroeconomics cannot simply be built on microfoundations. Microeconomics itself has to be founded; and it has to be based on extra-economic foundations. It is here that the idea provided by 'political economy' offers the challenge, by undertaking links with sociology, psychology, anthropology, political science and history. It is not simply a matter of adding a few appendages to the discipline. The rethinking of economics must plan to rebuild its foundations as a social science.

IN CONCLUSION

Among the primary tasks of scientific analysis are taxonomy and classification: the assignment of sameness and difference. Classification, by bringing together entities in discrete groups, must refer to common qualities. For classification to work, it must be assumed that the common qualities themselves must be invariant, even if reality itself has a fuzzy or 'dialectical' quality (Georgescu-Roegen, 1971).

The problem, then, is to develop meaningful and operational principles of invariance upon which analysis can be founded. In social science there are various traditions that share a common approach to this problem: the attempt to locate invariance by analysing social mechanisms and the institutional settings that sustain the formation and behaviour of *social* agents. There are plenty of examples of theories of social agency in the history of economic thought, from the social classes of the classical economists and Marx, to the collective agents and groups of the institutionalist, Keynesian and Schumpeterian schools.

Workers, capitalists, entrepreneurs, managers, speculators, consumers and so on are all sets of individuals who share a common position in a given societal and institutional structure and thereby follow common behavioural patterns. In these approaches it is impossible to study the structure and dynamics of an economic system by abstracting from the existence of such social agents and the institutional settings in which they act and interact. Note in contrast the quite opposite approach of mainstream theory.

Social agents and institutions, in short, are taken as the entities and units of analysis. This should apply to both microeconomics and macroeconomics. Theories focused on aggregates become plausible when based on a valid analysis of collective behaviour and social institutions. Money is a legitimate unit of account because money itself is an institutionally sanctioned medium. Aggregate consumption functions should relate to a set of persons with strong social interactions and institutional links, and so on. This contrasts with the approach based on reasoning from bare axioms based on the supposed universals of individual behaviour.

We warmly support a reorientation of economic theory in that direction. We could be wrong, but we are convinced that such a development may be able to rescue economics from its implicit atomist ontology and reductionist obsessions.

NOTES

1. The editors wish to thank Marco Dardi, Alan Kirman and Stefano Zamagni for their helpful comments on an earlier draft of this Introduction. Of course, the usual disclaimer applies. Much of the editorial work was carried out whilst Geoff Hodgson was a Research Fellow at the Swedish Collegium for Advanced Study in the Social Sciences, Uppsala, Sweden – for which he wishes to record his warm appreciation.
2. 'Non chiederci la parola', from *Ossi di Seppia* ('Cuttlefish Bones') (1925). Translated from the Italian by the editors.
3. Note the recent attempt by the institutional economist Philip Mirowski (1990a, 1991) to develop and formalize the foundations of a social value theory.
4. For a survey of the present state of economic research, see Screpanti and Zamagni (1992, chs 9–11).
5. This is not to deny the innovatory capacity of contemporary American institutionalism. Note, for instance, Philip Mirowski's (1986, 1989) original critique of the physics metaphor of neoclassical theory.
6. In the 1970s there were attempts in several Australian universities to set up separate departments of political economy. Amongst other things, this provoked an informative controversy of the use of the term 'political economy' (Arndt, 1984; Groenewegen, 1985). One author forcefully asserted that 'there is absolutely no historical justification to argue for distinct meanings of political economy and economics, by associating the

latter with positive value free science on the lines of Robbins' (Groenewegen, 1985, p. 749).

7.   Ironically, Marshall (1920, p. 36) saw economics as a 'broad term', in contrast to the 'narrower' political economy.

8.   Late in the nineteenth century (1883) the physicist Joseph Bertrand discovered that, if out-of-equilibrium trading was incorporated into a Walrasian model, then it could lead to indeterminate and path-dependent results that are inconsistent with the Walras's general approach. Likewise, in a prescient essay, Nicholas Kaldor (1934) saw the possibility of path dependency in economic models.

PART I

Prices, Markets and Production

2. Contributions to an Institutional Theory of Price Determination

Marc R. Tool[1]

Since all modern economies are, and will remain, monetary exchange economies, theoretical explanations of ratios of exchange – prices – and their determination must constitute a major area of inquiry in any encompassing examination of the economic process. This chapter is a part of a more extensive inquiry into the character and explanatory capabilities of an institutionalist theory of price determination. My general concern is to help formulate a logically coherent and empirically grounded theory of discretionary pricing. 'Discretionary pricing' here refers to the use by individuals of achieved economic power significantly to specify or to influence monetary terms of exchange.

Following Eichner (1987, p. 1558), I distinguish at the outset between *prices*, which as ratios of exchange refer to numerical values indicating the amount of funds that must be given up for a good or service, and *pricing*, which refers to the behaviour and judgements that determine prices. This chapter is addressed primarily to *pricing*, that is, to matters relating to the *formulation* of prices.

In this chapter, I examine (a) the theoretical context of price determination; (b) the institutional context of price determination; and (c) contributions of institutional economists to a theory of discretionary pricing, especially with regard to the corporate oligopolistic sector. I give particular attention to the views of Thorstein Veblen, Walton Hamilton, Gardiner Means, John Kenneth Galbraith, and to contributions of Alfred Eichner and Arthur Okun that are correlative with institutional economics.[2]

1. THE THEORETICAL CONTEXT

Neoclassical economists have long understood the significance of price determination as a part of the exchange process. Indeed, their primary interest has been to offer analyses of market pricing in differing settings on the assumption that to explain market-price determination is tantamount to ex-

plaining virtually all that is of importance in the economic process. Their
universe of inquiry has typically been confined to an analysis of pricing
phenomena tending to market equilibria that define economic efficiency. The
model of a free competitive market system is advocated as the most efficient
allocative mechanism. Unfettered price determination within such markets,
as explained through marginal analysis, accomplishes the efficient allocation.
This perspective reflects the 'intuitive belief', as Nicholas Kaldor (1985, pp.
13–14) characterizes it,

> that the price mechanism is the key to everything, the key instrument in guiding
> the operation of an undirected, unplanned, free market economy. The Walrasian
> model and its most up-to-date successor may both be highly artificial abstractions
> from the real world but the truth that the theory conveys – that prices provide the
> guide to all economic action – must be fundamentally true, and its main implication
> that free markets secure the best results must also be true.

Here 'truth' is a matter of logical and rhetorical affirmation, not of comprehensive evidential demonstration, and 'best', in a typical case, is an
approximation of Paretian optimality. The better-off–worse-off calculations
in such Paretian judgements are undergirded by a tacit acceptance of utility
as the meaning of social value and utility maximization as the preferred
social goal (Hodgson, 1988, pp. 73–4; Tool, 1986, pp. 89–94). Prices paid in
unfettered markets are the valuation measures.

This *a priori* focus of neoclassical inquiry has defined the discipline of
economics for mainstream scholars for most of this century. Its advocates
have generated 'market mentalities' (Polyani, Kindleberger) as the products
of their instruction and dominion. Neoclassical orthodoxy constitutes the
'conventional wisdom' (Galbraith) on all manner of policy options. Vigor-
ous advocacy of shrinking governments, deregulation and enterprise zones
are among recent policy reflections of this view. Moreover, positivist claims
notwithstanding, such price determination is presumed by such market mentalities to have both practical and *moral* significance (Ayres, 1944, pp. 3–38).
The neoclassical 'price system' is alleged to be *concurrently* a pervasive
characterization of how prices *tend to be* determined in most markets *and* a
stipulation of how prices *ought to be* determined in virtually *all* markets.
Departures from price-competitive market determinations are examined as
pathology. The abstract ideal defines the *proper* price system. The normative
use of this competitive model remains endemic in orthodox neoclassical
theory generally (Tool, 1986, pp. 87–103).

But within the sometimes contentious house of orthodoxy there is widespread recognition that the postulated theory of automatic, mechanistic price
determination in free competitive markets is not necessarily *descriptively*
adequate. Orthodox economists do not contend that free-market pricing under

conditions of pure or perfect competition actually and comprehensively prevails in any economy. The earlier literature on monopolistic competition (Chamberlin, 1948 [1933]) and imperfect competition (Robinson, 1969 [1933]), and the more recent literature on externalities and market failures (Spulber, 1989) are troublesome contributions, among others, that confirm extensive behaviour at variance with the general model (Tool, 1986, pp. 104–25). They suggest that neoclassical theory does not provide the *general* theory of price determination after all (Joskow, 1975, pp. 270–9). One can hardly claim generality when confronted with substantial nonconforming conduct and events.

As I explore below, managers, at least of large-scale enterprises, are increasingly perceived as *price makers* rather than *price takers. Fixprice* models usually come closer to reality than *flexprice* models. As Arthur Okun (1981, p. 23) observed, 'models that focus on price takers and auctioneers and that assume continuous clearing of the market generate inaccurate microeconomics as well as misleading macroeconomics'. Even so, it appears that neoclassical theorists assume that the *general* theory is one of free-market price determination, regarding which there are occasional departures. Institutionalists, in contrast, argue that the more inclusive and descriptively accurate theory must be one of discretionary pricing and that instances of free-market determination are exceptionally rare.

2. THE INSTITUTIONAL CONTEXT

All social orders, of necessity, provide for the *function* of exchange to occur. Institutional arrangements are everywhere used to facilitate the reciprocal activity of trading money in some form for goods or services. Monetary exchange typically involves the transfer of discretion over the objects of exchange.

'Institutions' are often defined by institutionalists as 'socially prescribed patterns of correlated behavior' (Bush, 1987, p. 1076). Institutional arrangements comprising markets condition and correlate behaviour in the exchange process. Such patterns of correlation do include the establishment and publication of prices. Markets are defined by Hodgson (1988, p. 174) as 'a set of social institutions in which a large number of commodity exchanges of a specific type regularly take place, and to some extent are facilitated and structured by those institutions'.

In the neoclassical market model, the primary institutions facilitating exchange are private ownership and legally enforceable contracts. Ownership consists of a legally sanctioned area of discretion over the possession, use and disposition of an item. Ownership is transferred with agreed-upon exchange; contracts stipulate the terms of the exchange; governments ensure compliance with contracts. But in the neoclassical formulation, markets themselves remain largely unspecified; they are accorded no other structural character (Hodgson, 1988, pp. 182–3). The neoclassical analyses do not reflect the breadth and complexity of behaviour actually correlated in markets, nor the roles of customs and habits in conditioning market conduct, nor the patterns and varying criteria of choice-making exhibited. Market motivations are simplistically affirmed as profit and/or utility maximization; market participation reflects 'constrained maximization'.

Institutionalists recognize that modern markets are comprised of a large number of usually complex correlated patterns of behaviour, all of which, though typically habitual, are initially creations of people as discretionary agents. Such correlated patterns organize and structure exchange activity. They specify behaviour not only with reference, at times, to property and contract, but also, for example, to acquisition of information, communication among participants, and transportation of items exchanged (Hodgson, 1988, p. 174). Customary, legal, political and economic patterns of behaviour are all present to regularize exchange practices and to provide some measure of predictability or security of expectations for participants. *Customary*: tradition may stipulate who in a family or a corporate firm is (are) the power-wielding, and status-bearing, market participant(s). *Legal*: laws specify the place, time, character, media and terms of exchange. *Political*: stipulations of governing bodies define where, and to what extent, discretion over market exchange shall reside, and whose economic interests are to be served. *Economic*: organizations of market participants – unions, megacorps, cartels, marketing co-ops, trade associations, business 'clubs' – impinge on and help shape market conduct. In brief, 'markets are organized and institutionalized exchange' (Hodgson, 1988, p. 174). But the customary and conventional character of market institutional structures, including prices, requires emphasis. Established exchange arrangements, once created, tend to persist. Habitual patterns of behaviour as conventions in price-setting are commonplace (Hodgson, 1988, pp. 125–34, 182–7). G. L. S. Shackle (1972, p. 227) suggests a reason:

> Prices which have stood at particular levels for some time acquire thereby some sanction and authority. They are the 'right' and even the 'just' prices. But also they are the prices to which the society has adapted its ways and habits, they are prices which mutually cohere in an established frame of social life.

We shall see this recognition also in the contributions of Galbraith and Okun below.

As with other facets of the economic order, both the *structures of prices*, the lists, schedules and patterns of relative prices, and the *price-setting practices* vary widely among economies and among sectors within economies. The customs and conventions of pricing in the National Health Service in Great Britain, for example, will reflect indigenous judgements somewhat unique to that culture; they will diverge from the pricing of socialized medicine on the Continent, or from fee-for-service medicine and private health insurance in the United States. Similarly, pricing patterns and practices in agriculture, accomplished by subsidies and management of aggregate supplies, or in the learned professions through fee schedules, will differ dramatically from price leadership and mark-up pricing in industry, and control of prices by regulatory commission in public utilities. There is extensive variation among political economies and among economic sectors within a political economy both in the structure of prices and the correlating patterns through which the determination of prices is accomplished. But the generalization that virtually all significant prices are set as discretionary acts of identifiable persons – that existential markets are, in large part, shaped and staffed by *price makers* rather than *price takers* – is an argument I make here and through the rest of the chapter. As Galbraith (1967, p. 190) observed:

> We are profoundly conditioned by the theology of the market. ... A price that is fixed by the seller to a singular degree does not seem good. Accordingly, it requires a major act of will to think of price-fixing as both normal and having economic function. In fact, it is normal in all advanced industrial societies.

Why, from an institutional perspective, is price *fixing* 'normal' in all major economies? Why has *discretionary price setting* become endemic? *Market participants seek and acquire control over price-setting in order to reduce uncertainty of judgement.* The reason one looks virtually in vain for examples of an actual pure or perfect market in the real world is that no market seller, in such a setting, can get sufficient relevant information to make informed economic judgements. The continuing uncertainties are destabilizing. Continuous actual unfettered competition, where markets actually determine prices, would be traumatic and intolerable. The inability reasonably to predict and control the character and direction of exchange phenomena, most particularly price changes, and the difficulties of influencing price elasticities of demand, makes reflective, means-consequence judgements concerning the level and character of production, the nature and extent of investment, the creation and/or employment of new technology, hiring policies and practices, and the like, exceedingly difficult, if not impossible. The most critically significant variables are unpredictable. Having to adjust to prices determined elsewhere narrows one's own choices; gaining the ability to adjust one's own prices widens choices. An observation made by Jan Kregel (1980, p. 40) with regard to investment decision-making in Keynesian theory, applies, in my view, more generally:

> The information required for rational decision making does not exist; the market mechanism cannot provide it. But, just as nature abhors a vacuum, the economic system abhors uncertainty. The system reacts to the absence of the information the market cannot provide by creating uncertainty-reducing institutions: wage contracts, debt contracts, supply agreements, administered prices [and] trading agreements.

I would modify this view only by attributing the reaction to the absence of market information, not to the 'system', but to those in the polity and/or economy who have achieved discretionary control over institutional adjustments, and are willing and able to use it. The discretionary agent(s) responsible for any significant economic organization (public or private) must gain and retain some appreciable control over prices charged and, if possible, over prices paid.

The quest for increasing security of expectation is unending. To seek and acquire as much control as possible over the forces and factions which ultimately determine the extent of discretion, the character of discretion and the duration of the organization, constitute the *real* 'bottom line'. Among such 'forces and factions' price setting powers figure prominently. Price fixing is and must continue to be 'normal', meaning typical, habitual and, in some considerable measure, predictable.

Having now considered the institutional character of markets and pricing, and why discretionary control over price determination is sought, I conclude this section with a brief illustrative exploration of institutional configurations in and through which pricing judgements are made.

In most advanced economies, the modern large corporation is the major institutional complex through which industrial goods and major services are produced and distributed. Although its specific form varies, it is usually created only with governmental permission. As a legal *person* in the eyes of the law, it has legal-entity status and standing; it can sue and be sued. Ownership is nominally 'private' but private owners' discretion may or may not be a viable instrument of attaining and retaining control. In most megacorps, through fragmentation and wide dispersion of shares, discretion for ordinary stockholders may well be limited to a passive claim to dividends. Ownership is dispersed; control is concentrated, as Veblen observed (1904) and Adolf Berle and Gardiner Means demonstrated (1932).

The modern large corporation is, in effect, a legally sanctioned private government usually run by a self-perpetuating dynastic management. Its government-like powers include the abilities to impose, deny and manipulate behaviour of persons subject to its hegemonic power. It is subject to constraints of competitive rivalry but normally not price competition. It defines cultural tastes; it creates demand for its own products; it influentially participates in the determination of what higher education consists in; it significantly shapes the social life of its employees (Dugger, 1989). It exhibits a continuing participatory role in bringing pressure and influence to bear on political processes at all levels.

The modern oligopolistic corporation is subject, in varying degrees, to public constraints of environmental compliance, labour laws and anti-discrimination and fair-employment rules, among others. Firms may confront governmental price constraints (general or industry-specific), negative political responses to pricing judgements made, and government macromanagement policies, fiscal and monetary, that help importantly to define the context for price administration. The megacorp may be a recipient of public largess through subsidies (including tax expenditures), trade protections, public education of its employees and, at times, mandated exemption status to regulations (pollution controls, safety standards), and the like.

In their unique concerns with price determination, in a typically oligopolistic organization, the corporation's price setters do not necessarily have an easy time of it (Hamilton, 1974, essay no. 3). They must, of course, set prices which cover their continuing costs of materials and labour, and a mark-up margin to generate the pecuniary options which residual balances provide. But also, they must function in a difficult, risk-filled, institutional environment that may well include intra-industry concerns over retaliatory pricing responses from industry rivals at home; accommodation to or adjustment of pricing judgements of material suppliers; negotiation of wage agreements under collective-bargaining rules and regulations; and market sharing agreements, among others. In addition, they may face inter-industry pressures from aggressive, state-subsidized and -supported rival contenders from abroad and negotiation of pricing accords (cartel or otherwise) with international firms.

Given the foregoing, and the significance and complexities of price-making in large corporations, it comes as no surprise that corporations have developed highly trained specialists as price-setters who work in specific and sophisticated agencies (bureaux or divisions) within the corporate or conglomerate complex and concentrate solely on the price-determination responsibility (Kaplan *et al.*, 1958, pp. 220-47).

When one asks, then, where discretionary prices are determined, the loci of discretionary determination of prices must be sought among the complexities and intricacies of the institutional fabric through which pricing power has been achieved, retained and exercised. In any problematic context, where access to such information is crucial, *only enquiry into the complexities of the structural fabric involved can disclose the particular pricing power centres, who the price-setting agents are, the criteria reflected in their decisions, and the consequences that flow therefrom.*

At this point, the focus of this chapter narrows, given space constraints, to consideration of price determination mainly in oligopolistic enterprises. It is in this realm that disarming apologias for price-setting power, rooted in neoclassical price theory, are most persistent; it is in this area that many of the major price-fixing decisions are initiated, with wide repercussions through the economy.

3. INSTITUTIONALIST CONTRIBUTIONS TO A THEORY OF DISCRETIONARY PRICING

Institutionalists have been contributing to a theory of discretionary pricing for nearly a century. That contribution began with Thorstein Veblen, and involves two largely complementary and converging approaches: the older tradition encompasses a literature on *administered* pricing, to which Walton H. Hamilton, Gardiner C. Means, John Kenneth Galbraith, among others, contributed. The more recent and more technical tradition is reflected in writings on *mark-up* or *cost-plus* pricing of Alfred Eichner and other such heterodox-leaning and empirically orientated scholars as Arthur Okun. After touching base with Veblen, I canvass selected examples of the work of these contributors, seeking conceptual tools, analytical formulations and synthetic characterizations for an *institutional* theory of discretionary pricing.

Thorstein B. Veblen

Although Veblen certainly was among the first American scholars to observe and explain the nature and significance of the corporate revolution in the organization of the economy, he did not dwell at length on the pricing power of the then newly emerging giant corporations. He did, however, see a general trend toward the development of 'business coalitions' that had an important bearing on price setting:

> 'Cutthroat' competition ... can be done away by 'pooling the interests' of the competitors, so soon as all or an effective majority of the business concerns which are rivals in the market combine and place their business management under one directive head. When this is done, by whatever method, selling of goods or services at competitively varying prices is replaced by collective selling ... at prices fixed on the basis of 'what the traffic will bear'. (Veblen, 1904, p. 258)

Moreover,

> [W]hen the coalition comes effectually to cover its special field of operations, it is able not only to fix the prices which it will accept ... but also in a considerable measure to fix the prices or rates which it will pay for materials, labor, and other services (such as transportation) on a similar basis. (Ibid., p. 261).

For Veblen, the drive to create monopolies, what he called 'business coalitions', is motivated by the quest for pecuniary gain, is prompted by the need to employ and control newly emerging technologies, and is required to provide 'the only refuge from chronic depression'. The incorporation of newer machine technology 'makes competitive business impracticable ... but it makes coalition practicable' (ibid., p. 263). At the time he wrote, the trend to concentration was already well-advanced: 'it is doubtful if there are any successful business ventures within the range of the modern industries from which the monopoly element is wholly absent' (ibid., p. 54).

With Veblen, then, we get an early characterization of a corporate-dominated, administered-price, industrial economy.

Walton Hale Hamilton

In the published writings of the distinguished lawyer and economist, Walton Hamilton, which cover more than 40 years, is to be found some of the most penetrating and significant analyses of the emergent corporate economy. In analysis less sardonic and somewhat more empirically grounded than Veblen, Hamilton explores the evolutionary transformation of the locus and use of economic power by corporations in labour relations and wage-setting (Hamilton and May, 1968 [1923]), in the use of patents and their protection (Hamilton, 1957, p. 63–99), and in administered-pricing judgements and practices (Hamilton, 1938), among others. Attention here is necessarily confined to his concern with administered pricing.

Heading a small research staff for the Cabinet Committee on Price Policy, appointed by President Roosevelt in 1934, Hamilton guided an inquiry into the actual pricing practices of a number of basic American industries. At issue was consideration of industrial policy which he defined as 'an aggregate of the measures contrived for the guidance of industry by all the agencies which operate upon it' (Hamilton, 1938, p. 528). Of the completed studies, those on the automobile, tyre, gasoline, cottonseed, dress, whiskey and milk industries were published in the collection edited by Hamilton, *Price and Price Policies* (1938). In the 'Preface' he observes that

> the literature of industry was inadequate to the demands of price policy. Accounts of how in general industry is organized and how in the abstract prices are made were available in abundance. Yet, with notable exceptions, little was at hand upon the structures of particular industries, their distinctive habits, their unique patterns of control, and the multiplex of arrangements – stretching away from technology to market practice – which give magnitude to their prices. (Hamilton, 1938, p. vii)

Hamilton and his fellow researchers sought to fill that gap in knowledge and therewith to contribute to policy deliberations.

In his concluding chapter, Hamilton (1938, pp. 525–56) does not presume to draw general principles from this sampling of industrial practice. He distils no synthetic summary of price determination. What he finds in these empirical studies, rather, is an extraordinary complexity of institutional structure bearing on pricing practices. Each industrial area studied revealed an idiosyncratic fabric of diverse interrelations and interdependencies. Each had a different history of emergence; each exhibited a somewhat unique pattern of customary behaviours; each had its own way of arriving at pricing decisions and of implementing pricing judgements. Although cost considerations were of some significance in virtually all pricing judgements, nowhere were they an exclusive concern. Loci of discretion over price varied widely among the industries studied, but nowhere could one presume or show that atomistic, automatic, freely competitive market forces were determining prices in auction markets. Hamilton recognized the cultural origins of demand: tastes are acquired; preferences are learned; industries must lead in creating markets for their goods. They must also adapt to changes induced by the growth of knowledge and new technology. Custom influenced the cost structure too: he was aware of the differing habits and practices which impinge on workers' wages and salaries; acknowledging the complexity of production programs, he recognized the difficulties of assigning cost in joint-product firms.

In sum, 'a touch of the motley rests upon the ways of price making. ... Price bears the marks of the process from which it emerges' (ibid., p. 530). 'The business unit is not content to leave its affairs ... and its survival to the arbitration of an impersonal market. It must bestir itself to hold its own' (ibid., p. 549). 'Price, quality, service, blarney, guile, and the creative touch are alike weapons of promotion and devices of accommodation' (ibid., p. 550). But the *manipulation* of price, in quest of market control or shares, may be 'too dangerous a mechanism to be employed'. (That is, discretion over prices *is held* but prevailing circumstances in the industry may discourage its use.) Industrial leaders will then seek a formal or informal understanding to shift to non-price forms of rivalry (see ibid., p. 542). 'Thus price – and the costs which attend it – are a pecuniary reflection of the usages which impinge upon the making and marketing of a good. These usages run through the whole industrial process. ... They are embedded in the ways of an industry just as the folkways are embedded in the culture of a primitive or a civilized people' (ibid.).

Hamilton's contribution to an institutionalist theory of discretionary pricing, then, consists of: (a) his recognition and demonstration of overt and pervasive pricing power in industry; (b) his showing of the role of convention and custom in actual industrial pricing practice; (c) his demonstration of the remarkable variability and complexity in pricing practices; and (d) in his recognition of the probable need for an industrial policy to impinge on industrial leaders' discretion over pricing, his implication of the need to examine and appraise criteria of pricing judgements.

Gardiner C. Means

For much of Gardiner Means's professional life, his research ambition was to provide a 'new paradigm for macrotheory'; it was to be a 'new macrotheory based on the realities of our modern economy' (Means, 1975a, p. 154). It would differ fundamentally from the neoclassical and Keynesian approaches. He had, early in his career, 'laid down basic postulates for the new theory'. Two are of special significance here: one 'is that a large part of production is carried on by a few great corporations in which final ownership is widely dispersed, ownership and control are largely separated, and management is largely a self-perpetuating body'. A second 'is that most prices are administered privately (or by agencies of government) and behave in a fashion quite different from that indicated by traditional theory' (ibid., p. 152). While the 'new paradigm' evidently was never completed, Means's contribution to a theory of discretionary pricing is revealed principally in his empirical demonstration of these two postulates.

Means was not academically trained as an institutional economist; his early empirical research into corporate structure and agricultural pricing drove him, as a fledgling scientist, to seek a theory that would better explain the factual realities he perceived. His heterodoxy was fuelled by his experience as a scholar. His research (with Adolf Berle) that culminated in *The Modern Corporation and Private Property* (Berle and Means, 1932) generated the first postulate; a long series of statements, incorporating his empirical research, and prepared as testimony for Congressional hearings, undergirded the second postulate (Means, 1963, pp. 213–39).

Means is the principal formulator of 'the theory of administered pricing'. Following is one of his more illuminating presentations of this idea:

> An administered price has been defined as a price which is set, usually by a seller, and held constant for a period of time and a series of transactions. Such a price does not imply the existence of monopoly or of collusion. However, it can occur only where a particular market is dominated by one or relatively few sellers (or buyers). It is the normal method of selling in most markets today. Its significance ... rests, first on the fact that it lies entirely outside traditional economic theory and, second, that where the area of discretion in price administration is large, administered prices produce economic results and problems of economic policy quite different from those dealt with by traditional theory. (Means, 1959, p. 4)

The theory of administered pricing was the basis for some partially successful federal policies (Means, 1975a, pp. 14–22). Also it has been the object of considerable professional controversy (Stigler, 1963; Adams and Lanzillotti, 1963; Blair, 1972; Kahn, 1975; Samuels and Medema, 1990), yet its credibility has survived (Kefauver, 1965). Price administration *is* accomplished in large corporations through the technique of target pricing, among other techniques. As perceived by Means (1975a) and John Blair (1975, pp. 33–67), price determination is customarily accomplished by the calculation of a 'target rate of return on capital'. What is sought is the highest rate of return on capital 'consistent with a healthy growth of the business'. Calculations of such target rates require decisions on the level of operation, estimates of the costs of production at various operating levels, determination of prices which will yield the desired target rates and, given costs and operating rates, the setting of discretionary prices in view of actual market conditions (Means, 1963, pp. 220–1). Recourse to this pricing technique was earlier confirmed in the Brookings study on *Pricing in Big Business* (Kaplan *et al.*, 1958) and later by John Blair (1976).

Finally, it is interesting to note that, although Means did not make explicit use of social-value theory, he does recognize that judgements of appropriateness or propriety must be made concerning prices administratively set. In this particular context, he argues that target rate prices which yield returns on capital no greater than 'the competitive cost of capital' may be considered as consistent with the public interest. A rough approximation of such a rate is that allowed public utilities by effective regulatory commissions (Means, 1963, p. 222). Any 'form of regulation should ... bring about the same type of economic behavior that would prevail if the industry were competitive' (Means, 1975a, p. 66). In this latter deference to the normative use of the competitive model, Means's break with orthodoxy is clearly incomplete.

Means, however, did not believe that market forces would provide a sufficient constraint on the power to administer prices. Although his specific policy recommendations shifted over the years as the problems to which he addressed himself changed, he consistently advocated public government supervision sufficient to ensure that the public interest was served. He argued, for example, that: 'inflation in the concentrated industries can be restrained only by the imposition of direct price and wage controls', and that 'restraints should be imposed on sudden and substantial increases in the target rate of return' (Means, 1975a, p. 66).

In sum, Means repeatedly demonstrated, to his own satisfaction if not that of his neoclassical critics, the continuing fact and practice of administered pricing in American industry. He posed, but did not adequately answer, the question of how to decide when judgements reflected in private price determination are in the public interest.

John Kenneth Galbraith

Perhaps no American economist in this century has been confronted with a more dramatic or significant test of applying institutional analysis to an area of critical public policy than was John Kenneth Galbraith upon his appointment, in 1941, as head of what later would be called the Office of Price Administration (OPA). This 'Price Czar Novitiate' (Galbraith, 1981, pp. 124–44) had the task of introducing and managing a comprehensive programme of price control and rationing for the wartime American economy. As preparation for that task, a long tradition of market-deferential, neoclassical analysis was, in his view, largely irrelevant. Orthodox economists thought it was unwise for him to undertake such a responsibility and impossible for him to achieve the goal sought (Galbraith 1980 [1952], pp. 2–7). In an important, if small and unfortunately neglected, book reflecting on this experience, *A Theory of Price Control* (1980 [1952]), Galbraith explains how his understanding of actual corporate pricing behaviour was comprehensively expanded and empirically reconfirmed by his experience as head of the OPA. In brief, he could generate his own tautology and assert that 'it is relatively easy to fix prices that are already fixed' (ibid., p. iv).

Here he distinguished between markets that were imperfectly or monopolistically competitive (oligopolies) and those that still resembled price competitive markets. This becomes a distinction between the 'planning' sector and the 'market' sector in his later work (see Galbraith, 1973). Imperfect markets could be controlled directly and with greater ease than was anticipated. Price competitive markets could be controlled but with more difficulty and only if rationing was also employed.

In imperfect markets, OPA-administered price control was easier because a comparatively smaller number of firms were involved, enforcement was facilitated, prices were already relatively inflexible and had become institutionalized (Galbraith, 1980 [1952], pp. 10–19). Supply-price conditions were also relatively stable at the time. Given unused capacity, production, except for agriculture and extractive industries, generally was expanded for war purposes without increasing fixed costs, and thus without creating major pressures for increasing prices. In a few instances, subsidies were used to 'offset higher "marginal" costs in increasing-cost industries' (ibid., pp. 20–5).

But even in efforts to control prices at the retail level, Galbraith came to realize that customary and conventional pricing was the rule. The price charged for the product or service is strictly a conventional mark-up. Profit *maximization* is not an operational option. The small seller 'has neither the information nor the capacity to adjust his margins commodity by commodity, week by week, or season by season, in such manner as might maximize his returns'. He relies on rule-of-thumb. 'The effect of a well-designed system of price control in markets of this kind is merely to continue accepted rules' (ibid., p. 18). In sum, price control in imperfect markets is comparatively easy and can be quite successful; price control in price competitive markets – markets where market shares are small and pricing power is more limited than in oligopolistic firms – can also succeed but is more difficult. What is confirmed for our purposes, however, is the pervasiveness of administered pricing in the so-called private sector, and the fact that comprehensive public control of privately administered prices, in this instance at least, was demonstrated to be both feasible and successful.[3]

For Galbraith, the 'technostructure becomes the commanding power' in the modern giant corporation. As organized management, it is the locus of discretion over pricing decisions and much else that effects the character and continuity of the large corporation. Its decisions are collegial, but authoritarian (Galbraith, 1973, pp. 83–6). The technostructure consists of the technical specialists who exercise *de facto* power and are placed hierarchically just below the *pro forma* executives and directors of the organization. These specialists generate and pool the specialized and technical knowledge that is required to fashion the productive process, and generate and update technological innovations and product improvements. 'For the exercise of this power – for product planning, to devise price and market strategies, for sales and advertising management, procurement planning, public relations and governmental relations – specialists are also needed' (ibid., p. 82). Governance of a megacorp is necessarily conjoint; members of the technostructure respectively contribute their expertise and insights in reaching judgements. 'Collective intelligence' guides managerial decision making; the positions of hierarchical 'heads' – president, chairman, director – are often status-conferring, anachronistic relics of an older order from which power is eroding. But members of the board can, if they are aggressive, sometimes influence the power of the technostructure and the direction in which it moves by eliciting sufficient support to change leadership officers (for example, the chief executive officer), 'directing the decision-making process into new areas', and/or by calling in outside experts to appraise the performance of the directive cadre (ibid., p. 89).

The purposive goals which drive the technostructure – the uses to which its *de facto* power are put – are twofold: to protect 'the autonomy of its decision-making primarily by seeking to secure a minimum level of earnings' and to reward 'itself affirmatively with growth' of the firm. Incident to these quests, technological innovation and *increasing* earnings may also be pursued. Profits will be sought; they are not typically maximized, orthodoxy notwithstanding (ibid., p. 107).

If these 'protective and affirmative purposes of the technostructure' are to be realized, prices must be set and must remain under the tightest possible control.[4] Productive technology is specialized, complex, time-consuming to create and expensive. Corporate planning of price setting must be such as to ensure that the necessary materials and equipment can be acquired. Prices must be firmly under discretionary control so that they can be revised, as necessary, to cover costs not wholly under control of the technostructure – as with the wage bill. Increased wages can be (and are) readily covered with increased prices. Prices must be firmly controlled to permit management and manipulation of demand.

Discretionary agents in megacorps must control prices to maintain their position *vis-à-vis* other firms. They must participate in a communal effort to preclude unplanned or pre-emptive price cutting. 'Oligopolistic cooperation'[5] with others is required to *avoid* losing control over their own enterprise. They must maintain a necessary level of earnings through adequate sales promotion. Prices must be set low enough to ensure adequate expanding sales. They must accommodate to existing price elasticities. Otherwise growth and its benefits for the technostructure cannot be realized. Roughly uniform prices will be commonplace in an industry. If there is a dominant firm, the technostructure of that firm will serve as price leader and its affirmative purposes and protective patterns will serve as the model for the industry. Given the complexity and interdependencies of the pricing patterns set, the intent is to leave most prices unchanged for an extended period of time. Each participant gains predictability and is able to sustain control more adequately.

In sum, Galbraith reconfirms the pervasiveness of discretionary pricing in the industrial sector, identifies the dominant price setting group or cadre, and explains the protective and affirmative criteria which guide their pricing choices.

Alfred S. Eichner

Although Alfred Eichner generally described himself as a Post Keynesian, there is a great deal of commonality between his critique of neoclassical orthodoxy and his recommended alternative approach, and that of institutionalists. Indeed, he sought to bring the two approaches into closer analytical congruity with his edited volume on *Why Economics is not yet a Science* (1983). He considers the neoclassical tradition, and especially its price theory, 'intellectually bankrupt'; its claims to generality and scientific status are without foundation. Because of its vacuousness, it is an unreliable guide to policy-making (Eichner, 1983, pp. 205–6). In these judgements, institutionalists concur.

Eichner sets the familiar institutional context: 'commodity markets have been largely superseded by industrial markets and the family business by the megacorp as the representative firm within those markets' (Eichner, 1987, p. 1555). Megacorps, by 'virtue of their size and dominant market position, have considerable discretion in setting prices'. These firms, 'with their administered pricing policies for financing growth and expansion, have become the locus of decision-making within the decentralized system of private planning that operates within the U.S. economy'.[6]

It is Eichner's central purpose to explain 'how prices are determined in the oligopolistic sector of the American economy, and how those prices, so determined, affect the growth and stability of the economy as a whole' (Eichner, 1976, p. 1). He seeks to provide a new micro foundation for Keynesian macroeconomic theory. The explanation offered may be characterized as a dynamic, extended cost-plus model in which the 'plus', as it varies over time and among industries, is also explained (ibid., pp. 4–5).

Two attributes in particular distinguish this pricing model from orthodox approaches. First, 'it is predicated upon realistic assumptions'. Secondly, it yields determinate solutions; empirically demonstrable accounts of pricing can be derived.

The realistic assumptions are rooted in institutionalist contributions: megacorps are characterized by a separation of ownership and managerial control. 'Production occurs within multiple plants or plant segments' in which the factor coefficients are fixed by both 'technological and institutional constraints'. 'The firm's output is sold under conditions of recognized interdependence'; oligopolistic co-operation prevails (ibid., p. 3). Indeed, Eichner's 'operational definition of an industry' is 'that group of firms which share a day-to-day interest in the same set of price quotations for a class of goods they are each capable of producing' (ibid., p. 10).

The deterministic solutions, as explanations, become evident 'only from the long-run perspective of the industry as a whole, with one megacorp, the price leader, acting as a surrogate for all members of that industry'. The long run view does not explain the 'absolute price level but rather the change in that price level from one period to the next ... the marginal adjustment'. The megacorp price leader 'will vary the industry price so as to cover (1) any change in per unit average variable and fixed costs, and (2) any increased need for internally generated funds' (ibid., p. 4). What is demonstrated is that the pricing decision for a price-leader megacorp 'is ultimately linked to the investment decision. ... prices are likely to be set so as to assure the internally generated funds necessary to finance a firm's desired rate of capital expansion'. The substantial convergence of this view with the 'target return' arguments of Means and Blair above are now apparent.

Eichner (1987, p. 1582) summarizes his discretionary pricing theory as follows:

Thus, once the institutional context in which firms find themselves has been correctly identified, it is possible to explain the price observed in any industry ... according to the change in cost ... or the change in markup ... from the preceding time period. The prices actually observed are therefore the outcome of a historical process, with the change in cost ... reflecting the changing input–output relationships that define the reigning technology, and the change in mark-up ... reflecting the need for investment funds relative to the pricing power of firms.

To pursue his more inclusive goals of inquiry, Eichner extends his analysis to a corollary microeconomic consideration of factor pricing, in the course of which he finds the neoclassical marginal productivity theory to be largely irrelevant. His own reformulation, in addressing the cost structure confronting megacorps, draws on the institutionalist literature on economic power, the sociologist focus on social norms, the Marxian interest in surplus value and the Keynesian stress on aggregate demand factors (Eichner, 1976, pp. 5–6). Beyond observing that factor prices are also largely administered, we need not, for present purposes, follow Eichner on this conceptual path.

In addition, Eichner explores the significance of his altered microeconomic theory for macroeconomic analysis. Here, given the megacorp's concern with price setting and investment to assure growth, and consequent concern with aggregate demand, Eichner's analysis 'lends theoretical support to the accelerator model of investment', and to the recognition of the significance for the economy generally of the megacorps investment spending from retained earnings. The megacorps play a central role in determining the secular growth rate for the economy (ibid., pp. 7–8). Economic power, reflected in discretionary pricing, matters.

Finally, in exploring policy implications, Eichner must address, as do other scholars, the character and consequences of price judgements made by megacorps. He concludes that 'effective social control over the individual megacorp can be achieved by no more and no less than regulating both the rate of growth, and the composition of aggregate investment'. The economic welfare of both individuals and the economy generally cannot otherwise be served. His major recommendation then is 'that a system of national indicative planning be established' (ibid., p. 9).

Arthur M. Okun

I have found nothing to suggest that Arthur Okun ever characterized himself as an institutionalist. Yet he, like institutionalists, was a theorist and a realist. I construe his analysis of pricing, with minor exceptions, to be both compatible with, and an extension of, earlier institutionalist contributions to a theory of discretionary pricing. More specifically, his work may be viewed as a plausible explanation of the conventional and customary mark-up pricing Galbraith found in administering comprehensive price controls in non-oligopolistic markets during the days of OPA.

Okun appears to have been committed to the premiss that theory ought actually to explain what it purports to explain. For him, mainstream orthodoxy has long since ceased to offer an adequate explanation of the pricing process; it does not provide the *general* theory of market behaviour.

As noted in section 1 above, Okun distinguishes between the realm of price *makers* and that of price *takers* in the modern economy. The portion of the economy exhibiting price takers in 'auction markets' is

> a small and shrinking sector of the U.S. economy. ... Most of our economy is dominated by cost-oriented prices and equity-oriented wages. Most prices are set by sellers whose principal concern is to maintain customers and market share over the long run. ... Prices are set to exceed costs by a percentage markup that displays only minor variations over the business cycle.   (Okun, 1979, pp. 1–5).

The realm of price makers, then, is not confined to oligopolistic sellers only. It includes most of the economy except for 'active auction markets' reported on the financial pages of the daily newspaper: financial assets, agricultural commodities, some primary metals and the like (Okun, 1981, p. 134).

In a fairly elaborate analysis of the complexities price makers must face in determining the mark-ups to be reflected in selling prices, Okun demonstrates, as earlier institutionalists have shown, that actual markets are institutionally complex. Of particular importance for Okun are the conventions and expectations that develop between sellers and buyers. Sellers offer stable prices, continuing services, access to credit, refund prerogatives, advanced sales notices and the like to secure customer loyalty and repeat purchases (ibid., pp. 138–48). Such 'implicit contract' arrangements 'economize on a variety of information and transaction costs' (ibid., p. 154). Predictability, dependability and fulfilment of expectations through such correlated patterns give the firm some measure of control over its own demand, and insulation from the competitive rivalry of other firms. Decisions on the size and frequency of price changes, then, are of critical significance. Alienating or disruptive changes in the continuity of expectations regarding prices is to be avoided. Firms regularly engage in price fixing as a routine effort to maintain their market shares. Their achieved market power is reflected in the degree to which their desires in that quest can be implemented.

Discretionary managers, in Okun's view, are more influenced in their pricing decisions by supply-side costs than by changes in demand:

> The setting of prices by marking up costs is a good first approximation to actually observed behavior in most areas of industry, trade, and transportation. Firms not only behave that way, but also condition their customers to expect them to behave

that way. ... Price increases that are based on cost increases are 'fair', while those based on demand increases often are viewed as unfair. (Okun, 1981, p. 153)

A significant hazard, however, in using 'cost-oriented pricing' as a standard in setting prices is that customers do not, and cannot, observe the price setting deliberation process. They must take on faith any contention that price increases were caused or validated by cost increases.

The conceptual dilemma facing the price setters is itself quite complex. The definition and measurement of costs that are to become part of the bases for price determinations require price setters to take account of such standards or constructs as historical costs, replacement costs, valuation adjustments, standard volume unit costs, full or direct costs, and material costs (Okun, 1981, pp. 154–64). Even so, 'the empirical evidence for the United States suggests that cost-oriented pricing is the dominant mode of behavior' (ibid., p. 165).

Okun has one main reservation concerning the Means-Blair theory of administered pricing: his own model

> allows for various causal factors to determine the pricing behavior of an industry, while the administered-prices view focuses on the single explanation of industrial concentration. ... Markup rigidity seems to me simply too pervasive across the U.S. economy to be attributable to oligopoly. ... The aggregate evidence on pricing in private nonfarm business accords closely with the mark-up model. (Okun, 1981, pp. 175–6)

Okun's pricing theory, concerning customer–seller attachments, expectations and conventions, does appear to account for this limitation in the Means-Blair position. Recall, in addition, that Okun reconfirms Galbraith's earlier characterization that smaller, private non-farm businesses employ mark-up pricing practices and reflect price rigidity. Discretionary price determination is not confined to oligopolies.

Finally, though only passing reference is made, Okun does regard his 'customer-market' view of inflexible prices as implying an approvable and acceptable market structure. It is 'an inherently desirable institutional arrangement' because it 'economizes on the expenses of shopping, trying out products, and otherwise engaging in transactions'. There are significant 'benefits of customer attachments' (ibid., p. 178). Accordingly, these pricing conventions serve what are, for Okun, economically defensible purposes; they are normatively approvable.

4.   CONCLUSION

While no elaborate summary is provided, the following generalities summarizing institutionalist, and quasi-institutionalist, contributions to a theory of discretionary pricing may be noted:

- Exchange occurring in non-auction markets is not simplistic and reducible to maximizing tenets and singular behavioural constants. It is accomplished by a complex, and widely divergent, pattern of institutional arrangements that facilitate the making of pricing judgements. In all economies, these arrangements continue to evolve as new problems and their consequences are identified and new pricing judgements and structures are instituted to resolve them.
- To these institutionalists, the mainstream neoclassical theory of pricing does not explain the overwhelmingly dominant phenomenon of discretionary pricing in advanced industrial economies. In their view, the explanatory capabilities and policy relevance of that approach continues to erode as empirical inquiry and theoretical critiques undermine its claim to significance.
- At the level both of oligopolistic megacorps and of smaller non-auction market sellers, prices are determined as deliberate decisions by price setters to serve a variety of individual and firm goals. The presumption that a Walrasian-like price mechanism – structure-free, atomistic auction-house – is the vehicle through which prices are determined becomes even more conjectural, in their view.
- Such discretionary pricing typically reflects the use of one or another variant of mark-up, cost-plus, target or similar pricing rule. Actual pricing rules as conventions are set; pricing judgements are made; markets are institutionally ordered; and market behaviour is correlated.
- Price-making decision bodies vary with industry structures, custom and conventions, and extant power bodies. The technostructure – an information, organization and/or technology-dominating managerial élite – appears to be a typical locus of price-making power in megacorps. But only extensive inquiry will disclose the particular loci of power the pricing rules and structures employed and the character of pricing judgements made.
- All contributors acknowledge, but do not extensively address, the fact and need for external standards or criteria with which to judge the propriety of pricing decisions made. Such standards reflect conditioned views of what is a fair, proper, right or just price. Public appraisals of private pricing decisions, of course, have long been a common practice. But there is no agreement among these contributors on what standards or

criteria should be used for such appraisals or what social-value theory to employ in quest for such standards. An agenda for further inquiry is suggested.

NOTES

1. The author wishes to thank Paul Dale Bush, Harry Trebing and John Henry for instructive suggestions on an earlier draft of this paper. The comments of the editors of this volume were also most helpful in preparing the final version.
2. These contributions are presented as illustrative and indicative of what I characterize as institutionalist, or institutionalist-compatible views, not as a definitive treatment of the subject field. The latter would require, in addition, consideration of contributions of Post Keynesian theories of the firm and of macro analysis, and other heterodox theories.
3. The foregoing does not address Galbraith's views concerning the loci of price-setting power in imperfect markets as such, nor explain how, among oligopolies, prices are determined, nor consider criteria in terms of which pricing judgements are made.
4. I draw heavily on Galbraith (1973, pp. 112–21) in this and the following paragraph.
5. See also Munkirs and Sturgeon (1985).
6. Eichner here cites Munkirs (1985), who presents a general theory of 'Centralized Private Sector Planning'.

3. The Nature of the Market: a Structural Analysis

Frederick C. v. N. Fourie[1]

1. INTRODUCTION

Although the market is at the core of conventional economic analysis, the question 'what is the market?' has hardly been satisfactorily answered. At most, the question has received indirect or implicit treatment, primarily in discussions of the nature of competition, most often atomistic or perfect competition between individualistic agents.

Notable efforts to rectify this oversight are the contributions by Scott Moss (1981, 1984), Geoff Hodgson (1988) and Malcolm Sawyer (1991). Moss (1984, p. 80) provides a theory of the structuring of the interior of the market, with particular attention to the institutions that fulfil the role of intermediaries 'inside' markets. In this way the configuration of markets becomes endogenous, unlike in conventional theory (p. 108).

Sawyer (1991) points out that the conventional theoretical conceptualization of the market appears to be similar to that of the firm; that is, that of a mental construct not intended to correspond to real world markets, but rather, to help generate predictions (or explanations). Moreover, there is the uncertainty as to what is meant by market in the real world, in addition to what is denoted by market in theory and the correspondence between the two.

Hodgson (1988, esp. chs 7–8) offers building blocks for an institutional analysis of the market by defining it, and the reasons for its existence, in relation to a wide set of social institutions, such as legal institutions, customs and practices of exchange, property rights, transportation and communications institutions, and so forth. A central element is the economic activity of exchange.

2. THE MARKET, EXCHANGE AND INSTITUTIONS

This chapter is concerned with the following question: What is the distinctive or *typical nature* of the market as societal phenomenon? What is market and what non-market? For example, the market has something to do with exchange, but not all exchanges are market exchanges. And is the market a real thing, or merely a 'behavioural relation', an abstraction, or just a figure of speech?[2]

Methodologically the idea of uncovering a typical or intrinsic nature of the market is based on the following reasoning. Actual markets can and do occur in a variety of forms: different types of markets, in different contexts and configurations, in different places and economic systems, and in different historical periods. Yet all these varieties of market are observable, recognizable and identifiable *as markets*. This suggests that they must have something in common. To ascertain that common element of markets is the objective of this contribution.

While the implications of identifying this common element will be discussed below, it has to be said that the idea of such a common nature must not be understood in the sense of an ideal type towards which all existing forms must strive, or against which they must be measured.[3] Its significance is that, as a common element in all markets, it may be the clue to something intrinsic or generic.

The implicit theoretical point of departure is the existence and nature of a differentiated society: a society where identifiable, and identifiably different, kinds of communal structures are intuitively observable – where the term communal is used to include all kinds of organizations or institutions or collectivities or societal units.[4] In a modern differentiated society these normally include families, churches, the state, schools, universities, business organizations, trade unions and a variety of other voluntary associations. It is due to this conception of 'structural pluralism' that the analysis presented here can be called a structural approach. In this analysis a key concept, directly linked to the idea of a typical nature, is that of a 'structural identity principle' (SIP).

This structuralist point of view implies a rejection of an individualist conception of society, in which society is regarded as merely a multitude of individuals-in-interaction, normally in a contractual fashion, with organizations or communal structures being no more than a combination of such individuals.[5]

Given these points of departure, the crux of the argument is that the market as societal phenomenon cannot be understood without acknowledging and explicating two essential features:

(a) that the market, and the exchange relations concerned, are typically economic relations (amidst having other, non-economic dimensions as well);

(b) that the market is inextricably interwoven with various societal organizations and communal structures (firms, families, the state, schools, churches, clubs and so forth).

2.1 The Structural Identity Principle of an Economic Exchange

That markets and related exchanges are economic phenomena may appear to be obvious. However, what actually makes an exchange identifiably an *economic* exchange? What determines its *character specificity*?

Hodgson (1988, pp. 148–9) tries to pin down a sensible, circumscribed understanding of the term 'exchange'. He positions himself against an excessively wide, 'meaning undermining' conception of exchange that also includes a bee depositing pollen 'in return for' gathering nectar, or production as an 'exchange with nature'. He identifies the transfer of property rights as an important qualification and method to narrow down the concept. This is helpful, but I do not think sufficient. While most economic transactions may involve a transfer of ownership titles, an exchange of gifts also involves a transfer of property rights. In addition, many market transactions only involve a transfer of the right to access to, or to the use of, a commodity or service (although this is perhaps conceivable as a 'property right to use').[6]

An important characteristic element of economic exchange is the idea of *quid pro quo* – 'something for something'. While in some societies the giving of gifts may imply a converse social obligation on the recipient, it is not an essential element of the general phenomenon of gifts. On the other hand, in economic exchange or interchange the presence of a mutual understanding of reciprocity is essential, a necessary condition.

Secondly, the obligation is for a counter-offering at an *agreed-upon exchange ratio* or price. Prior agreement on, and making the terms of the *quid pro quo* explicit, is something absent from, for example, an exchange of gifts.

But this is not the whole story. An essential element of what makes an exchange an economic exchange must simply be that its *qualification* is economic. Although an economic exchange always has many other dimensions (social, historical, symbolic, ethical, legal), the economic aspect can be seen to be the dominant, qualifying or leading aspect, impressing its indelible stamp on the way the other aspects are realized or actualized.[7] This is what makes the parties to an economic exchange *buyer* and *seller*.

One can distinguish a variety of aspects of exchanges or markets, such as numerical (number of buyers or sellers); spatial (geographical space; product space; market share); physical (the idea of market equilibrium; dynamism); biotic (market growth; product development and differentiation; competition as a process); psychical (market sensitivity; elasticity); historical (process of market formation; market power and control); symbolic (prices; product image); social (economic intercourse; fashionable products); juridical (exchange contracts; justice in exchange; a justified or legitimated price) and ethical (honesty; trust; fairness). In each case the actual form and functioning of an aspect is decisively 'coloured' by the dominant economic aspect: the concept of 'product space' clearly is an economically qualified spatial concept; the concept of 'economic intercourse' is obtained by economically qualifying the idea of social intercourse, and so forth.

The character specificity or *structural identity principle* (SIP) of an economic exchange relation can be formulated as follows:

> An economic exchange is an economically qualified purposeful interchange of commodities on the basis of a *quid pro quo* obligation at a mutually agreed upon exchange ratio.

The term 'commodity' here is understood comprehensively, so as to include services and the utilization of commodities and, of course, money. In most cases an exchange of property rights will be involved.[8]

The idea captured in this SIP appears to be central to, and decisive for, the distinctiveness of the phenomenon of economic exchange in all its appearances and forms (and therefore eventually also of the market). On the other hand, it has no pretensions to be a complete description, for that would involve other, secondary (including non-economic) aspects, and in practice would depend decisively on historical and institutional context (the distinction between a structural identity principle and a definition of the market is discussed in section 2.6 below). *The idea is to capture the kernel or nucleus of the distinctiveness of economic exchange in contrast to otherwise qualified exchanges or interaction.*

There is a particular contrapositioning of interests (or the way interests are served) in an economic exchange. Typically exchange implies the voluntary participation of two parties that do not act within the context of one communal structure with a common purpose. Rather, they act with more or less independent, even incongruous considerations in mind, and often with diverse or contrary interests. Also, the determination of the exchange ratio or price affects the interests of the parties diametrically, in that a higher price favours the seller at the expense of the buyer.

On the other hand, this diametry typically does not constitute an absolute divergence or antagonism. The two parties to an exchange are, for the moment, dependent on one another; therefore the contrapositioning can be described as 'mutualistic' (cf. section 2.3 below). Moreover, despite the intrinsic elements of contrariety, mutual benefit from a voluntary exchange is of course not precluded.

However, the idea that the rate of exchange is *agreed upon* should not be regarded as implying that all exchanges therefore are 'good' or fair, or that the contrapositive, diverse interests of all are served equitably. Although there is equivalence between the price of a commodity and the money paid for it by a buyer, in many exchanges a buyer or seller may have strong reservations about the real economic value of the commodity he or she is buying or selling. Nevertheless, if an actual exchange takes place it does mean that buyer and seller have agreed to some 'exchange value' or price, and that both have decided to engage in this transaction.

In a monetary economy price acts as a symbolic expression of the 'consensus' exchange ratio implied by a completed economic exchange. A price can exist if, and only if, there is an agreed-upon exchange ratio. Therefore the phenomenon of price is peculiar to economic exchange: it captures and symbolizes the specifics of the *quid pro quo*. (Other functions of prices are discussed in section 2.5).

2.2   The Institutional Context of Exchange - 'In the Beginning There Were Markets'?

The market has to be seen in its institutional context, that is, in relation to the entire spectrum of societal organizations and communal structures, notably firms, households and the state. This institutional context appears in various ways.

First, why do exchanges take place? In general, needs and desires cannot be understood outside the context of the societal structures in which individuals are involved. Needs necessarily are socially contextualized and institutionally embedded. An individual buyer typically does not act as an isolated person, but within the context of a societal structure.

Secondly, exchange is an *inter*relation, a relation *between* two parties. Therefore commodity exchange relations cannot occur without being linked to firms, households and so on. Thus the market is not an isolated phenomenon. Furthermore, markets cannot themselves produce commodities (Fourie, 1989a). Markets presuppose the existence of firms (or other organizations) producing the commodities that merely are transferred and allocated by market transactions.

Therefore exchange relations comprise interrelations that link firms, households and other institutions *externally*. In a differentiated society, exchange relations typically cannot occur without finding their counterpart in communal structures like firms and households. Exchange relations, being inter-individual or inter-organizational in character, cannot be correctly conceived of without explicit acknowledgement of the nodal interlacement between interrelations and societal structures like firms and households (with their own internal relations and authority structure). Likewise there is an unbreakable correlation and interlacement between the internal relational structure of the firm/household and the external interrelations in which it is involved.[9]

That there is an unbreakable correlation and coherence between communal structures and interrelations, and that neither of these two kinds of societal forms can be conceived of without the other, appears to be a general structural principle. However, despite and amidst this structural interwovenness, each relation or structure retains its own identity. Despite the efforts of some contractarians (for example, Alchian and Demsetz, 1972; Jensen and Meckling, 1976) to depict firms as fictitious abstractions, as nothing but clusters of inter-individual market-like contractual relations, firms and markets remain distinguishable – although not separable (Fourie, 1989a). Neither can be reduced to the other; in addition neither becomes a part of the other. The interwovenness is external and 'character-preserving'.

Being *inter*relations, exchange relations are very different from the relations within organizations or communal structures – for example, the internal relations between managers and workers in a firm. Interrelations have the characteristic that the linking of individuals and/or firms does not unite them in any way. Whereas one finds a certain coherence, a certain inner unity of will and purpose within organizations like firms, interrelations merely constitute an external, non-integrating contact (exchange, agreement) in order to reach typically different and often diverse goals.[10] Although the parties in inter-party relations are in a sense dependent on one another, their actions can interlock in several ways, in co-operation or in antagonism. But never does the interaction as such bind them together in a relatively solidary internal unit. The structure of these relationships typically is not confined within an organization or communal structure.

This difference in intrinsic nature also is apparent from the fact that an exchange intrinsically is a momentary phenomenon, while organizations or communal structures like firms typically display a significant degree of durability and an existence independent of the turnover of managers or employees.

This structuralist-institutionalist approach contrasts strikingly with much conventional economic analysis. For example, Hodgson (1988, p. 148) points out that for Ludwig von Mises (1949) exchange becomes a broad and universal category, also covering Robinson Crusoe in exchanges 'with nature'. This clearly is untenable. Exchange is a bilateral concept, whereas in 'autistic exchange' there can be no mutual understanding of *quid pro quo*.[11]

This is but part of the problem of an entirely non-institutional and individualistic conceptualization of individual behaviour – found, *inter alia*, in the so-called 'new institutional economics' – where the denial of the existence of communal structures and institutions repeatedly leads the analysis into inconsistencies and problems.

For instance, Oliver Williamson's (1975, p. 20) assertion that 'in the beginning there were markets' is invalid – logically as well as historically. Apart from the fact that one can argue that markets can only exist if there are products to trade – that is, if firms already exist (Sawyer, 1991; Auerbach, 1988, p. 121) – the presumed relation between markets and firms is contrary to the historical development process (see Fourie, 1989a).[12] But the real point is that it is futile to engage in this kind of chicken-and-egg argument. The existence and development of firms and markets are unbreakably correlated.

An important disclaimer is necessary. While much of the argumentation here is set up in opposition to individualistic approaches, the intention is not to replace an 'individuals-only' approach with a 'structures-or-institutions-only' approach. A very important principle of the 'structural' analysis presented here is that individual persons always are involved, but never individualistically or discretely; rather, always in a context of simultaneous interwovenness with a variety of communal structures of which individuals are part. A structures-only approach would be equally fallible and unsustainable. Going from one polar extreme to the other is not a solution.

2.3   From Exchange to Market Relations: the Structural Identity Principle of the Market

The exchange relation, interwoven as it is with communal structures like firms and households, is not the only interrelation that constitutes a market. Market relations typically entail much more than exchange. While exchange *is* central, the market appears to be a layered and structured set of relationships, only some of which are exchange relationships. Although the degree of complexity will depend on the degree of development of the market, some basic distinctions can be made.[13]

Non-exchange relationships come into existence when multiple sellers or multiple buyers are present, explicitly or implicitly. These are (a) the relation between different sellers of a product; and (b) the relation between different buyers of a product. Following standard terminology, these two types of interrelations can be viewed as horizontal relations, in contrast to the exchange relation as a vertical relation (being between successive steps in the economic production and distribution process).

Although the horizontal relations in the market also are interrelations, and also economically qualified, they differ intrinsically from the exchange relationship – first of all because *quid pro quo* is critically absent. More specifically, the nature of selling is *mutually exclusionary or substitutive*: selling by one agent excludes another from that particular act of selling. In contrast to *quid pro quo*, the substitutive between-seller relationship can be indicated by the Latin phrase *alterius loco*: 'one in the place of the other'.[14]

Fundamentally this is another way of saying that between-seller relations inherently are competitive or rivalrous: the contrapositioning of interests is mutually exclusionary and adversarial (in contrast with the 'mutualistic' contrapositioning between a buyer and a seller – in an economic exchange relation each party is dependent upon the other). This does not exclude the formation of co-operative or collusive agreements between sellers – such agreements indeed presuppose the prior existence of a rivalrous relation.

The same analysis applies to between-buyer relations, since buying also is mutually exclusionary – although in practice inter-buyer relations often are less competitive or interactive.[15]

Diagrammatically one can depict the set of interrelations as in Figure 3.1. The market relations are illustrated together with the correlated internal relational structure of the involved firms.

Figure 3.1: The basic relational structure of the market

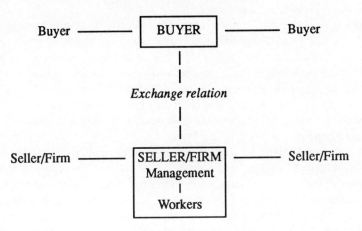

The important points are twofold: (a) exchange is at the core of the market, but (b) the market is more than exchange, and indeed is a layered *cluster* of both exchange (*quid pro quo*) and rivalry (*alterius loco*) relations. The market is not one relation, nor an entity in the sense of being an organization or communal structure like the firm. It is not an identifiable unit or societal whole. It is a collection of interrelations linking individuals and communal structures, but always in a non-collective, non-communal, independent sense.[16]

The vertical and horizontal relations are perforce linked and correlated. The emergence or existence of an exchange relation necessarily implies the existence of correlated horizontal between-seller and between-buyer relations. Since the economic exchange relation is at the core of the market phenomenon, it is foundational to the other relations in the market. Its relationship to the two horizontal relations can therefore be described as a foundational interwovenness.

One can thus formulate the structural identity principle (SIP) of the market as follows:

> The market is a structured and interwoven cluster of economically qualified exchange and rivalry relations foundationally interwoven with, and centred around, the economic exchange relations, all externally (or nodally) interwoven with firms and other communal structures.

Above it was noted that exchanges intrinsically have only a momentary existence. Despite this, it appears that markets do tend to exhibit a relative continuity and significant elements of stability and cohesion. What explains this, and why is there no disintegration into discrete exchanges? That is, why do markets actually exist and endure?

Interwovenness provides the clue. The relative structural stability of a modern differentiated economy is founded not in the nature of the interpersonal or market relations themselves, but in the interwovenness with the organized institutions and natural communities. The intrinsic durability of, first of all, families and households, and then also of firms themselves, provides the stability and relative continuity of markets. Since these institutions do not exist in isolation, but in linkage with external relations, they impute a certain 'durability' to markets.

In addition there has been a tremendous increase and differentiation in the individual person's needs, and thereby in his reliance on others. The mere increase in the *number* of buyers and sellers in modern society also provides a foundation for continuity. Furthermore, non-economic bonds may also provide integrating forces. Nevertheless, any market continuity is very different from the integrated durability and unity found in a communal structure like a firm.[17]

This also reflects on the question as to the reasons for the existence of markets, specifically in the sense of an interrelational complex with some continuity. Compared to fragmented or isolated exchanges, markets provide a basis for the reduction of transactions costs: 'All the reasons that are cited by Coase to explain why market arrangements are more costly than the firm, serve perfectly well as reasons why the market is less costly than atomized exchange' (Hodgson, 1988, p. 181). Consequently, markets often are constituted so as to economize on transaction costs (often via specialized intermediaries, as highlighted by Moss). Such reductions in transactions costs depend critically on the horizontal relations in markets, and therefore on the degree of market extension.

Note that it is precisely because of the economic qualification of market relations – the dominance of the economic aspect – that costs are so decisive in the way actual markets are constituted. The same is true of the positive form in which a firm is constituted – in contrast to, for instance, a family, where economic considerations appear to be non-dominant (although present).

Lastly, a notable characteristic is that actual, existing markets, like firms, are a product of human activity. Markets are not natural phenomena: 'If markets too are social institutions which have evolved through time then the naturalistic or ethereal view of the market is flawed' (Hodgson, 1988, p. 178). Market relations generally form part of, or depend on, the historical formative and organizational activities of people, including the organization of firms. It is part of the historical actualization of societal relations and structures. In this sense the market can be said to have a *historical foundation*.

2.4   The Structural Complexity of Developed Markets

The phenomenon that relations in a market are differentiated, interwoven and layered is inescapably implied by the idea of a differentiated society, and vice versa. The differentiation of the market into a complex bundle of relations implies and presupposes the existence of corresponding and corre-lated organizations (communal structures).[18] Similarly, the existence of a differentiated variety of producing, distributing and buying institutions nec-essarily implies the existence of a complex set of market interrelations.[19]

From the formulation of the structural-identity principle two additional things are apparent. First, the dichotomy between free markets and con-straining institutions must be rejected, as Hodgson (1988, p. 178) has ar-gued. Markets typically do not and cannot exist without being interwoven – often in rather complex ways – with institutions, organizations and other communal structures, many of which are of an intrinsically non-economic nature. This also explains why the market has ineradicable social and "collectivist" aspects' (ibid., p. 178).

This does not imply any normative judgement on the form of such in-volvement in real market relations; merely, that it is not useful – perhaps especially for normative purposes – to start with a 'structurally separatist' conception of a 'pure', detached, individualistic market.

Secondly, it is not helpful to think in terms of a perfect or pure case, such as perfect markets or perfect competition (Sawyer, 1991). While the corre-spondence of actual markets with the structural-identity principle of the market may possibly be used as the foundation for a normative evaluation – and this would be no simple issue – there is no such thing as a perfect form of a market. In particular, the structural-identity principle of the market can be actualized in a variety of ways, all of which still reflect – perhaps with less or more distortion – the intrinsic or generic structural identity of the market as a societal institution.

Generally the positive form and operation of markets can vary according to (a) the positive form of the vertical and the two horizontal relations; (b) which of the three types of relations is dominant in a particular situation; both of these may in turn depend on (c) the degree and actual nature of the interwovenness of firms and other organizations, in particular the relative economic power of participants in these relations.

Clearly, the factual nature of market relations will be strongly influenced by firms and their objectives. On the other hand, market relations can often be markedly determined by non-economic societal organizations with which they are interlaced, such as the family, trade associations, or the state. Relative dominance by a communal structure – for example a (large) firm or the state – can project an indelible imprint on the actual form of the market relations.

More generally the nature of the 'economic system' must be understood, *inter alia*, as a reflection of the positive form of the market, notably the extent to which the state is interwoven with the market, or to which market relations are dominated by large firms. Obviously, this can occur in various degrees and in a rich variety of ways. This reinforces the argument above that one must not think in terms of pure forms, such as the polar extremes of a decentralized pure market economy or a centrally planned economy.

Especially, two structural linkages must be noted. First, the state is pivotal in the establishment and upholding of a public legal order. One part of this is the function of the state juridically to protect and guarantee the civil law sphere, within which private economic exchange relations are carried out (and contractually enforced).[20] This indicates that the idea of a separation of the 'sphere of the market' from 'the sphere of the state or politics', as in the theory of limited government, is not sustainable.[21]

Secondly, and fairly obviously, the state acts as buyer and seller of commodities and services. Thus the internal relational structure of the state – between government and citizens – is nodally (that is, externally) linked to the market and thereby with, notably, selling organizations (firms).

In general, variations in positive form can be understood in historical context, notably the transition from undifferentiated to differentiated society. Here it is helpful to conceptualize a 'stylized' evolutionary history of markets. Beginning from simple markets involving trade between craftsmen or firms and households, one can perceive the increasing differentiation of all the types of market relations (vertical *and* horizontal, exchange *and* non-exchange).[22] This process is inextricably linked to a coincident differentiation of societal institutions.

The change from simple (embryonic) markets to sophisticated, differentiated markets in modern society can be described as an *unfolding* process progressively realizing the latent structure and characteristics of the market as a societal phenomenon. In this process the market's institutional content and interwovenness with other institutions may vary considerably – but not its intrinsic nature.

2.5 The Horizontal and Vertical Roles of Prices

As noted above, one function of price is as a reflection or symbol of the exchanged value in an economic exchange. In the context of a market, where an exchange does not occur in isolation, additional functions can be distinguished.

One can distinguish between the vertical and horizontal roles of price: the former refers to its symbolic function as a manifestation of the exchange ratio in a single economic exchange, whereas in the latter case it functions as a transmitter of information between multiple exchanges in a market. This explains the observation by Hodgson (1988, p. 174) that the market is a forum in which consensus over prices can be established – something absent in isolated transactions.

This horizontal function of price is founded in and presupposes the vertical, exchange-specific function of price. In addition it presupposes the interrelational involvement of firms and other communal structures in market relations. Therefore this function of prices is a necessary counterpart of the societal and economic differentiation process (part of which involved the replacement of barter by moneyed exchange).

The differentiation of societal institutions in the modernization process also explains the appearance of another class of (horizontal) interrelations. With the multiplication of firms and traded commodities, markets (and the firms producing the commodities) became specialized and differentiated, simultaneously becoming increasingly interlinked. In such a context buyer and seller knowledge of, and access to, specialized and differentiated markets bring horizontal *between-market* relations – likewise economically qualified – into play. Standard concepts like complementarity, supplementarity and cross-elasticity describe the nature of the inter-market relations that can exist between products, and therefore between the (buyers and sellers in) markets where those products are traded.

This inter-market context is where the allocation function of markets can be structurally located and analysed. Market allocation of resources between the different products is based on opportunities to channel buying power to alternative markets (and the sellers operating in them).[23]

The integral role of price can now be appreciated. Its horizontally extended, between-market information signalling role, founded in its vertical exchange-specific (symbolic) role, is central to the allocation function of differentiated markets. It also implies a differentiation (and deepening) of the role of price itself.[24]

2.6 So What Else is New?

A comparison with the Moss and especially the Hodgson definitions of the market is instructive. Moss (1984, p. 10) defines the market as: 'A set of mutually independent agents who produce and use a commodity together with all other mutually independent agents whose activities are required to get the commodity from its producers to its users.' Hodgson (1988, p. 174) sees the market as: 'A set of social institutions in which a large number of commodity exchanges of a specific type regularly take place, and to some extent are facilitated and structured by those institutions.' He thus sees markets as 'organized and institutionalized exchange', with stress on 'those market institutions which help to both regulate and establish a consensus over prices and, more generally, to communicate information regarding products, prices, quantities, potential buyers and potential sellers'.

Both Moss and Hodgson appear not to distinguish sufficiently and systematically between the organizations in the market, the interrelations at the core of the market, and the relationship between these. The term 'institution' is often used too structurally undifferentiated or unspecified to enable finer distinctions: for example, it could apply equally to interrelations or to communal structures, or even to regularized behavioural patterns. In addition, the typically economic character of all these phenomena is not really explicated. In general it appears that the theoretical grip on the nature of the complex of relations involved has to be tightened somewhat. Doing that in a systematic way is a central purpose of the 'structural' analysis presented here.

However, what is clear – and here they are very correct – is that one should not attempt to define the market without explicit reference to the interwoven institutions and organizations.

Perhaps the issue here is a subtle difference between a definition and a structural identity principle (SIP). The latter is understood always to attempt to capture the characteristic kernel or nucleus of a phenomenon *amidst and despite* a variety of actual forms and actualizations and degrees of differentiation or interwovenness with various institutions or organizations in different historical situations. Stated differently, the intention is not to describe existing markets, but to circumscribe or define *conditions for being a market*. In contrast, many 'definitions' describe the configuration of actual, existing (often modern) markets. For instance, the formulations of Moss and Hodgson may make it difficult to distinguish between simple, 'unextended' markets where the horizontal relations are relatively undeveloped, and complex, horizontally 'developed' markets. In this sense the definitions of both Moss and Hodgson seem too historically contextualized to capture the intrinsic, nuclear nature of markets in all phases of development (or even in different economic systems).

This does not mean that the intention is to avoid historical context: on the contrary. But a market in historical and institutional context is always seen as but a contextualization and realization of an underlying structural identity principle, that is, of the intrinsic conditions for being a market. Context does not determine the intrinsic or generic nature of the phenomenon at hand, only the particular form it is given. Indeed, an 'empirical' requirement – and test – for a satisfactory formulation of the structural identity principle is that the variety of actually existing markets must be seen to be but different actualizations of the structural-identity principle. In this particular way the theoretical conceptualization – the structural-identity principle – has a direct counterpart in real world markets; real markets provide the intuitive basis for the theoretical derivation of the structural identity principle.

3. CONCLUSION

This paper has been concerned with two recurring themes: (a) the idea of the *economic qualification and character-specificity* of market relations (among other societal phenomena); and (b) the idea of *structural interwovenness* between societal relations, interrelations and communal structures.

In this analysis the idea of an underlying or generic nature of markets – of which the variety of observed forms are manifestations and realizations – is central. Indeed, it appears to be critical for a dynamic theory of society. Without some recognition of the structural identities of relationships and communal structures – without a conception of structural identity which captures an underlying constancy in the generic nature of the involved entities and relations – it is indeed impossible to identify any *changes*.

Two broad conclusions can be formulated, both concerned with proper regard for the intrinsic nature of the market. First, given the intrinsic nature of the market as societal institution, both markets and theoretical market analysis are only appropriate where exchanges or related societal interaction that are *economically qualified* take place (also see Sawyer, 1991; Hodgson, 1988, pp. 175–6). Therefore markets and market analysis are not applicable in all areas of social interaction or every instance where choices have to be made. Markets cannot regulate all social activities because not all these are economic exchanges. On the other hand markets *are* the appropriate societal structures to facilitate economic exchanges. This should be acknowledged and appreciated – whilst continually bearing in mind that actual market configurations can be better or worse, more or less equitable, or more or less efficient, implying a clear need for an appropriate normative framework for evaluating markets.

Following from the first conclusion, one thing that is wrong with both radical free marketism and absolutist state socialism with an all-embracing central plan is that each distorts the market as societal structure, *inter alia* by separating it from the complex and differentiated institutional interwovenness in which it is unbreakably embedded and which ultimately determines both its relative importance and relative *un*importance. In addition, its economic qualification and typicality – which again determine both the potential and the limitations of its applicability – are denied.

Secondly, the ideology of the free marketeers parallels much of neoclassical economics, by dislodging the market from its institutional interwovenness and conceptualizes it in an institutionally disembodied and (methodologically) individualistic way. While this purportedly is aimed at strengthening the market by fortifying the 'pure' or 'free' market against 'institutional contamination', the result is the opposite; by severing the market from its structural-institutional context, it is reduced to nothing but inter-individual relations. In a modern differentiated-economy context, this 'mental construct' clearly is inapplicable. In any case, such markets are not feasible, and any effort to institute such 'insulated' markets is misguided. In addition, the market is seen as a super societal organizer capable of regulating almost any societal activity or sphere. While this clearly overstretches the market, the economic role and impact of firms and, in particular, of non-economic organizations in markets and in society as a whole, are largely denied.

In the centrally planned state socialist economy, state domination of the market leads to *its* distortion and denigration. Centrally planned socialism (and its supporting theory) absolutizes one particular communal structure, the state, to the exclusion and distortion of the market and all the other organizations and linkages with which the market is interwoven in a differentiated society. In effect, the market (and by implication all involved firms) is transformed into a subordinate part of the 'state society' as larger whole.

Market relations and firms are equally constitutive and equally important in a modern differentiated economy. This is what is really meant by the phrase 'keeping the market in its place'. By disregarding the typical and inherent nature of the market, both ideologies fundamentally distort it – conceptually, theoretically and in practice. As a consequence, the distinctive nature and contribution of the firm (and other organizations) is denied.

NOTES

1.   The contribution of the Institute for Research Development of the South African Human
     Sciences Research Council towards the financing of the research leading to this chapter
     is gratefully acknowledged. Viewpoints expressed are those of the author alone.

2. Paul Auerbach (1988, p. 122) states that markets are largely figures of speech in economics. He argues that 'a market is not a thing but a behavioural relation' which is made into a thing, in conventional theory, by a process of 'reification'. Sawyer (1991) remarks that this merely reinforces the definitional difficulties.

3. Such an interpretation would be mistakenly to identify this approach with that of essentialism.

4. As used here the term denotes only a societal structure that is not 'interacting individuals only', not non-integrating, not a mere aggregate of discrete individuals. In this sense both organized institutions (organizations) and natural entities like families can be described as communal.

5. For critiques of individualistic, transactions and contracts approaches to the nature of the firm, notably of Alchian and Demsetz (1972), and Jensen and Meckling (1976), see Fourie (1989a), and Hodgson (1988, ch. 3).

6. The role of property rights in exchange needs further investigation. One question is whether property rights are necessary for economic exchange, or whether it simply is that property rights are conducive to exchange, or highlight incentives for exchange.

7. A similar idea is contained in Hodgson's (1984, pp. 85–109; 1988, pp. 167–71) 'principle of dominance' and 'impurity principle', that is, that in addition to a predominant aspect, each system or subsystem contains 'impurities' which are not typical of the whole, but which are nevertheless necessary for the system to function. For example, 'all so-called "economic" exchanges exhibit "social" aspects to some degree' (Hodgson, 1988, p. 169). This also suggests that something like 'pure' exchanges or markets, in the sense of involving only contractual elements (ibid., p. 167) is not possible, if only because the contractual element already is a legal aspect functioning under the qualification of the dominant economic aspect. Also, the view of 'pure' markets implicit in general equilibrium theory (Sawyer, 1991), where the only contact between parties concerns exchange, actually is impossible. There always is more involved than pure exchange relations, for example, trust relations. As Sawyer (1991) argues, the analysis of market economies cannot be adequately undertaken solely in terms of arms-length exchange transactions.

8. Labour markets may present a snag here, for the idea of an agreed-upon exchange ratio is problematic where the work to be done by an employee is not specified in advance (i.e., an open contract). I would suggest that it still is a moot question whether labour should be regarded as being traded in markets, just as another commodity. Being employed can alternatively be regarded as becoming a member of a firm (Fourie, 1989a), in which case a different analytical framework may be applicable.

9. Another important illustration of the unbreakable coherence between firms and markets is that the *purposes* intended in the formation of a voluntary association like the firm is necessarily dependent upon and directed towards the inter-communal market relationships in which it is involved.

10. This characteristic of firms and other organizations does of course not exclude differences of opinion and purpose amongst members, nor does a quarrel between a husband and wife nullify the typical inner unity and coherence of a marriage – in contrast to the typical non-integrating character of interaction between foreigners, say. On the other hand the fact that persistent and unreconcilable differences actually threaten the continued existence of both marriages and firms just proves how integral this element is. (Also see footnote 5.)

11. As noted above, in Hodgson's view (1988, p. 148) the absence of an exchange of property rights is the main problem in this conceptualization.

12. Historically more individualistic inter-individual or inter-communal relationships followed on periods where communal relationships (sibs, ancient villages and mediaeval cities, guilds or religious communities) dominated society.

13. While the entire spectrum of societal entities (and individuals involved in them) can and do take part in market transactions, for exploratory purposes the analysis will be in terms of the conventional, prototype seller–buyer pairing of firm and household.

14. This is shortened version of *alter loco alterius*. An equivalent phrase is *quis loco cuius* ('somebody in the place of another'); alternatively one can refer to an *aut-aut* ('either-or') relation.

15. That buying typically is mutually exclusionary does not necessarily imply mutual exclusivity in consumption, as the public-goods case illustrates.

16. There is the question whether or why an economic exchange is not sufficient to constitute a market. In the context of an actually existing differentiated economy, and in contrast to Hodgson (1988, p. 177) it is suggested here that all economic exchanges form part of some market. Except when isolated, an exchange always takes place in awareness of some alternative buyer or seller options, so that some direct or indirect interaction or independence is implied, that is, sufficient interrelatedness actually to constitute a market context. Although the horizontal relations in the market may have a very specific actual form, they still exist.

17. Of course, markets can be formally institutionalized, as in organized farmers' markets or stock markets. In this case the structural picture is somewhat more complicated, for it involves the formation of an organization to provide the facilities in which market transactions can take place. It is an example of structural interwovenness, as discussed below. Still, the intrinsic nature of the market relations that are actualized within this organizational context is unchanged. Each societal relation or structure retains its individuality amidst any interwovenness.

18. Moss (1981, 1984) has demonstrated how modern, intermediated markets are filled with institutions operating at different levels of the economic process.

19. This explains why Auerbach (1988, p. 121) can argue that firms have been at the same time devices for the avoidance of the market mechanism as well as for its extension: 'The option of avoiding internal organisation by the use of the market is only possible if other entities have been organised in sufficient depth that a "market" appears for the services at hand.'

20. The other part can be found in the public-law sphere, in which relations between citizens/subjects and the government are legally governed, protected and guaranteed. The existence of these different spheres of law, in turn interwoven with each other, is an integral element of differentiated society. On this see Fourie (1989b) and Hodgson (1988, p. 153).

21. This explicates Hodgson's (1988, p. 150–3) point that in any developed system of commodity exchange there must be an appropriate legal system enscribing and protecting property rights. It also becomes clear that the implicit or explicit contractual aspect of market transactions is an inseparable element thereof. Also, that the extension of property rights and commodity exchanges to more commodities and areas of social life – as propounded by free marketeers – does not reduce the role of the state, as intended. As Karl Polanyi (1944) has observed, increased transacting and contracting in freer markets necessarily imply greater state involvement to guarantee relevant rights and legal interests, and to provide the infrastructure for potential litigation.

22. In this process it appears that the horizontal (often rivalrous) relations and tendencies gain in importance relative to the vertical exchange relations, impacting on their actual form and realization.

23. Actually, the allocation function of markets can be seen on two levels: one is *within* a market, where buying power is allocated between competing sellers in that market, allocating resources within that product sphere; the other is where buying power is allocated between different commodities/markets.

24. The allocation function is only possible if sufficient social and economic differentiation has taken place, or only develops in so far as such differentiation occurs. Therefore the exchange versus allocational functions of markets must be understood in the context of the historical unfolding process described above. Compared to the exchange function of markets, the market's allocational function – a 'horizontal' function – emerges, and becomes more significant, only as markets become more differentiated or relatively more sophisticated or mature (that is, the process whereby horizontal relations gain in relative importance in the first place). This implies that, while allocation is important, it

is not the only or even primary function of markets, and not the only measure of effectiveness or optimality. See also the discussion of the role of prices by Sawyer (1991).

4. The Pertinent Levels of Analysis in Industrial Dynamics

Dominique Foray and Pierre Garrouste[1]

Economic analysis has long faced, and continues to face, the problem of selecting the pertinent level at which to study the industrial system. Alternatively, either the firm or the industry can be considered as the basic unit of analysis. One of these two concepts then constitutes the fundamental unity, the atom, so to speak, from which the theory of industrial reality is constructed.

With this apparent dilemma, the obverse concept is relegated to a secondary status. If analysis is centred on the concept of the firm, then industry becomes nothing more than an aggregate of firms. Conversely, if the industry is considered to be the conceptual key to the industrial system, then real firms, with all their diversity and complexity, become no more than the analytical abstraction of the 'representative firm'. Several authors, such as Richard Nelson and Sidney Winter (1980), have discussed the reductive nature of such an approach, and attempted to 'reconcile' the industry and the firm. In this chapter we address the same central problem, but on the basis of a different approach.

A method is here proposed which permits a designation of the pertinent level of analysis in 'industrial dynamics',[2] in the light of the nature and structure of the relations between firms and industries. Crucially, whether it is the firm or the industry which represents the fundamental element of stability within the system depends upon the precise nature of these relations in the productive system under analysis.

We further postulate that whether firms or industries represent the fundamental element of stability depends particularly upon the conditions and processes of technological change. Firms as well as industries may possess a degree of autonomy, and thus be analysed as an autonomous system. Either productive form can possess a strong internal coherence and a trajectory of evolution constrained by this coherence. Regarding the industry, our argument is based on our previous work (Foray, 1985; Foray and Garrouste, 1991). With regard to the firm, the argument derives from the work of Winter (1964), who developed the idea of the firm as an autonomous system.

Accordingly, the concept of autonomy can be applied either to the firm or to the industry, depending on the 'locus' (the sector) of the productive system under investigation. One productive form may exhibit the behavioural characteristics of an autonomous system, and hold the central position in the analysis, while the other productive form remains in a secondary position. This method allows us therefore to adjust the centre of gravity of analysis by focusing behavioural studies on the particular productive form that is selected.

Both productive forms (firm and industry) can coexist as autonomous systems in certain sectors of the productive system. This case, particularly regarding multi-product firms, will be addressed below.

Finally, the construction of a certain number of different mappings between firms and industries (according to the location of the autonomous unit) permits us to formulate different patterns of firm behaviour and relations and to revisit some central theoretical conceptions in this field.

1. AUTONOMOUS SYSTEMS AND INDUSTRIAL STRUCTURES

We have found it useful to conceptualize industries and firms in terms of the notions of organization and structure such as deployed by Francisco Varela (1989),[3] where the organization of an autonomous system covers the ensemble of relations which defines it as a unity. The system's structure, that is, the set of relations between the identifiable elements of that system, will vary in response to perturbations emanating from its environment. However, with a given, identifiable system it is assumed that such perturbations are sufficiently small to ensure that the essential elements of this structure remain intact. Otherwise such perturbations will involve the transition from one type of system to another. Varela's definition of a system thus encompasses both continuity and change.

1.1 Industry as an Autonomous System

The conception of an industry as an autonomous system is thus equivalent to the notion that the industry has an identifiable and invariant network of relations, defining its identity and internal coherence. Along these lines, we shall make use of the following analytical decomposition of products into three sets of characteristics:

a product could be described as the combination of two sets of characteristics, called technical (X_i) and service (Y_i) characteristics respectively, and by a pattern of mapping, relating the two sets of characteristics mentioned above. ... A second mapping is introduced from the technological characteristics X_i to the process technology characteristics Z_i, from which one can define types of technological change just as with the service characteristics mapping. (Metcalfe and Saviotti, 1984, p. 144)

Table 4.1: Product and process characteristics

Process characteristics		Technical characteristics		Service characteristics
Z_1		X_1		Y_1
Z_2		X_2		Y_2
.		.		.
.	$\longleftrightarrow$	.	$\longleftrightarrow$	.
.		.		.
Z_p		X_m		Y_n

Source: Metcalfe and Saviotti, 1984.

At the point at which it is introduced into a productive system, a given product possesses an ensemble of technical characteristics $(X_1, \ldots X_m)$, which do not necessarily correspond to an ensemble of service characteristics $(Y_1, \ldots Y_n)$, nor to an ensemble of production method characteristics $(Z_1, \ldots Z_p)$. Take, for example, a foundry product (Foray, 1985). At the beginning, neither its uses nor its production methods are necessarily specific to it. This product's uses may be indistinguishable from those of other products (of the forge or of, say, a pottery). As for the methods of production, they are particular to the iron and steel industry. However, production methods could be borrowed from elsewhere, as in the case of the recent development of fibre optics depending upon production methods borrowed from glass manufacturing (Massard, 1988).

In the light of this discussion we address the general question of the autonomization of productive activities. The degree of autonomization is expressed by the level of internal coherence between the three ensembles of characteristics evoked above. An initial situation where the ensembles of characteristics Y and Z are not yet specific is often followed by a search for internal coherence between X, Y and Z, which may continue until the activity becomes autonomous, that is, until the activity establishes its own peculiar production and service characteristics. Productive systems which have thus become autonomous may be called industries.

Once this stability has been identified on the basis of the organization of the industry, it becomes possible to define structural change as a set of transformations that allow the industry to respond to perturbations arising from its environment, within the constraints imposed by the maintenance of its organization. Structural changes can thus be identified merely as the evolution of the elements of the three sets of characteristics.

Facing global changes in terms of demand functions, technological systems and macroeconomic regulation, an industry may preserve its unity if the structural changes it is able to generate are sufficient for its adaptation to the new environment. If, in contrast, this adaptation is impossible without changing the organization – the relations of internal coherence – then the industry may no longer be identifiable as an entity.

It would be a mistake to regard autonomization as a direct goal of firms themselves. Rather, firms seek improvements in efficiency which, at certain points in time, can no longer be achieved except by the development of coherence between the three ensembles of characteristics and therefore by autonomization of the particular activity. Autonomization is normally an unintended, rather than an intended, outcome.

In previous works (Foray and Garrouste, 1991) we have attempted to discover, for a given series of activities, the decisive technological change that completes the process of autonomization. This technological change most often concerns the notion of specificity of a piece of productive equipment. For example, the foundry industry cupola provided a means of 'exit' for the industry from its steel-manufacturing origins, and the 'VAD' system appears today to favour the autonomization of optical-fibre production by enabling independence from glass-manufacturing equipment.

However, industries thus defined are not immutable or eternal. They can themselves speciate into different industries. They can disappear whenever a particular perturbation in their environment calls their organizational integrity into question.

Finally, there normally coexist groups of productive activities as yet without an autonomized industrial coherence. These latter tend to be emerging activities, developed initially on the basis of production methods and service characteristics not properly belonging to them, and which yet function efficiently without recourse to internal coherence between the characteristics X, Y and Z.

In the sectors of the productive system where activities are not yet autonomized, and therefore do not yet possess the elements of stability enabling them to evolve as a unity, the localization of autonomy and therefore the study of behaviour should be directed at another (lower) level of organization of the productive system: that of the firm.

1.2   The Firm as an Autonomous System

Like the industry, the consideration of a firm as an autonomous system boils
down to the identification of an invariant network of relations defining its
identity. This is what we believe Winter (1964) is doing when he distinguishes between two characteristics of a firm: its organizational form and its
routines. By adopting this particular distinction it is possible to address the
question of whether a firm is an autonomous system. According to Winter,
the organizational form characterizes the firm. The invariability of this form
is necessary to the maintenance of a firm's existence.

An organizational form is a functional relationship between the state of
the world and the actions of a firm. This relationship may be broken down
into two stages: (a) an information-acquiring stage, in which the information
available to the firm is determined as a function of the state of the world; and
(b) an action-taking stage in which the firm's action is determined as a
function of the information available to it and of the firm's internal state
(Winter, 1964, p. 237).

Faced with the invariable character of a firm's organizational form, its
routines possess a certain plasticity. Winter (1964, p. 264n) clarifies this
point by observing that he uses the word 'routine' to mean 'a pattern of
behavior that is followed repeatedly, but is subject to change if conditions
change. If the patterns of behavior were *not* subject to change, the description of it would be a description of the firm's organization form.' One can
interpret this difference between organizational form and routines as representing, at the level of the firm, the distinction between the organization and
structure of an autonomous system: the routines fix the modifications which
are acceptable by the organization form; they define the frontiers of the
structural changes of the firm.

1.3   On the Internal Coherences of Industries and Firms

Comparing the firm and the industry, it is useful to stress that the type of
internal coherence – the foundation of autonomy – is of a very different
nature. If they were similar, it would be impossible to distinguish analytically between these two kinds of productive forms, and to construct meaningful mappings between firms and industries.[4]

A previous work focused on the nature of the internal coherence of the
industry (Foray and Garrouste, 1991). Addressing the firm, the concept of
internal coherence relates closely to the important distinction between the
decision-making process and the (routinized) procedures of action. This
issue is at the core of the notion of organizational form, according to Winter's (1964) account.

In sum, behavioural autonomy can be situated either at the level of the firm or at the level of the industry. The determination of the appropriate structural entity indicates the pertinent level for the analysis of the dynamics of technical change.

2.   TOWARDS A UNIFIED FRAMEWORK OF ANALYSIS

In this section we analyse the established relations between the firm and the industry in light of their appropriate designation as autonomous systems. These relationships lead us to the notion of the structural plasticity of firm assets. This plasticity varies according to the localization of autonomy at one or the other of the two levels of analysis.

2.1   Structural Plasticity

Armen Alchian and Susan Woodward introduce a distinction between firms, according to whether their assets are more or less 'plastic'. The degree of plasticity relates to the range of discretion for asset-related decisions. To illustrate, they compare the cases of a pharmaceutical research laboratory with a steel-manufacturing firm. In contrast to the laboratory, 'there are fewer options for discretionary behavior in steel manufacturing. The technology is largely determined by the nature of the plant' (Alchian and Woodward, 1988, p. 69).

This approach, like Winter's, is reminiscent of Varela's conception of the relations between an autonomous system and its environment. As Varela (1989, p. 112) writes:

> the continued interactions of a structurally plastic system in an environment with recurrent perturbations will produce a continual selection of the system structure. This structure will determine, on the one hand, the state of the system and its domain of allowable perturbations, and on the other hand will allow the system to operate in an environment without disintegration. We refer to this process as structural coupling. If we can consider the system's environment also as a structurally plastic system, then the system and the environment will have an interlocked history of structural transformations, selecting each other's trajectories.

Thus it is on the basis of a consideration of the environment of the firm – the stability or instability of which is a function of the existence of an industry as an autonomous system – that we are able to specify a firm's degree of structural plasticity. The pertinent level at which the study of firm behaviour must be carried out is derived from this specification.

To clarify the point, two extreme cases can be identified. First, the case where the firm's environment is stable and where an industry has been clearly constituted, and secondly, the case where the environment is unstable and activity at the industrial level is emerging, but as yet without the internal coherence that is characteristic of an existing industry.

2.2 The Case of Environmental Stability

In this first case, productive activity is organized in the form of an industry, as the result of the development of a sufficiently high degree of internal coherence. In this situation, what matters (in terms of industrial dynamics) is the capacity of the industry to maintain its unity (internal coherence) in the light of the overall transformation of the productive system. The evolution of the industry, within the limits imposed by the maintenance of its internal coherence, provides significant stability in the environment faced by firms.

Accordingly, the 'structural plasticity' of these firms is weak; their capacity to modify the trajectory of structural transformations of the industry is limited by the constraints pertaining to the internal coherence of this industry. The behaviour of individual firms is not intelligible without consideration of the properties and movement of the industry as a whole.

Thus, for a business enterprise operating *exclusively* within the framework of a constituted industry, the range of possible decisions is confined to the different levels of already implemented processes and to the technical characteristics and services of products thereby obtained. In this case, the firm possesses the characteristics of Marshall's representative firm. This point is derived from the observation, in this particular case, that a knowledge of structural modifications in an industry is sufficient to inform us of the evolution of the routines of firms operating *exclusively* within the framework of that industry. In effect, the identity of the firm becomes nothing more than the unitary expression of the evolution of the industry. Thus, as a trivial example, it is 'the foundry industry' that matters in terms of industrial dynamics, since the principal problem depends on the manner in which this industry evolves as a unity, whereas 'foundries', considered as so many black boxes, simply record the structural changes generated by the industry within the framework of its evolution as a unity.

This extreme case becomes complicated as soon as the firm is confronted by an environment which results in the overlapping of several industries. A possible approach here is to break the 'real' firm down into sub-units,[5] each of which is considered as a firm with respect to a specific environment, and which in turn is limited to a single industry. As each of these sub-units therefore possesses a weak structural plasticity, we then rediscover the theoretical characteristics of Marshall's representative firm.

However, the above approach fails to recognize that a firm composed of sub-units can increase its structural plasticity by operating upon its own centre of activity distribution. The behaviour of the large firm consequently represents 'something more' than the sum of the behaviours of its sub-units. The global behaviour of the large firm cannot be reduced therefore to the mere record of the structural modifications of the different industries, corresponding to the sub-units of this firm. This case implies an increase in the range of possible routines (Teece, 1982), and is similar to the situation we shall now examine with respect to unstable environments. This case also allows us to emphasize that our approach avoids a determinism of industrial structures on the behaviour of firms: even in a constituted industry a firm may, by 'destabilizing' its environment, increase its structural plasticity and acquire the characteristics of autonomous behaviour.

2.3 The Case of an Unstable Environment

When there are no enduring constraints in a firm's industrial environment, the given activity can be considered as not yet being constituted within the form of an industry, that is, no internal coherence exists with respect to the ensembles of characteristics X, Y and Z. Here we no longer speak of industries but rather of emerging groups of activities. The analysis of industrial dynamics should therefore focus on the firm. Relative to the environment, the firm's structural plasticity is stronger.

In this case, the selected trajectories, pertaining to the structural transformations of firms as well as of the environment, are very open and unpredictable. To the extent that the characteristic structural coupling of the interactions between the firm and its environment depends essentially on the firm's capacity to 'choose' a structure rather than to see one imposed on it, a firm's behaviour should be understood and analysed in the light of its character as an autonomous system. Its routines are not here constrained by the preservation of the unity of an industry, but rather by maintenance of the firm's own organizational form. This organizational form therefore represents the pertinent level of analysis and it is consequently out of the question to regard the firm simply as a black box.

Rather, we have to take a good look at the theory of the innovative firm (Amendola and Bruno, 1990; Gaffard, 1990) as well as the micro-micro theory of Harvey Leibenstein (1979). For example, in the case of the currently emerging group of activities around fibre optics, it is the (glass-manufacturing) firms that matter, in that they strive to preserve their organizational form by integrating a new activity (the adaptation of glass-manufacturing equipment to the fabrication of fibres) in their routines.

CONCLUSION

In presenting their 'evolutionary' theory, Nelson and Winter observe that the adequacy of an analysis cannot be examined independently of the kind of object to which it is applied. Thus 'special theories aimed one narrow class of phenomena may involve different assumptions, have different structure, than theories aimed another class of phenomena' (Nelson and Winter, 1980, p. 181). Nevertheless, in order to keep theoretical disparity within limits, they still believe it to be advantageous to construct a 'unifying framework' within which all specific theories may be integrated.

We endorse this outlook. Indeed, the approach outlined above allows for the localization of the preponderant elements of stability within the productive system. It further encourages us to adjust continually the centre of gravity of our analysis by successively qualifying one or the other of the two basic productive forms (firm or industry) as the autonomous system and thereafter centring our behavioural studies upon the appropriate productive

Table 4.2: The pertinent levels of analysis in industrial dynamics

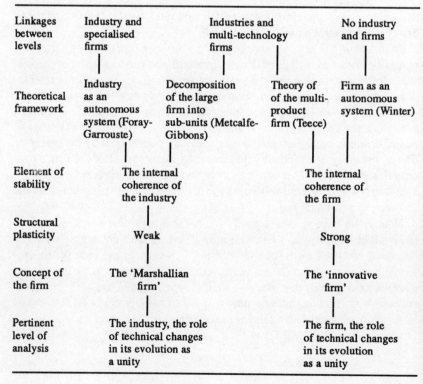

Linkages between levels	Industry and specialised firms		Industries and multi-technology firms	No industry and firms
Theoretical framework	Industry as an autonomous system (Foray-Garrouste)	Decomposition of the large firm into sub-units (Metcalfe-Gibbons)	Theory of of the multi-product firm (Teece)	Firm as an autonomous system (Winter)
Element of stability		The internal coherence of the industry		The internal coherence of the firm
Structural plasticity		Weak		Strong
Concept of the firm		The 'Marshallian firm'		The 'innovative firm'
Pertinent level of analysis		The industry, the role of technical changes in its evolution as a unity		The firm, the role of technical changes in its evolution as a unity

form. The approach is therefore one based upon a general theory of *'eigenbehaviour'* (Varela, 1989) and a unifying framework of analysis. It may be applied alternatively either to the firm or to the industry, depending on which may at a given moment be appropriately analysed as an autonomous system.

NOTES

1. We are indebted to Fabio Arcangeli and Geoff Hodgson for helpful comments on an earlier version of this paper.
2. B. Carlsson (1987) usefully distinguishes between two research programmes in industrial economics: industrial organization versus industrial dynamics.
3. The general theory of systems is divided between autonomous and heteronymous approaches. In Varela's opinion this divergence is a result of the competition between two research programs, one based on the works of Norbert Wiener, which Varela intends to reactivate and which gave rise to cybernetics, and the other based on von Neumann's proposal, which interprets cognitive functioning in terms of the running of a program.
4. The taxonomy of Keith Pavitt (1984), for instance, could be applied indifferently to both the firm and industry levels.
5. For example: 'Finally, the firm is defined as an organization articulating a knowledge base to generate a particular revealed technological performance in pursuit of certain objectives. This is not codeterminous with the firm as traditionally defined in terms of control over the disposition of capital assets. Rather, in contemporary conditions, our "firm" is to be interpreted typically as a business sub-unit of a larger enterprise often being multi-technology in nature. The relation between the "firm" and the larger "umbrella enterprise" often constitutes an important part of the operating environment of the former' (Metcalfe and Gibbons, 1989, p. 158).

5. Production Flexibility

Mario Morroni[1]

1. INTRODUCTION

Particular attention will be devoted in this chapter to one aspect of flexibility which in recent years has aroused increasing interest: *the flexibility of production processes*. With the rapid evolution of market conditions, efficacy – which indicates the ability to meet consumer demand – becomes a complex goal and assumes a predominant role in affecting the competitiveness of a firm. In the presence of uncertainty, efficacy requires production flexibility.

As will become clear, production flexibility is not an exclusive prerogative either of small or of large firms (or production units) and the need for flexibility greatly differs from one sector to another. Production flexibility is even independent of the technology adopted, since it can be achieved in firms through the flexible organization of rigid equipment or production units. Nevertheless, the new information technology is proving a formidable tool for cutting flexibility costs, and thus for encouraging further development of flexible organizational systems. Hence the potentialities offered by this technology will undoubtedly be a strong incentive to apply flexible organizational systems to large as well as small production units.

The implementation of flexible production systems leads to a drastic reduction in the duration of the production process, response times, and the quantity of goods lying in inventories and goods in progress. Consequently, the analysis of production flexibility needs a representation of the production process which takes account of the organizational and temporal dimensions of production.

The chapter consists of four sections. In the second section the different meanings of production flexibility are discussed and a taxonomy devised. Section 3 deals with the link between uncertainty and production flexibility, and analyses briefly the organizational aspects of production flexibility. Section 4 examines the main effects of computer-based technology on production flexibility. Information technology reduces set-up times, which makes economies of scale compatible with economies of scope. Notably, sections 3 and 4 involve applications of the analysis to recent developments in industrial capitalism. Finally, some general conclusions are drawn in the last section.

2. PRELIMINARY DEFINITIONS

Flexibility expresses the capacity for adjustment to variations in external conditions; in other words, it is the ability to learn from experience and change plans over time. The greater the uncertainty, the greater, of course, is the need for flexibility. 'True uncertainty' depends upon the inability or

Table 5.1: Flexible production systems: a taxonomy

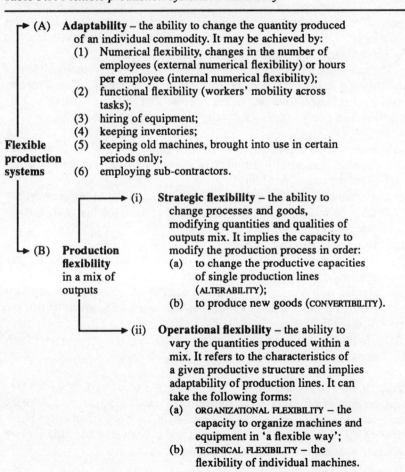

Flexible production systems

(A) **Adaptability** – the ability to change the quantity produced of an individual commodity. It may be achieved by:
   (1) Numerical flexibility, changes in the number of employees (external numerical flexibility) or hours per employee (internal numerical flexibility);
   (2) functional flexibility (workers' mobility across tasks);
   (3) hiring of equipment;
   (4) keeping inventories;
   (5) keeping old machines, brought into use in certain periods only;
   (6) employing sub-contractors.

(B) **Production flexibility** in a mix of outputs

   (i) **Strategic flexibility** – the ability to change processes and goods, modifying quantities and qualities of outputs mix. It implies the capacity to modify the production process in order:
   (a) to change the productive capacities of single production lines (ALTERABILITY);
   (b) to produce new goods (CONVERTIBILITY).

   (ii) **Operational flexibility** – the ability to vary the quantities produced within a mix. It refers to the characteristics of a given productive structure and implies adaptability of production lines. It can take the following forms:
   (a) ORGANIZATIONAL FLEXIBILITY – the capacity to organize machines and equipment in 'a flexible way';
   (b) TECHNICAL FLEXIBILITY – the flexibility of individual machines.

impossibility of considering all future contingencies and their probability distribution.[2] Hence, in the presence of uncertainty, a *flexible action* tends to reduce the degree of irreversibility of economic decisions, facilitating an improved reaction if something unforeseen or unforeseeable occurs.[3]

Production flexibility permits output flows to be regulated in line with the evolution of market conditions. Within this general definition, it may be useful to distinguish between flexibility in relation to absorbing quantitative variations in the demand for a *single* commodity, and flexibility in relation to a *mix* of outputs. For the sake of simplicity I call the former adaptability and the latter production flexibility (see Table 5.1).

A mono-product plant is more adaptable the less its unit costs vary with the quantity produced (that is, the lower the elasticity of unit costs is in relation to the volume of production). It is generally assumed that there is a trade-off between adaptability and efficiency. Since greater adaptability makes plant more efficient over a large range of products, it reduces efficiency at the optimum technical output level.[4]

The indivisibility of production elements and sunk-cost irreversibility of investment in capital goods generally imply a low adaptability level. Hence, firms pursue adaptability by increasing the divisibility of plants and by reducing their fixed cost. In short, adaptability may be obtained by:

(a)   numerical flexibility that involves changes in the number of employees (external numerical flexibility), or of working hours per employee (internal numerical flexibility);

(b)   functional flexibility which refers to the capacity to adjust workers' skills in order to change the required tasks (mobility across tasks, changing job assignment, retraining);

(c)   hiring of equipment;

(d)   keeping inventories that serve to compensate for quantitative fluctuations in demand;

(e)   keeping in-house old machines and equipment, which are already fully amortized and which are brought back into use only when the demand is particularly high;

(f)   employing sub-contractors, so that variability of demand is largely transferred to suppliers.

If we take into consideration the production of a mix of goods, *production flexibility* may refer to, first, the capability for modifying the mix, changing processes and goods produced (strategic flexibility); or secondly, the possibility of varying the quantities produced within a given mix, using a given productive structure (operational flexibility).[5]

Strategic flexibility implies an innovative capacity; that is to say, the ability to change production processes, production element endowment and the qualities of outputs in relation to changes in environmental conditions. Strategic flexibility may involve widening the mix of products and variations in product quality. Thus, strategic flexibility implies alterability, that is, the ability to modify the productive capacity of single production lines; and convertibility; the ability to introduce new products. In a changing environment a certain degree of strategic flexibility may be achieved, for instance, by buying less-durable equipment.[6]

In contrast, what is termed *operational flexibility* is related only to the characteristics of a given productive structure in relation to the possibility of adjusting the quantities of various outputs within the same range. Hence, operational flexibility depends on the degree of adaptability in the single processes belonging to the production mix. Operational flexibility includes both organizational flexibility and technical flexibility. The former refers to the capability for organizing rigid machines in a 'flexible way'; the latter refers to the degree of flexibility of individual machines, in order to guarantee variability in the quantitative composition of the mix of outputs.

It should be noted that the need for production flexibility may differ greatly from one industry to another. On the other hand, no deterministic relationship exists between technical flexibility and organizational flexibility, in the sense that technical flexibility does not require organizational flexibility, because it is conceivable that versatile machines or plants may be utilized within a rigid organizational structure. Conversely, a production unit can achieve a degree of organizational flexibility through the combination and organization of inflexible (highly standardized mono-use) machines. Likewise, a firm can secure organizational flexibility by arranging the activity of several (mono-product) production units (or firms). In conclusion, the analysis of flexible production systems requires the technical aspects of production processes to be considered together with the organizational dimension.

3. UNCERTAINTY AND FLEXIBLE ORGANIZATION

Consider the particular relevance of this issue to the evolution of industrial systems. During the 1950s and 1960s the economic development of industrialized countries was based on stability and a highly standardized demand, ready availability of unskilled labour, and technical changes allowing large economies of scale, through the application of *rigid automation* in the production process. These first two decades after the Second World War were characterized by mass production and corporate development at the microeconomic level, and by what were labelled Keynesian policies, at the macroeconomic level.[7] During the 1970s these conditions were progressively transformed. Market structures and production organization were influenced by a number of factors, which gave rise to uncertainty in many industries.[8] Among these factors, the following may be mentioned:

(a)   increasing instability of demand and increasing product differentiation;
(b)   notable increases in the prices of raw materials and wages;
(c)   floating exchange rates and recurrent financial disturbances;
(d)   labour unrest; in particular, variations in expectations over levels of skill and job satisfaction;
(e)   increased competitiveness of developing countries in mass production;
(f)   the spread, since the late 1970s, of computer-based technology.

All these changes have certainly induced many enterprises operating in industrialized countries to seek greater production flexibility. In fact, as already noted, production flexibility is required if environmental conditions change rapidly and if there is a low degree of predictability with regard to the direction and magnitude of changes (bounded rationality). If there is a trade-off between production flexibility and efficiency, the firm's choice (as to which plant and organizational scheme to adopt) depends on the level of flexibility required by the environmental conditions in relation to flexibility costs.

Furthermore, the saturation of mass markets (which have increasingly become substitution markets) and the associated evolution of consumption models lead to the spread of more and more personalized and differentiated commodities, with a larger service component. Consequently many firms become more market orientated. Efficacy, linked to the capacity to evolve in response to changed market conditions, begins to be an increasingly important aspect of competitiveness for many firms.

The need to produce differentiated goods may also derive from reasons of international competitiveness. Standardized production, based on rigid automation technologies, becomes less and less competitive in industrialized countries as it spreads among developing countries, which often have considerably lower direct costs. In these mature sectors, international competitiveness is maintained only in those market segments where the differentiation of the product is very important, and where the products have a large service content, with the capacity to respond to the evolution and growing differentiation of consumption models.

In many cases this flexibility was obtained even before the advent of new information technology, through the adoption of various organizational structures able to adapt to a differentiated and rapidly evolving market. A certain degree of operational flexibility is obtainable by increasing the adaptability of single production lines, without recourse to computer-based technology. In this case, production flexibility is mainly achieved through:

(a) in-house organizational systems, such as:
    (i) multi-production by juxtaposing many production units within the same firm and or several product lines within the same production unit;
    (ii) just-in-time method of production;
(b) agreements between specialized firms (groups or constellations of independent firms, subcontracting, etc.).[9]

Consequently, flexibility can be increased, while still using rigid technologies, by combining individual, inflexible machines and organizing them in a 'flexible way'. With rigid automation technology, agreements between independent firms and/or in-house multi-production involve simply the sum of specialized elements that produce the different goods.

The just-in-time method of production can be seen as a production philosophy aimed at achieving production flexibility while still using inflexible technology. A certain level of flexibility is obtained, on the one hand, by trying to reduce set-up times, and on the other hand by producing small batches using the Kanban system.[10]

The just-in-time production model is not applicable to all operations. In fact, it requires a particular set of technical and organizational environmental conditions. For example, suppliers must be near at hand, because delays in delivery would make it advisable to have large reserve stocks despite the costs of locked-up semi-finished products. Another important condition is a stable demand – sudden changes can create a crisis for a production system with no reserves. Lastly, there should be no bottlenecks in the flow of production, which means that the productive capacity must be well-proportioned along the various intermediate stages.

The spread of computer-based technology helps to remove some of the constraints limiting the diffusion of the just-in-time production model. In fact, new technology, by cutting down set-up times and providing an information network from the final consumers to the suppliers of materials and semi-finished goods, through the different units which go to make up the production *filière*, reduces the volume of the minimum economic batch and hence the need for intermediate warehouses.

Flow-fund models, based on Nicholas Georgescu-Roegen's production analysis, provide a useful applied research tool into the economic effects of changing degrees of organizational flexibility. These models address the time profile of production processes and the quantities of intermediate goods lying in inventories.[11]

4.   THE ECONOMIC IMPACT OF COMPUTER-BASED TECHNOLOGY

The development and promulgation of computer-based technology provides another useful set of examples to which the above analysis and taxonomy may be addressed. The main property of computer-based technology is the *automation of information processes*. This has several important consequences:

(a)   increased flexibility and efficiency of organizational processes by reducing the specificity and complexity of information management;[12]
(b)   changes not only in the quantity of inputs in relation to output, but especially in their quality. In particular, with regard to the labour market, skill requirements and work patterns (shifts, hours of work, and so on) undergo a drastic change.[13] In many industrialized countries, the growth of service employment leads to a displacement of the demand for labour from traditional industrial occupations to new service occupations even within the manufacturing sector itself;
(c)   increased (technical) flexibility of equipment through cutting down the duration of the production process, response time and set-up times (hence reduced quantities of goods held in warehouses and reduced working capital).

The following pages focus on the effects of computer-based technology on *technical flexibility*, in particular on the shortening of production processes and their set-up times, and on the associated removal of the trade-off between economies of scale and economies of scope.

The duration of the production process has a double nature: it can be seen on the one hand as a *sort of input*, objectified in the quantity of stocks and semi-finished goods in process, and on the other as a contributory factor in determining the quality of the goods. The influence of process duration on product quality can be understood in two different ways. In the first place, response time (based on the process duration) is generally included among the qualitative characteristics of the product. Duration also affects the degree of strategic flexibility in qualitative changes of the product mix. In fact, the shorter the production process duration, the easier it is to vary the output qualitative characteristics in relation to market changes. For example, CAD/CAM can drastically reduce the time required for planning, design and production of a given product.

In certain industrial sectors that are strongly influenced by fashion (where the evolution of design plays a crucial role in orientating demand), as well as in service sectors, the overall process duration and response times are particularly important in determining the efficacy and efficiency of a production unit. Hence they have a decisive influence on its competitiveness.

Differentiation involves a cost when it leads to a loss of *economies of scale* inherent in standardized productions. Basically, differentiated production is more costly than standardized production when the loss of *economies of scale* is greater than the *economies of scope* that can be obtained when the different processes are carried on within the same firm or production unit. There are economies of scope when it is less costly to 'combine' the productions of two or more commodities than to perform them 'separately';[14] in other words, if it is possible to economize on some shareable production element or intermediate stages by saturating their production capacities.

Economies of scope make multi-production within a single microeconomic unit desirable, but they do not determine its degree of flexibility. This is determined by the adaptability of the production processes of single goods. On the other hand, it is possible to produce, in a 'flexible way', a vast range of outputs without enjoying economies of scope. In fact, a wide mix of products may be obtained by using subcontractors rather than by producing all the commodities in-house. We have seen that in some cases the use of subcontractors reduces fixed costs and hence increases the adaptability of the processes.

Cutting down set-up times is a key element in reducing the cost of producing differentiated goods with the same equipment. Greatest flexibility is obtained when the same degree of economies of scale can be enjoyed in producing single-unit lots (that is, one-of-a-kind) as in producing a single homogeneous product. In this case, it is possible to enjoy economies of scope and economies of scale at the same time.[15]

With the spread of information technology, industrial production acquired some of the elements typical of traditional artisan production (high flexibility and trade specialization). This has been brought out by the literature on flexible specialization.[16] Alongside these *similarities*, however, there are two important *differences* between artisan production and flexible industrial production. These are due to the fact that the latter, unlike the former, permits a reduction in idle time, and allows economies of scale. Artisan production has three basic characteristics: high flexibility, long idle time for tools, and long training time for workers (high specialization). The long idle time for tools is due to the fact that the craftsman moves from one operation to the other, using his tools one at a time. The more operations performed by one craftsman, the longer the idle time of the tools will be. Generally the craftsman's tools are simple and the incidence of idle time on total unit costs is relatively low. The great advantage of handicraft production is, of course, its flexibility, which allows very small batches, or indeed single units, to be produced. The importance of this advantage is such that in many activities handicraft has never been completely supplanted by cheaper industrial production, but has survived alongside the latter. On the other hand, industrial production, based on the factory system, permits the excess of equipment productive capacity to be reduced. In particular, this may involve a decrease in the time that individual machines and tools lie idle.[17]

The possibility of reconciling economies of scope with those of scale is leading to the spread of a new model of industrial organization for firms and markets: *large-scale flexible production*. In fact, 'on-line' linkages between markets and producers, and flexible technology, allow 'custom-made' production in large establishments.[18]

Large-scale flexible production is destined to coexist with other forms of production and market organization: small-scale flexible industrial production, industrial production based on rigid technologies and flexible organizational systems, mass production, traditional artisan production. The prevalence of one form of production over another in a geographical area or sector of activity depends on the interaction of environmental and institutional elements.

Microelectronics may reduce the minimum investment cost. This lowering of the entry barriers, which allows new firms access, is essential but is not sufficient for the formation and development of a large number of small, flexible, specialized firms. Other determining factors are: the characteristics of financial markets and financial availability; the spread of entrepreneurial abilities; trade-union regulations and industrial relations; central and local governments' industrial policies; and laws on taxation and social security contributions.[19]

However, flexible automation production systems usually require high investment per operator, which makes it indispensable to keep the plants running 24 hours a day.[20] Therefore the production process tends to be organized according to principles similar to those in the continuous-process industries, such as the iron, steel, chemical and paper industries (ECE, 1986, p. 135). With increased capital intensity, idle time must be reduced through flexible utilization of working hours and shifts.

In small and medium companies, the application of flexible automation production systems still faces considerable difficulties. In particular, the diffusion of computer-integrated manufacturing (CIM) or computer-aided manufacturing (CAM) involve the following main problems:

(a) higher investment cost per employee than old technologies based on rigid automation;[21]

(b) the need to produce a large total volume of differentiated products in order to benefit from the economies of scale allowed by flexible equipment;

(c) in-house technical expertise;

(d) resistance to modifying the existing organization and distribution of skills;

(e) the technical difficulty of making compatible the software used in different areas.

The spread of computer-based technology within firms usually begins with islands of automation with very little interconnection between them. The search for a common language permitting communication between different areas of automation may prove technically difficult, and therefore economically burdensome. At the present stage of software development this difficulty may discourage the planning and realization of computer-integrated manufacturing (CIM).

The application of information technology within firms through islands of automation and the coexistence of a variety of organizational and technical solutions correspond to the nature of the technical change highlighted in the works of Christopher Freeman (1974), Nathan Rosenberg (1976, 1982), Richard Nelson and Sidney Winter (1982) and Giovanni Dosi (1984, 1988). The capacities of the workers in a firm develop gradually with the introduction of new techniques, according to the way in which these new techniques are translated into practical knowledge. All these capacities together determine the specific nature of the firm itself, which is more than the sum total of the different experiences and skills.

5. CONCLUSIONS

In changing market conditions, efficacy, which indicates the ability to produce the right thing for the market, becomes a complex goal and assumes a predominant role in affecting the competitiveness of a firm. In the presence of uncertainty, efficacy requires production flexibility.

Production flexibility involves workers being subjected to turbulence and changes in productive activity, since it implies that workers are actively involved in the production process and are rapidly adapting their own skills to changes in products and processes. In many situations the demand for greater organizational flexibility is met by compensation mechanisms that make changes more acceptable to workers and to society. Thus it happens that some forms of flexibility are counterbalanced by forms of rigidity. For example, functional flexibility may be accompanied by a low numerical flexibility, so that functional flexibility is compensated (and limited) by the stability of the worker–firm links. This is the case in the large Japanese firms where there is a high degree of functional flexibility in the use of labour power, but little external mobility (employees are said to have 'a job for life') and with a strong dualistic flexibility in labour market. Moreover, in some contexts the workers' direct involvement may be achieved or simply encouraged by forms of participation, co-management and co-operation which can result in a reduction of external mobility. In yet other situations strategic and operational flexibility can be obtained through numerical flexibility, within the context of a social system that guarantees a network of protection (such as unemployment benefits and opportunities for retraining). In conclusion, *each specific context* features a combination of rigidities and flexibilities that varies according to the evolution of institutional conditions which differ enormously from one sector of activity to another (namely, the financial structure, economic policies, social security system, industrial relations and market characteristics).

The emphasis often placed on computer-based technology, and on the opportunities it provides for making production processes more flexible, may induce people to forget that flexibility can arise from the way in which the elements of production are organized, regardless of the technology being used. In fact, flexibility in production is first and foremost an economic phenomenon, which may even be independent of the technology adopted. The theoretical treatment of flexibility and applied studies of the phenomenon both need an analytical representation of production which takes account of organizational and temporal dimensions of production processes. Moreover, while there is no doubt that conditions of uncertainty demand greater flexibility, there is no close link between the pursuit of greater flexibility and the size of production units or firms. In fact, in some cases new technology allows a high degree of flexibility in large-scale production, while in other cases it favours the economic potential of small firms or production units. This encourages the coexistence of different technical and organizational structures.

NOTES

1. This chapter discusses some arguments developed in Chapter 12 of the author's forthcoming book *Production Process and Technical Change* (Cambridge University Press). He is indebted to Cliff Pratten, Sandeep Kapur and the participants at the European Association for Evolutionary Political Economy (EAEPE) 1990 Annual Conference in Florence for useful comments. The research received financial support from the National Research Council (CNR, Rome, 89.05143ct10).
2. On true uncertainty and probability, see Keynes (1921, ch. 6; 1936, pp. 148, 152, 168, 316; 1937, pp. 112–14); Knight (1921); Carabelli (1988, pp. 47, 58–9, 199, 212–22).
3. On different meanings of flexibility see: Stigler (1939) who discusses flexibility in the context of static decision-making; Marschak and Nelson (1962) where flexibility makes subsequent actions less costly or preserves more choices; Koopmans (1964) on flexibility of future preference; Jones and Ostroy (1984) who consider flexibility in relation to the probability distributions of payoffs over time in a sequential decision context. See also

the interesting discussions in Merkhofer (1975), Mills (1986), Del Monte and Esposito (1989), Amendola *et al.* (1990).

4. Stigler (1939) represents the trade-off between adaptability (flexibility in his terminology) and efficiency by the position and the slope of the short-period average-cost curves: the unit-cost curve of a more adaptable plant is flatter, but with the minimum point higher, than the unit-cost curve of a less adaptable plant. Generally the literature on production flexibility concentrates on adaptability (Marschak and Nelson, 1962, pp. 42ff.; Mills, 1986).

5. There is still no definitive taxonomy concerning flexibility in economics. Strategic flexibility is also called dynamic flexibility, while the concept of operational flexibility is similar, in many respects, to the definition of short-run flexibility or static flexibility (Cohendet and Llerena, 1988).

6. See Rosenberg (1982, p. 109).

7. Minsky (1982, 1985); Vercelli (1988, p. 105); Boyer (1988, pp. 84ff.); Duijn (1982).

8. For a thorough analysis of these factors see Piore and Sabel (1984); Boyer (1988); Barca and Magnani (1989).

9. On the development of industrial districts, the renaissance of small firms and inter-firm forms of collaboration, see Becattini (1989); Bellandi (1989); Brusco (1982, 1986); Mariti and Smiley (1983); Piore and Sabel (1984); Russo (1985); Vercelli (1988); Lorenzoni and Ornati (1988); Tinacci Mosello (1989); Goodman *et al.* (1989); Barca and Magnani (1989); Phillimore (1989); Storper (1989); Amin (1989a, 1989b); Capecchi (1989); Mariti (1991). On the role of small firms on innovative processes, see also Rothwell and Zegveld (1982); Oakey (1984); Oakey *et al.* (1988); Vercelli (1989).

10. The just-in-time model was tested by Toyota in car production at the beginning of the 1960s. The philosophy of just-in-time production could be summed up as 'the smallest possible quantity [of production elements] at the latest possible time'. Just-in-time is a system whereby materials are bought and components are built only at the moment when they are to be used, without any intervening storage period. Using special order-cards (Kanban system), various orders come from the market and pass successively back through the different work-cells of the production cycle to the suppliers of inter-mediate goods and raw materials (the pull system). The literature on this subject is vast; see, for example, Monden (1983); Lubben (1988); Hay (1988).

11. See Georgescu-Roegen (1966, 1971, 1976); Tani (1986, 1987, 1988, 1989); Scazzieri (1983); Zamagni (1987, 1989); Landesmann (1986); Leijonhufvud (1986); Piacentini (1987, 1989); and, for an attempt to apply a flow-fund model to empirical research, see Morroni (1992, Part II).

12. See Perez (1985, pp. 453–4), Rullani (1988, pp. 96–8).

13. A large body of literature examines the social and labour-market implications of computer-based technology. Among the main contributions, see Rothwell and Zegveld (1979); Blattern (1981); Stoneman (1987, ch. 14); Cooper and Clark (1982); Bosworth (1983); Freeman and Soete (1985, 1987); Leontief and Duchin (1986); ECE (1986); Cyert and Mowery (1988); OECD (1988). There is general agreement that, in analysing the impact of introducing computer-based technology, an approach that integrates the microeconomic and macroeconomic dimensions must be adopted.

14. Panzar and Willig (1981, p. 268). Given two output vectors y_1 and y_2, we have economies of scope if we can assume the following relation between the cost functions: $C(y_1, y_2)$ $C(y_1, 0) + C(0, y_2)$. See also Teece (1980, pp. 225ff.). On production diversification, see Grant (1988). Generally, the literature considers only the combination of different production lines within one firm. However, the economies of scope may operate not only at firm level but also at other operational levels, such as at production unit, plant and production line level.

15. On this point see Bailey and Friedlaender (1982, p. 1026); Del Monte and Esposito (1989, p. 23).

16. 'Flexible specialization leads back to those craft methods of production that lost out at the first industrial divide' (Piore and Sabel, 1984, pp. 6, 27–8, 124). For a critical analysis on flexible specialization, see, for instance, Minsky (1985); Landes (1987); Williams *et al.* (1987); Archibugi (1988); Hyman (1988); Amin (1989a).

17. Georgescu-Roegen (1976, p. 68) writes that the factory system, for this extraordinary property to achieve the maximum time economy, 'deserves to be placed side by side with money as the two most fateful economic innovations for mankind'. This innovation is 'economic' and not technological, 'because the economy of time achieved by the factory system is independent of technology. Nothing prevents us from using the most primitive technique of cloth weaving in a factory system'.

18. Perez (1985, p. 46, n. 23).

19. The impact of 'regional institutions' on the spread of new technological and organizational solutions is stressed, for instance, by Sabel and Piore (1984, pp. 264–5); while on the role of financial structure credit institutions, see Minsky (1982, 1985); Storey (1983); Vercelli (1988).

20. With the introduction of information technology, some large-scale production may become so capital-intensive that production in Europe will be competitive, even if the labour costs are higher than in developing countries.

21. Northcott and Walling (1988, p. 11), reporting the results of thorough empirical research on the impact of microelectronics in British industry, observe that more than one-fifth of the user factories have experienced economic difficulties due to high development costs (particularly for product application), and lack of finance for development. On diffusion of CIM, CAM and CAD see ECE (1986, pp. 24ff., 45ff.); Gaibisso *et al.* (1987); Edquist and Jacobsson (1988); OECD (1988); Vickery and Campbell (1989).

PART II

Innovation, Technology and Economic Evolution

6. Reflections on the Present State of Evolutionary Economic Theory

Ulrich Witt[1]

---

1. INTRODUCTION

The idea that evolutionary economics is a new field of research has been promoted by an increasing number of writers in recent years.[2] Yet the problems investigated by these writers and the theoretical approaches they use differ considerably. Indeed, evolutionary phenomena and evolutionary concepts seem to attract the interest, and are akin to the 'world-view', of different schools of thought in economics. The recent wave of papers and books is rooted in four quite different intellectual traditions: the Austrian school, the Schumpeterian tradition, institutionalism, and, to a lesser extent, the Marxist school. The present state of evolutionary economics is thus best characterized as being a new heterodoxy in economic thinking. The new heterodoxy has in common opposition to the neoclassical world-view which at present dominates economics. The 'hard core' of the latter is a synthesis of the constrained maximization calculus and equilibrium concepts. The opposition's main criticism is that this hard core prevents the neoclassical approach from gaining proper access to the understanding of process and change, the crucial features of modern economic history. There is no doubt, indeed, that neoclassical equilibrium theory has, until recently, had serious problems in explaining even what the theory itself had identified as the most prominent driving force of economic development: technical progress.[3]

Unfortunately, however, the diverse contributions to evolutionary economics have been better at launching criticisms of neoclassical concepts than at developing the reasons for their opposition into a more constructive consensus about alternative core notions. Much of the neoclassical paradigm's attraction, and many of its recent successes in taking up new topics,[4] appear to spring from the simple but very general analytical structure provided by its hard core. It would seem desirable, therefore, to develop evolutionary economics into a more coherent approach based on principles of comparable generality. The present paper explores the prospects for such an endeavour. The argumentation proceeds as follows.

Section 2 reviews the synthesis of constraint maximization and equilibrium concepts in more detail in order to point out its shortcomings in explaining process and change. It is because it is a fruit of an analogy to classical mechanics that the synthesis has no access to the phenomenon of endogenously caused change. The idea that change may be generated in a systematic way within the economy is, however, a core notion shared by all currents of evolutionary economics. Starting from this basic proposition, section 3 focuses on the role of novelty and innovations and discusses some principles that could explain the motivation and the capacity to create innovative change on the level of the individual.

Section 4 then looks into how innovations diffuse through the economy. This phenomenologically most obvious part of an evolutionary process is often considered as the economic evolution *per se*. As such, innovation diffusion has elicited a lot of contributions in evolutionary economics. What seems to have found less attention is the institutional background. The generation and propagation of novelty – itself a driving force in the emergence, change and decay of markets and other institutions – is strongly dependent on whether the predominating institutions are innovation-inhibiting or innovation-encouraging. The diffusion of novelty is, of course, only a partial aspect of the more general co-ordination problem in which economic theory is traditionally interested. Section 5 therefore explores the consequences of the principles previously derived with regard to the theory of market co-ordination and its allocative predictions. Section 6 offers some tentative conclusions.

2. THE CRUCIAL OBJECTION TO THE NEOCLASSICAL PARADIGM

The evolutionary approach to economics is still awaiting a discussion of its general principles – ideally, principles comparable, in their generality, to the standards of the neoclassical hard core. This discussion would certainly help increase the coherence between the heterodox contributions. Yet it may have been precisely because of the rather specialized research interests of the different schools contributing to evolutionary economics that a need for such a discussion has not yet been felt. In the tradition of Schumpeter (1934[1912], 1942), for instance, important objections to neoclassical economic thought have been formulated (Winter, 1971; Nelson and Winter, 1982; Day and Eliasson, 1986; Dosi *et al.*, 1988; Hanusch, 1988). In the constructive work, however, the focus of this school is quite narrowly on the firm, on industrial development and growth in long waves, technical progress, innovation and market structure (Nelson, 1987; Rahmeyer, 1989). Little attempt has yet

been made to develop a more general background which would cover the
level of individual behaviour, the industry level, and phenomena at a more
aggregate level.

Institutionalist writers have provided a thorough criticism of neoclassical
economics (see Hodgson, 1988; Gordon and Adams, 1989, for recent surveys).
But, by its very nature, this approach tends to de-emphasize all aspects
related to individual behaviour in economics while focusing on patterns of
change in institutions and aggregate phenomena in a rather eclectic manner
(Langlois, 1986a). It is not entirely clear whether a more general theoretical
foundation, if compatible with the institutionalists' conception of a theory,
would be seen as desirable. (See, however, Hodgson, 1988, pt 3.) The
Marxist school relies in its critique as well as in its own theoretical contribution on the classical, that is, pre-neoclassical, way of thinking and categorizing
(see Goodwin, 1986, for a recent assessment). It has therefore never assessed
the general individualistic foundation of economics during the marginalist
revolution as an achievement and hence has never been interested in providing something comparable.

There are disproportions too between the criticism and constructive
achievements of the Austrian and subjectivist contributions.[5] Despite considerable methodological quarrels about the Misesian heritage of apriorism
and, more recently, about hermeneutics, the writers within this camp have
tried to develop a coherent theory of expectations (Shackle, 1972; Lachmann,
1977), of capital and interest (Lachmann, 1978; Faber, 1986) and of the
market process as guided by discovery and arbitraging activities (Hayek,
1978, pp. 179–90; Kirzner, 1979; Lachmann, 1986; Streit and Wegner, 1991).[6]
With these broader research interests and with its methodological individualism the Austrian/subjectivist school perhaps comes closer, in its compre-
hensiveness, to neoclassical economic theory than the other currents contributing to evolutionary economics. Moreover, both the Austrian and the neoclassical school originate from the same major upheaval in the history of
economic thought: the marginalist revolution of the previous century. The
basic ideas pursued by the Austrian/subjectivist school, and particularly the
reason that it departed from neoclassical economics from the very beginning
(see Streissler, 1972; Mirowski, 1989, ch. 5), may therefore provide a good
starting point for the present exploration of some more general principles for
evolutionary economics.

Jevons and Walras, the neoclassical protagonists of the marginalist revolution, were inspired by an analogy to the contemporaneous ideal of the physical
sciences – classical mechanics. Jevons (1879, p. 23) expressly wrote of a
'mechanics of utility and self-interest'. For Menger, the Austrian protagonist,
this model from physics played no role at all. His efforts were directed
towards a psycho-economic foundation for economic theory (Witt, 1986a).

Consequently, he elaborated on issues such as subjective foresight, expectations, uncertainty, fallibility of knowledge and the role of time, while playing down the role of equilibrium (Menger, 1981[1871]). These ideas have since then been developed further, the most recent of the subjectivists' notions being ignorance and constant flux in a world of kaleidics (see Shackle, 1958, 1972; Loasby, 1976; Wiseman, 1983). Menger's psycho-economic speculations, published at a time when psychology was still a rather backward field, may appear amateurish today, but the problems were perceived with a genuinely economic understanding. Thus Menger's approach did not run the risk of being led astray by subscribing to an analogy with doubtful consequences.

This is precisely, it is submitted here, what happened to Jevons, Walras and their neoclassical successors in their eagerness to interpret economic problems in terms of the model borrowed from mechanics. The neoclassical paradigm is, in this way, based on a latent misconception which prevents it from reaching an adequate understanding of process and change in economics. The problem is not so much one of whether dynamic models are used as a means of dealing with time as an essential dimension of economic phenomena. This is perhaps one of the misunderstandings underlying more recent semantic expansions of the neoclassical approach to evolutionary phenomena. The crucial objection is rather that using the mechanical model necessarily involves breaking up the historical flow of events and creating a dichotomy between exogenous disturbances on the one hand and endogenous restorations of equilibrium states on the other.

In mechanics, disequilibrium is caused when some outside force creates free energy within the system under consideration. In the process of restoring equilibrium this free energy is dissipated. The first element of the neoclassical hard-core synthesis – the constrained utility maximization hypothesis – carries this basic concept over to economics. The economic analogue to free energy is psychic energy, drive or motivation to act on the part of the individual (Wolfson, 1987; Mirowski, 1988, ch. 1). It is measured by the difference between the utility obtained from the presently realized combination of choices and the utility that might be gained from other feasible combinations of choices, if outside forces – that is, exogenous data changes – make more-preferred choices feasible. The analogy suggests that the drive is dissipated once the individual has achieved the constrained maximum.

Prerequisite to the constrained utility maximization hypothesis is a particular theoretical representation of the individual's cognitive situation. The individual is portrayed as already having a complete overview of all possible choices and at least a rough understanding of their consequences. This is the complete opposite of the Austrian idea of partial ignorance and fallible knowledge creating room for discovery and learning. In particular, the fact, emphasized over and over again by Shackle and other subjectivists, that decision problems are not something given, but first have to be created in the mind of the individual, is completely left out of the neoclassical representation. Cognitive creativity is, of course, at odds with the very spirit of the neoclassical synthesis of constrained maximization and the notion of equilibrium.

At a time when the tools of dynamic analysis were little developed, the synthesis seemed to provide a means of getting rid of the need actually to examine the intricate dynamics of the hypothesized interactive individual adjustments. If all individual plans, which have been maximized on the basis of market prices, production functions and initial endowments, are mutually compatible in equilibrium as required by definition, then there is, by virtue of simultaneous optimization under perfect information, no further incentive to deviate from the chosen individual plans. If there is any further change in the individual's behaviour, this must, quite logically, be attributed to factors not explained within the theory. In this interpretation, any kind of changes that occur must necessarily be either unexplained 'data changes' which disturb equilibria, or adaptation or convergence processes to a hypothesized new equilibrium state. It is only the latter that has to be explained.

The unfortunate implication is that individual behaviour cannot be conceived as other than responding to changing conditions imposed on them from outside. There is no idea that change can be created by the agents themselves. Hence, to the extent to which change is, in fact, caused endogenously within the economy, a theoretical approach which builds on the mechanical interpretation can, at best, provide a fragmentary understanding of the evolutionary economic process. This is not to say that an economy or any of its parts is never subject to effects originating outside the domain of economic theory, effects which therefore have to be treated as exogenously caused. The crucial question is whether all change in the economy has its cause outside the scope of economics. The new heterodoxy of evolutionary economics seems to agree that an answer in the affirmative would be a misperception (Dopfer, 1986). Important aspects of the changes which can be observed in modern, rapidly altering economies, changes which distinguish them from pre-modern economies, would simply be inaccessible to economic theory. This would, for example, be the case for entrepreneurial activities, technological progress, changing preferences and newly emerging institutions.

3. FEATURES OF INDIVIDUAL BEHAVIOUR REQUIRING EXPLANATION

Evolution can be defined in many ways. The definition underlying the following considerations is a very simple one: *evolution is considered to be the transformation of a system over time through endogenously generated change.*

In the previous section it was argued that this kind of change, and thus evolution, is systematically excluded from the basic explanatory pattern of neoclassical economics. The explanation of endogenously generated change can therefore be considered a distinctive task of an alternative, evolutionary approach. Where does this change come from and how is it projected into the economy? As has been submitted in more detail elsewhere (Witt, 1991a, ch. 1), the ultimate source of this kind of change is the human creation of novelty. New information emerges incidentally or is deliberately sought. Once its meaning has been revealed, this new information may diffuse throughout the economy and induce new kinds of action, that is to say, innovations. As crucial aspects in evolutionary economic theory, the emergence and dissemination of novelty will be discussed in turn in this and the next two sections.

Looking more closely into how novelty is generated, two features of behaviour, which do not seem to be sufficiently understood, show up: the motivation behind the search for novelty and the cognitive problem of the mental creation of novelty. The first feature can be characterized by asking why people search for novelty – something the meaning of which they cannot anticipate, and hence evaluate, during the search. The neoclassical optimization model cannot provide the answer. Optimal choice of actions can only be based on perceived or expected consequences. In the case of unknowable future outcomes, expectations cannot be formed and, hence, cannot motivate action, unless it is assumed that people systematically err with regard to the unknowability condition or deliberately ignore it.[7] What is needed in order to come to grips with the problem of motivation is a hypothesis of different character, one that explains the psychic energy, motivation or drive to act not by reference to future outcomes but by reference to a past or present state of mind.[8]

There are several candidates for such motivation hypotheses (Witt, 1991a, ch. 3). Consider, for instance, an individual who gets a feeling of thrill or pleasure from experiencing new, not previously known, cognitive stimuli. There is considerable empirical evidence that humans do have such feelings and these may be identified as the driving force behind curiosity. Their intensity varies with the degree of relative deprivation of the feeling: the more boring a life becomes, the more new cognitive stimuli are appreciated (Scitovsky, 1976). The motivation to search for something which is not yet known, apart from it being new, is thus explained by the present state of a personal disposition.

Another motivation hypothesis is associated with the concept of 'satisficing' (Siegel, 1957; March and Simon, 1958, pp. 47–52). Here the motivation to act results from dissatisfaction relative to a variable aspiration level, that is, a level that reflects earlier successes and failures in attempting to reach the current aspiration level. Imagine a situation in which the set of choices feasible to an individual – her 'entitlement rights' in the sense of Sen (1981) – is significantly deteriorating. This means that the best option feasible in the present is inferior to the best one in the past. According to the optimization model, the individual adjusts to the new, but inferior, optimum and, if this happens to be an equilibrium, that is the end of the story. Not so under the satisficing hypothesis where, in such a situation, the current aspiration level is not satisfied. The divergence generates a motivation to act, and the action may involve search for new, not yet known, options even though it is not known whether the search will be successful.[9]

In both motivation hypotheses, the present state of a personal disposition – the relative deprivation or the current aspiration level – determines the current motivation to search. Because of this property, these hypotheses imply a strong path-dependency, or historical contingency, of the individual motivation to search for novelty. The flow of earlier historical events forms the individuals' current curiosity levels or the levels of aspiration (Hagen, 1964). Even if a co-ordination equilibrium in the sense of the neoclassical approach has been successfully attained in the present, these levels may imply a continued individual inclination to look for and try out new possibilities of action and thus an endogenous distortion of the equilibrium state.

The second feature mentioned above as requiring explanation, the capacity to create novelty, plays a key role in subjectivist economics. A decision-maker's perception of choices and the conditions under which they are feasible is influenced by her imaginative power, that is, the capacity to create novelty (Shackle, 1972; Loasby, 1976). Imagination becomes more important the smaller the roles of routine and experience. The crucial fact now is that, by its very nature, novelty cannot be predicted. There is an ultimate 'bound of unknowledge' (Shackle, 1983) or, to put it more generally, an irreducible constraint to positively anticipating what will come out of evolution.

This is a trivial, but epistemologically momentous postulate. Despite its trivial character it is often violated so that paradoxical results follow, such as in the neoclassical 'innovation' research already mentioned. If the postulate is taken seriously, theoretical work cannot do more than rule out some specific outcomes whatever novelty will otherwise emerge (Hayek, 1964). That is, theory may claim that certain things will not happen. Such predictions can be tested. But, since the number of still-possible outcomes is unlimited, such theories do not positively anticipate evolution and its properties. Moreover, if the class of outcomes ruled out is small, such theories will have rather little empirical content.

Besides the problem of impossible substantive predictions of novelty there is, of course, the procedural question of how novelty is generated.

Hypotheses on regularities governing these processes are not subject to the epistemological constraint and may therefore be feasible. In fact, they should give a key for understanding why novelty cannot be positively anticipated. Novelty, as a product of human imagination, emerges from the brain's activities (see Popper and Eccles, 1977). Although the complicated processes taking place here are not yet very well understood, it seems that recombination of already known cognitive components plays a key role. Perhaps the processes are not different, in principle, from 'blind' – that is, unintended – variation which is responsible for generating genetic novelty in biology (Campbell, 1987). A possible interpretation would be that new cognitive constructs emerge from the recombinatorial processes and are compared and selected according to interpretative patterns (see Andersson, 1987).

To be frankly speculative, imagine cognitive constructs as points and interpretative patterns as attractors in a very high dimensional phase space. At a given point in time, out of an infinite number of existing attractors, a particular attractor which has been attained in a historical (that is, path-dependent) process is pre-eminent. As long as cognitive constructs newly produced by recombination remain within the same basin of attraction, the prevailing interpretative pattern is maintained. Once the bounds of a given basin of attraction are exceeded, however, a new attractor becomes relevant and the newly produced construct is conceived as novelty (Witt, 1991a, ch. 1). The complexity of these recombination processes increases so extraordinarily the further one tries to iterate them that the possible outcomes and interpretations are almost instantaneously lost from sight. This is the reason that novelty cannot be anticipated. The only way to keep track is by following up a sample of the infinite number of possible recombinations – which, of course, amounts to carrying out the very process of mentally creating novelty.

There may thus be a chance, though at present rather vague, of describing and explaining the process of generating novelty on the basis of formal models. The properties of such models confirm the non-anticipatability postulate: they cannot be used to predict positively the outcome, that is, what will be produced in the process of recombination. The non-anticipatability postulate can be related in this context to the problems resulting from a multiplicity of equilibria to which the extremely complex and thus opaque recombination process may be attracted. To the extent to which future economic developments involve novelty, as they now usually do, an interesting conclusion can be drawn. Difference and/or differential equations in economic variables with unique solutions cannot be expected to provide reliable predictive power. If novelty intervenes then predictions derived in that way are almost surely bound to fail. It may be conjectured that the common failure even of medium term econometric time series forecasts of economic activities is a case in point.

Now add the implications of the motivational aspect of individual innovative behaviour to this picture. The emergence of man-made novelty may then be described as a process which not only possesses a multiplicity of local attractors, but which also, given a continuing recombination activity resulting from the motivation to search for novelty, must have another significant property: the capacity to escape from any locally constrained basin of attraction as time elapses. This is simply another way of saying that change is endogenously generated.

4. INSTITUTIONAL FEATURES OF ECONOMIC EVOLUTION

Compared to the problem of emergence of novelty the dissemination of novelty and innovations has attracted considerably more interest in the new heterodoxy, particularly its Schumpeterian branch. A reason perhaps is that the context of dissemination may appear less loaded with epistemological problems. However, this impression is due, first of all, to the fact that the emergence and dissemination of novelty are more easily separable analytically than in the actual historical process. The usual assumption is that the properties of new items which diffuse in a population are already completely known to the scientific observer.[10] In actual fact, however, people have the capacity to make innovative modifications of the diffusing items in the very process of adoption, that is, they can create new variants which cannot be anticipated by the scientific observer. As previously argued, a systematic motivation to try to do so seems likely so that emergence and diffusion of novelties and innovations are actually interactive processes.[11] Nevertheless, an investigation of the dissemination context, on the premiss that novelty does not intervene, can contribute important insights into certain properties of evolutionary processes.

Two new dimensions show up here. First, the very fact of a diffusion requires an explanation of why everybody does not acquire the new information instantaneously. In general, in order to provide an answer one has to refer to institutional features such as communication networks with limited information transmission capacity, so that 'institutions indeed matter'. Secondly, while, as appropriate to the perspective of the Austrian/subjectivist school, in the previous section the level of the individual was predominant, the level of a population of individuals now carries a meaning of its own. This can be explained in more detail as follows.

Consider (as in partial market analysis) a particular class of individual choices in isolation – those associated with the diffusing item. In the easiest case this is just the bimodal choice between adopting or not adopting. Now think of individual behaviour as a frequency phenomenon occurring in a given population. The individual is, of course, still sovereign in making decisions, but the choice which is made becomes the marginal change in the relative frequency of choices of that class within the population. Finally, imagine that the individual makes her own decision in a way that in some respect depends on how many other members of the population have already made a particular choice. In that case, the marginal change in the relative frequency of behaviour within the population itself depends on the frequencies already achieved. Note that relative frequency is a variable which can no longer be defined in purely individualistic terms.

This kind of interdependency is called the frequency-dependency effect. It is a phenomenon already well-known from biological evolutionary theory (Murray, 1989) but has also gained increasing attention in various fields of economics.[12] Frequency-dependency effects are pervasive in diffusion processes in economics and the social sciences (Rogers, 1983). They are the central argument in diffusion models based on the analogy to contagious processes[13] as, for example, the early product life cycle models (Mahajan and Wind, 1986) and technology diffusion models (Iwai, 1984) with a logistic curve as diffusion pattern. Similarly, frequency-dependency effects are at the core of the recent work on network externalities, learning-by-using and technological 'lock in' (Arthur *et al.*, 1987; Arthur, 1988b, 1989; David, 1987; Gerybadze, 1991).

The various appearances of the frequency-dependency effect can neatly be illustrated if, under some idealizing assumptions, the dependency is expressed by a function. Consider the simplest bimodal case of choosing between adopting (a) and not adopting (b) a diffusing item when confronted with it, assuming for simplicity that there is only one such confrontation. Let the individual net benefit of choosing a over b be written as $u_a = u_a(F_a(t))$, where $F_a(t)$ is the relative frequency of adopters in the population at time t. For the probability f_a of choosing a over b assume that f_a is monotonically increasing with an increasing net benefit – a probabilistic version of opportunity-cost orientated behaviour (if the net benefit 0, then $f_a = 0$). Thus, a function $f_a = \theta(F_a(t))$ can be derived which reflects the frequency dependency effect of the benefit associated with choosing a. Imagine $u_a(0) > 0$ and $u_a' < 0$. The corresponding shape of θ is illustrated in Figure 6.1a. In this case, the benefit from adopting decreases as the number of adopters increases. This seems to be a very common pattern in markets where coming first is rewarded on the supply side because, for example, competitive pressure increases as F_a increases, and on the demand side because, for example, distinctiveness of consumption decreases with increasing F_a.

The particular time pattern of the corresponding diffusion process depends on a more specific assumption about how the individuals are confronted

Figure 6.1a

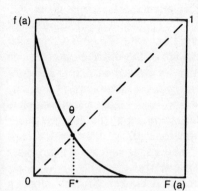

Figure 6.1b

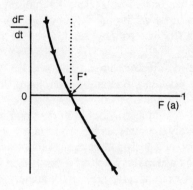

Figure 6.2a

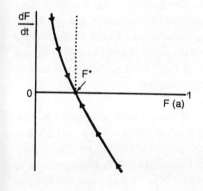

Figure 6.2b

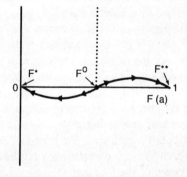

with the adoption opportunities over time and is therefore beyond the present outline. However, a phase diagram representation at least can be given with very little additional information. Since with probability f_a the number of adopters increases by one, f_a gives the marginal change of $F_a(t)$. Therefore, let $dF_a/dt = \emptyset(f_a - F_a)$. The qualitative properties of the diffusion process can then be illustrated as in Figure 6.1b, where for convenience, $\emptyset$ is a one-to-one mapping. As can be seen, the diffusion process is attracted to a unique equilibrium frequency of adopters $F_a^* < 1$. At this satiation level adopters and non-adopters coexist in the population. Surprisingly, the result is qualitatively the same, as the reader may confirm, for $u_a(0) > 0$ and $u_a' > 0$, at least for some specifications satisfying these conditions, as well as for many other cases where the graph of θ has a slope between -1 and 1.

A dramatically different situation emerges if the benefit from adopting increases in a non-linear fashion as in Figure 6.2a. Such a case may arise, for example, if two competing novelties diffuse simultaneously and positive externalities are present which increase with the number of adopters of either of the alternatives a or b. These alternatives may now, for instance, be new technical standards diffusing competitively as in Arthur's (1988b, 1989) technological 'lock in' phenomenon. As can be seen from the corresponding phase diagram in Figure 6.2b, an all-or-nothing situation emerges with two opposing attractors $F_a^* = 0$ or $F_a^{**} = 1$. This is the simplest possible example of a model with the characteristic features of non-linear dynamics: a process which can attain alternative multiple equilibria over time. If the process starts in the unstable state F_a°, as is reasonable in the case of competitively diffusing novelty, the historical path may initially be equally well attracted to F_a^* as to F_a^{**}. Once a tendency in one or the other direction has developed, however, the process is unlikely to return so that path-dependency shows up here once more as a significant evolutionary feature.

A difficult question that has been neglected in the diffusion literature is that of where the process of adoption or non-adoption of a given new item, or a set of competing items, does in fact stop or break off. The question is particularly pertinent, for instance, in the practical predictive use of life-cycle models. Sad experience (Tellis and Crawford, 1981) has taught us to be aware of the fact that saturation levels are difficult to determine and that what can happen after saturation is difficult to predict. Also, the diffusion process of a particular item may virtually die off long before the expected diffusion pattern has run its course, or unexpected jumps may occur during the process. The economically most significant reason for such imponderables may be that non-anticipated substitution processes are launched – either away from the diffusing novelty in the direction of its substitutes or the other way round. The causes for the initiation of such substitutions may often be rightly attributed to exogenous factors. But, in the absence of an appropriate motivation hypothesis, many cases may also be treated as exogenously caused, particularly in neoclassical contributions, although they are actually brought about by individuals responding to the effects of the diffusion process. This is certainly the case whenever the dissemination of novelty induces an individual motivation to respond by search and creation of further novelty.

The diffusion success of an innovation may, for example, induce substitution processes which drive a whole industry producing the substitute into crisis. Schumpeter (1942) called this 'creative destruction'. However, under the satisficing hypothesis, crisis is likely to generate the motivation to search for new possibilities of acting possibly – if cognitively anticipated – even before the crisis becomes virulent. If search is successful this may thus, under fortunate circumstances, indeed lead to an unforeseeable end to the substitution processes or even to re-substitution. An analysis of this phenomenon means, of course, jumping back and forth between the dissemination context and the context of emergence of novelty. Although this may appear difficult, the basic principles of individual motivation and the creative capacity to generate novelty, pointed out in the previous section, both require and permit the evolutionary approach to do so where appropriate.

Sometimes the novelty to be adopted or not adopted may be behavioural regularities such as rules, customs, habits and so on. The way in which the latter come into existence, that is, are adopted in a given population, can then be represented in the same way as diffusion processes (Witt, 1989b). Indeed, if behavioural regularities of any kind are interpreted as 'institutions' in the broadest sense, the theory of diffusing novelty, such as new technological or organizational devices and new consumption habits considered so far, can be used to represent 'institutional change' just as the diffusion of rules, customs or habits. The basic patterns induced by the frequency dependency effect can thus be generalized to govern the emergence of institutions, at least as far as the case of Figure 6.1 is concerned.

A certain difference may occur in the interpretation of the unstable fixpoint F_a° in Figure 6.2. In the case of competitively diffusing technological standards the diffusion process is likely to start in the neighbourhood of this point. In the case of institutions like rule, customs, habits and so on which usually have the character of conventions, institutional change may only take place by overcoming already established forms. The point of departure is then either F_a^* or F_a^{**}, and it turns out that F_a° becomes a 'critical mass point'. Accordingly, two different ways in which institutions can emerge must then be distinguished: spontaneous emergence associated with a diffusion profile like that of Figure 6.1; and an emergence which requires the organization of a coordinated adoption behaviour, that is, a collective transition of the critical mass, as in Figure 6.2. This insight can help to make sense of an old dispute in social philosophy about the nature of institutions (Vanberg, 1986; Witt, 1989b).

Suppose the rule, custom, or habit under consideration expresses the attitude towards innovativeness in a group or society – in this simple bimodal form thus either approval or disapproval. Then the case of Figure 6.2 may help to explain why highly innovative societies are historically rather rare cases. A transition has to be made from the primitive, innovation-averse institutions which threaten and punish all attempts to innovate to institutions which approve or encourage innovativeness. Once the critical mass point has been overcome, however, increasing innovativeness may expose ever more members in the society to competition and crisis and thus induce them to keep pace by searching for novelty themselves (Witt, 1987).

5.   COORDINATION AND DE-CO-ORDINATION: HOW SHOULD ALLOCATION THEORY BE MODIFIED?

The discussion on the dissemination of novelty has been confined to the 'partial' framework conventionally adopted in diffusion research. To the extent to which individual adoption decisions hinge upon the frequency-dependency effect, this engenders a peculiar form in which individual behaviour is co-ordinated, in regard to the partial setting concerned. This is drastically expressed in synergetics as the 'slaving principle' (Haken, 1987, ch. 1). In particular, an additional constraint is invoked on the decision-makers: the institutionally determined sequence of individual choices. People are not free to choose when to choose. By contrast, economic theory of co-ordination and the allocation of resources is traditionally orientated towards explaining co-ordination without paying much attention to the question of the historical sequence of interactions.[14] Furthermore, it is not the partial setting, for example a single market, which is considered, but the entire interdependent system of markets in the economy. It seems appropriate, therefore, to look also into the more generally posed problem of market co-ordination under conditions where novelty emerges and disseminates in the economy.

As is well known, the central propositions of neoclassical general equilibrium theory take a strong view on market co-ordination. Many of the propositions are obviously motivated by the desire to derive welfare-theoretic implications. It is claimed that a certain allocation of resources will have been achieved once all arbitrage and recontracting activities in the markets have been brought to an end. Under standard assumptions the allocation is determined to depend solely on initial endowments or, more generally, entitlement rights, on production technology and on preferences. Arbitrage and recontracting are thus viewed as producing what may be labelled 'perfect co-ordination' of individual, optimized plans. 'Perfect' here means that all opportunities for improving one's position through voluntarily achieved re-allocation have been exploited. The actual interactive adjustment process is rarely dealt with, and when it is, only under severely simplifying assumptions. Nevertheless, for a broad class of processes, it seems to be common understanding that exchange and production activities converge to a state of perfect co-ordination if 'no favourable surprise' turns up and interrupts the process of convergence (Fisher, 1983).[15]

Precisely at this point, however, the qualifications made earlier with respect to the role of equilibrium in evolutionary economic theory must be taken up again. Learning, contractual adjustments and arbitrage in the markets certainly tend to increase the co-ordination of individual behaviour in the economy. But, as discussed above, new possibilities of action do not just 'pop up' in an inexplicable way. There is a systematic tendency to search for and create them. Innovative activities not only cause new needs to inform and learn, that is, new problems of temporary ignorance; they also extend the choice set of the innovators in a 'non-co-ordinated' way, which is to say in a way where, by the same token, the position of other agents in the market may be caused to deteriorate through pecuniary external effects. The substitution processes which these innovative activities may trigger off have already been addressed in the partial framework of the previous section. In the present more general perspective they amount to effects which tend to de-co-ordinate the allocation of resources.[16] Since both the co-ordinating and the de-co-ordinating tendencies work simultaneously, the notion of 'perfect co-ordination' draws a one-sided picture.

For an evolutionary approach a generalization is necessary in which the systematically de-co-ordinating tendencies are accounted for. A way to achieve this may be based on the following consideration.[17] Imagine the situation of an agent who, perhaps due to a highly innovative environment, is not perfectly informed about all conditions relevant to her decision making. On the demand side of the markets, all that the agent knows for sure is that an ultimate budget constraint exists, so that each single item of her expenses competes with every other one. The precise form of the constraint depends on current prices, which are not known completely, and on the agent's entitlement rights. On the supply side of the market, the agent knows that there is an upper bound for the price she posts, where demand is zero, and a lower bound, where demand is greater than or equal to zero, but costs of supply can no longer be covered. Assume for convenience that, in the interval between the upper and the lower price, demand and costs co-vary in such a way that non-negative profits are possible.

A necessary condition for survival in the markets is to keep to the ultimate budget constraint on the demand side and to keep within the limits of the upper and lower price bound, that is, to avoid losses sufficiently frequently on the supply side. Hence, for all agents in the economy there are viability bounds which, via prices and entitlement rights, depend on the behaviour of other agents and thus are variable. Agents who do not manage to keep to these moving bounds do not survive – the analogue of natural selection. Losses and overdrawing of budgets alert the agents to the need to adjust their expenses and price and supply behaviour appropriately. The threat of being driven out of the market thus induces efforts on the part of all agents which, in effect, represent mutual co-ordination efforts.

In a hypothetical, perfectly competitive case in which all agents are able to adjust perfectly, the bounds are exactly met by everyone. The upper and lower price bound on the supply side would then simply collapse into the unique, zero-profit, competitive price. However, this case is systematically inhibited by the de-co-ordinating effects resulting from the search for and creation of novelty. Innovations tend to expand the innovator's viability bounds while contracting those of the innovators' competitors. They may be exposed to dwindling profits, or even losses, and to an interference with their ultimate budget constraints so that considerable adjustment or co-ordination necessities are newly induced.

Co-ordinating and de-co-ordinating tendencies in the markets thus jointly effect a 'viable co-ordination'. Neoclassical equilibrium theory labels this 'disequilibrium', but no concepts are offered to characterize more closely the regularities governing such a state. As a consequence, it is difficult to understand how such a state 'far from equilibrium' can be stable. The evolutionary interpretation just outlined offers such a concept. The two opposing endeavours, learning and adjusting on the one hand, and searching for and trying out of innovations on the other, establish opposing co-ordination tendencies with regard to the resulting co-ordination. Their effects may just balance and stabilize a situation of viable co-ordination as a persistent, though not necessarily unique or stable, pattern of prices and quantities.[18]

Agents experiment with prices and/or quantities in trying to learn about their environment. What happens as long as an agent manages to keep within the viability bounds may be subject to arbitrary individual dispositions and subjective, idiosyncratic experience. Selection pressure is not tight enough to eliminate this kind of variance (Witt, 1986b) – contrary to Friedman's (1953) assertion which is based on the fictitious conditions of perfect co-ordination.

Accordingly, the allocative picture is blurred by the particular, path-dependent mixture of ignorance, learning achievements and acquired skills, which is shaken up anew with every other innovation. Indeed, under viable co-ordination, markets where an equilibrium in the usual sense can be observed may be rare events. Even highly organized markets with very fast communication of information specific to that market may not achieve more than volatile short-term market-clearing conditions.

Yet viable co-ordination does not mean total disorder. The degree of co-ordination or efficiency is certainly lower than the 'perfect co-ordination' fictitiously presumed by general equilibrium analysis. But efficiency losses are constrained because of the sanction of bankruptcy. All – much worse – allocations not compatible with this constraint are thus excluded. On the other hand, given the potential of the productivity gains and quality improvements which may become feasible through innovative activities, viable co-ordination may be accompanied by faster growth of material wealth. In the longer run the growth effect may turn out to be more important than the (fictitious) efficiency losses. Indeed, this is the very basis of Schumpeter's (1942, ch. 8) growth optimism in spite of monopolistic industries, and of Hayek's (1978, pp. 179–90) plea for 'competition as a discovery procedure'.

Certainly not surprisingly, however, a theory of market allocation in which both the co-ordinating and the de-co-ordinating tendencies are simultaneously taken into account lacks the simplicity as well as the precision of neoclassical general equilibrium theory and is hardly predestined for welfare-theoretic applications. But, despite its rather vague allocative implications, the theory of viable co-ordination reproduces what has been the cornerstone of classical economic philosophy: the hypothesis that market co-ordination works as a self-regulating system. The classical view of the market process from which the hypothesis has been derived is no less vague in its allocative implications.[19] The price for the precision which neoclassical economics has injected into allocation theory by borrowing from classical mechanics is the over-stylized nature of the idealizations that had to be accommodated. Almost all propositions of general equilibrium theory which go beyond the self-regulation hypothesis basically refer to fictions.

The evolutionary notion of viable co-ordination implies perfect co-ordination as a hypothetical limiting case. What it may have to offer beyond this is a fresh look at theoretical controversies about aggregate phenomena such as persistent profit differentials as a necessary condition for a high pace of innovativeness (Helmstädter, 1990), unemployment rates and the business cycle. The opposing co-ordination and de-co-ordination tendencies within the markets can stabilize at different levels of aggregate output and employment. What needs to be better understood is how the interaction between the endogenous generation of novelty and the efforts to adjust to novelty can induce transitions between the different aggregate levels. It would not come as a surprise if here once more non-linear dynamics played a crucial role, now possibly in a very complicated, interactive form. However, work in this direction still remains to be done.

6.   CONCLUSIONS

In the present reflections, an attempt has been made to organize conjectures and insights of various heterodox contributions to evolutionary economics into a general and coherent line of argument. In the future this may well become a major research programme. The basic concern in all the contributions is with the fact that humans are able to create and alter their social and economic environment by coming up with new ideas, with novelty. The reason for this – the motivational aspect – and the capacity to do so – the creative aspect – must not be left out if an unbiased understanding of the common feature of evolutionary phenomena is desired: their endogenous causation within the economy.

Since the predominant neoclassical theory in economics sometimes denies the legitimacy of an alternative evolutionary approach, the paper started by outlining why the heuristic background of neoclassical theory in classical mechanics systematically prevents it from achieving an adequate interpretation of process and change in the economy. The motivation to search for novelty and the capacity to generate novelty were then discussed at the level of the individual. Considered more broadly, these two problems belong to the context of emergence of novelty. The paper thus went on to highlight some important elements and results from the context of dissemination of novelty.

A large body of research exists which deals with diffusion problems of diverse sorts. A unifying analytical category of this research was identified in the form of the frequency-dependency effect. Somewhat less attention has been given in the literature to the classical co-ordination problem which, as was pointed out, does require a genuinely evolutionary reinterpretation.

In many aspects and on many levels of evolutionary economic theory the same feature has been met with: non-linear dynamics and multiple equilibria. Associative brain activities, frequency dependency, path dependency, indeterminacy of future evolution and other phenomena mentioned, all point to these features. Unfortunately, the analytical tools for understanding the interaction of non-linear dynamics on many levels and in a very high-dimensional space are not yet sufficiently developed. Until work on this problem has made progress, theoretical investigations in evolutionary economic theory will have to treat the interacting levels basically as isolated partial domains, and a comprehensive view will have to be postponed.

Thus further efforts in developing the foundations of the evolutionary paradigm are urgently needed. They will help to understand better the puzzling fact that, despite the potentially unstable non-linear dynamics on the various interacting levels, the overall economic development appears as a rather stable historical process.[20]

NOTES

1. The author wishes to thank J. Irving-Lessmann, T. Kuran, and the participants at the European Association for Evolutionary Political Economy (EAEPE) 1990 Conference in Florence, Italy, for helpful comments on an earlier draft. Financial support by the Thyssen Foundation is gratefully acknowledged.
2. See Röpke (1977); Boulding (1981); Hirshleifer (1982); Nelson and Winter (1982); Gowdy (1985); Day (1987); De Bresson (1987); Foster (1987); Johansson, Batten and Casti (1987); Allen (1988); Silverberg (1988); Gordon and Adams (1989), Faber and Proops (1990); Lesourne (1991), to mention just a few.
3. Solow (1957); for an interesting criticism from the point of view of evolutionary economics, see Hesse (1991). Because of its total neglect of institutional factors the theory has moreover been unable to explain why soaring economic growth has historically always been confined to just a tiny fraction of the world population.
4. Neoclassical economics has caught up with many of its critics in recent years. Besides the countless formal attempts to come to grips with the non-static character of economic problems there are now neoclassical theories of technical progress and innovation (Binswanger and Ruttan, 1978), of differential economic growth and development (Lucas, 1988; Romer, 1989), of long-term institutional change (North, 1981), and so on. The success rate with which neoclassical economics attacks new problems once they have been identified and addressed by its critics may even take much of the momentum out of the critical heterodox movement of evolutionary economics some day. Symptomatically, efforts are already being made to develop elements of a neoclassical interpretation of economic evolution (Ursprung, 1988; Hansson and Stuart, 1990; Lehmann-Waffenschmidt, 1990).
5. See, for example, O'Driscoll and Rizzo (1985). Subjectivists are called here those writers who do not necessarily associate themselves with the Austrian school, but hold views closely related to it. See, for example, Shackle (1972); Lachmann (1976); and the authors in Wiseman (1983).
6. In a broader view the theory of societal evolution by Hayek (1979; 1988) is also relevant here.
7. In the more recent neoclassical literature on industrial innovation races (Kamien and Schwartz, 1982, chs 4–5; Reinganum, 1989) search for novelty is interpreted as a problem of optimal investment in competitive R&D activities. Not surprisingly, this representation is based on rather odd presumptions: all competitors are assumed to search for the same 'innovation' (which thus must be clearly conceivable for everybody), and they even anticipate the profits that will accrue from it. Quite obviously, such an 'innovation' hardly deserves the label.
8. It may be noted that there are many such mental states which potentially motivate action and which have no place in the 'rationalist' optimization model: dissatisfaction, anger, curiosity and so on.
9. The motivation to search declines the longer the search is continued without success, because the aspiration level declines. The latter may eventually converge to the presently feasible best option, the motivation to search thus fades away. If, on the other hand, search is successful, in the sense that an innovation improves the best available choice, then the aspiration level will increase to this new level.
10. They are then 'new' in a subjective sense only to the individual adopter who, in the diffusion process, is confronted with them for the first time, while the scientific observer is able to anticipate the effects which the items have. A distinction between 'objective novelty' (something not previously experienced by anybody including the scientific observer) and 'subjective novelty' (new to a particular person in question but known to others including the scientific observer) may be helpful to mark the difference; see Witt (1989a).
11. The growing number of neoclassical contributions to diffusion research (David, 1989) ignore this interaction by the device of treating novelty as something exogenously

given. Once having entered the economy in an unexplained way, the newly entered item triggers off adjustments to new equilibria, now in the particular form of diffusion processes.

12. See Schelling (1978); Hallagan and Joerding (1983); Granovetter and Soong (1986); Witt (1986a); Kuran (1987); Arthur (1988a); David (1989); Wärneryd (1989); Weise (1991); the effect has already been addressed by Veblen (1899), by the way, who made a major argument of it without, of course, labelling it that way.

13. According to the logic of these models the number of potentially contagious contacts in a population of non-infected individuals increases exponentially with the number of people who have caught the disease until the frequency of non-infected persons, which by the same token exponentially decreases, curbs the further spread. See Waltman (1974) for a survey.

14. Although it also becomes significant, for instance, in the non-tatônnement theory of market processes.

15. In an attempt to formalize ideas by Kirzner (1973, 1979) on how individual alertness in discovering new arbitrage possibilities affects the process of market co-ordination, Littlechild and Owen (1980) come surprisingly close to this conjecture.

16. Schumpeter (1942, ch. 7) called this de-co-ordination tendency the 'perennial gale of creative destruction', but he confined his discussions of the implications to a reassessment of competition policy.

17. For more details see Witt (1985) and Lachmann (1986).

18. See Fehl (1986), Lesourne (1989). Stable states 'far from equilibrium' are central to the theory of dissipative structures in thermodynamics. The theory inquires into how a varying inflow of energy into an otherwise closed system (e.g., a fluid in a bowl) may lead to different persistent patterns of motion within the system and to characteristic transitions between them (Prigogine, 1976). However, while in that theory the source of change (a varying energy inflow) may be treated as exogenous or may be left to the discretion of the experimenter, the explanation of how change is endogenously produced within the system is crucial in the present evolutionary theory of economic co-ordination.

19. See, for example, Adam Smith (1979, Bk. 1, ch. 7).

20. For a discussion of this point see the chapter by Hodgson in this volume (ch. 10).

7. Cultural Difference and Subjective Rationality: Where Sociology Connects with the Economics of Technological Choice

Mary K. Farmer and Mark L. Matthews[1]

1. INTRODUCTION

Students of empirical aspects of technical and technological change cannot avoid encountering the effects of different national cultures upon the rates of, and directions taken by, technical change.[2] Not only are there national variations in innovative accomplishment which can be (reciprocally) linked to more general economic performance differentials, there are also fairly distinctive national styles to technical advance, reflected both in technologically superficial (yet economically important) styling preferences, and in more technologically fundamental aspects of design. Recently, research on firm behaviour and competences has begun to place more emphasis upon where (nationally) a firm is based and from where it originates (Porter, 1990b). But to recognize national differences is not to explain them. To be sure, fairly easily understood processes involving spillovers between firms, labour force skills, the availability of specialized suppliers and the like can be identified in the attempt to explain the ways in which these culturally diverse technological solutions emerge and are maintained. But do these really tell us the whole story? More often than not, it might be argued, they are effects, not underlying causes of difference.

The problem of understanding and accounting for cultural diversity in technology is extremely important, and yet difficult to deal with, because it unavoidably brings to the surface fundamental differences between approaches to technical change, differences in particular between economists and sociologists. A number of developing theoretical traditions such as neo-institutionalism, subjectivism, evolutionary economics and socio-economics offer the prospect of more synthetic, or heterogeneous, approaches to understanding, modelling or theorizing the economy. This chapter is an attempt to clarify some of the methodological issues which they raise, and which we believe currently obscure and confuse attempts to make headway with the treatment of relationships between technology and culture.

2. 'SOCIOLOGICAL' VERSUS 'ECONOMIC' MODES OF EXPLANATION

Two very different sorts of response to differences in the technologies found in different national cultures are suggested by the literature. The first simply attributes differences – beyond those which can be explained by local differences in factor prices – to 'technological gaps', between users of technologies assumed to be at the technological frontier, and those viewed as lagging behind.[3] According to this view, the problem is reduced to one of explaining the speed of imitation. This may sometimes in turn be treated as a cultural residual-type effect – for example, the 'British Disease' – outside the scope of a formal explanatory model, a problem which the investigator would prefer to live with rather than investigate further.

The second approach treats the production and reproduction of cultural differences in technology as a crucial, if not one of the most crucial, issues in understanding technical change, and directs our research efforts to deconstructing them. In this view, differences are not 'temporary' disequilibrium phenomena, en route to being eliminated: rather, a variety of technological problem solutions is a persistent feature of the cultural diversity of the social world.

The former approach, which assumes a tendency for convergence of technological solutions within the economy, and puts any observed persistence of diversity down to 'exogenous factors', broadly characterizes the thinking of many mainstream economists.[4] The latter commonly reflects the approach of analysts influenced more by sociological traditions.[5]

A common perception of the difference between economic and sociological approaches is captured by James Duesenberry's well known aphorism that 'economics is all about how people make choices; sociology is all about why they don't have any choices to make'. On this view whilst economists emphasize choice, sociologists are more concerned with rule- or norm-guided behaviour.[6] Yet there is something odd about this characterization, which is revealed by reflection on the differing explanations of cultural diversity in technology. Wouldn't we expect a degree of diversity of outcomes to be the inevitable concomitant of the true exercise of the choice emphasized by the allegedly 'choice-theoretic' approach of the economists? And if sociology is all about 'why actors don't really have any choices to make', then why is the wide-ranging sociological literature on the social construction of technology transparently far more at home with the existence of a diversity of technological problem solutions in different cultures? (See MacKenzie and Wajcman, 1985; Bijker, Hughes and Pinch, 1987).

3.   RATIONAL CHOICE IN NEOCLASSICAL ECONOMICS

Modern neoclassical economics starts by assuming that individuals act as if they can rank their preferences over possible states of the world, and act consistently to produce their most preferred outcome, subject to whatever constraints they face. This is what orthodox economists mean by 'rational action'. The impression is given, not least by the common use of the term 'rational choice theory', that rational, maximizing behaviour plays the core explanatory role in the theory.[7]

However, in describing the microeconomic theory which is supposedly built up from the foundation of this account of individual action as 'choice theory' or 'rational choice theory', economists are engaged in something bordering on self-deception (see Hodgson, 1988, pp. 10–11). For, convenient as the label 'choice theory' is for reinforcing neoclassical economics' credentials as a liberal social theory, mainstream economists are actually implicitly trained to view the world, or at least the economy, in a deterministic way which parallels the model of the physical world found in Newtonian mechanics.[8] The starting point for their way of thinking may be a view of the world in which actors are described as rational, maximizing individuals, but these are actors who neither really 'act' in the ordinary sense, nor have much scope for being individual. Rather, they are 'atoms' who are assumed to act in predictable ways in response to given stimuli. Their preferences, reflected in a utility function the contents of which are deemed outside the scope of economic explanation, or even, according to one now quite widely accepted if extreme version, given and immutable (Stigler and Becker, 1977), determine their actions in a mechanical way. And whilst real actors may differ from each other in their preferences, the use of the concept of the 'representative actor' provides a convenient route to the development of economic models which can generate predictions analogously to those of classical mechanics.

It is thus the assumption that actors are rational maximizers which is the foundation for a belief in the predictability of actions on which economists place so much store. That which is the 'rational' course of action for such a maximizer could, it is believed, be in principle objectively specified by any outside observer who knew the actor's objective function and the state of the world they faced. The 'external' world is viewed as impinging on and affecting the actor as 'knowledge' (perfect or otherwise) and as 'constraints' on his or her action. It is important to note here that the theory neither allows a distinction between 'the world' and actors' (and analysts') knowledge of it, nor recognizes the social world as being continuously produced and reproduced by interacting human actors.

The same formal model of action which postulates an individual human actor maximizing subject to constraint, is also applied to the firm, in this case sometimes substituting profit for utility in the objective function.[9] Just as in the individual case this implies that there is a 'rational' decision in any given situation, and the theory requires that this is what the actor will do, so firms producing the same goods in the same markets must be expected not only to produce the optimal quantity, but also to use whatever technology is 'optimal' at reigning factor prices, unless something is producing imperfections in the market, such that, for example, they don't all face the same factor prices, or unless there are information asymmetries (a currently fashionable idea for mathematical economists addressing problems of incomplete information).

The account we have given is of course simplistic. There is a great deal of work, still broadly within the neoclassical tradition in economics, that develops more sophisticated models which recognize conditions under which there can be no uniquely optimal action for a given actor, or where a systemic equilibrium cannot be reached, or will not be stable, for example. But the starting point is still generally the same broadly deterministic framework we have described. A reason why a body of theory supposedly emphasizing choice is at a loss in trying to make sense of cultural diversity in technological solutions is that this diversity itself resides in differences between the expectations, capabilities, preferences and cognitive frameworks of the actors. These are a product of different life-histories, and cannot be captured by any model which starts from the representative agent. The problem lies not in assuming that human actors are rational – in some reasonable sense of that word – but in the assumption that all rational actors are the same.

4. RATIONALITY AND THE CRITICS OF ECONOMICS

Orthodox economic theory has many critics. These are generally united by their concern that such abstract formal theories do not translate into plausible accounts of the workings of real-world economies.[10] One of the most telling aspects of this criticism is the claim that modern mainstream neoclassical economists, focusing as they do on equilibrium in economic systems, cannot account for change, process and development in economies: issues which were, of course, at the very core of the concerns of their classical predecessors. This, it is argued, is why mainstream economics has so little to say about technical change, which it is forced to treat as an exogenous, rather than an economic, variable. Technical change may clearly involve the adoption of new and previously unthought-of solutions to old problems, yet this is not something which easily finds a home in the deterministic world of the orthodox economist. But as we shall indicate, the way in which innovative technical configurations arise is something which does not receive a much more satisfactory treatment from many influential critics, either. We believe this is because, blinded perhaps by the centrality neoclassical economists themselves attribute to the assumption of rationality, they pay too much attention to the shortcomings of the rationality concept, at the expense of real and deeper problems.

Located in a variety of heterodox traditions, it is striking how consistently critics of neoclassical economics focus on the assumption of rational maximizing behaviour as the source of the failure to account adequately for 'real world' economic processes, and proceed to build their alternatives out of an attempt to modify the rationality concept in pursuit of greater 'realism'.[11] Well-known examples include Simon's concept of 'satisficing', Leibenstein's 'X-efficiency', and Heiner's 'C–D' gap between the 'competence' of actors at using information and the 'difficulty' of their decision problems (Simon, 1959; Leibenstein, 1980; Heiner, 1983).[12] Some critics such as Geoff Hodgson (1988, pp. 123–4) go further, citing sociology as the potentially fruitful source of an alternative approach to explanation which supposedly rejects rational choice and replaces it with a conception of the actor as, for example, a follower of social rules or norms whose actions can frequently be viewed as habitual rather than rational.

Habitual action could of course be accounted for in a rational choice framework, for example by representing as ' "rational" actions which are repeated because the "cost" of changing them is perceived as too great' (Hodgson, 1988, p. 125). But, echoing other critics' responses to such claims, Hodgson (1988, p. 126) explicitly rejects this account on the grounds that it involves 'continuous overall monitoring and calculation to an extent which is impossible given the amount and complexity of the information received' and that it involves treating habits as 'being ultimately consistent with an over-riding preference function'.

5.   PROBLEMS WITH THE TREATMENT OF KNOWLEDGE

We want to stress here that the real source of the problem in the neoclassical approach lies deeper, in the idea that there is some theoretically imaginable full, complete or perfect knowledge of the external world – or of aspects of the external world – to which actors could conceivably aspire. If, as we shall argue, this idea is meaningless, then the theoretical coherence of the idea of a 'knowledge gap' captured by such concepts as 'imperfect knowledge', or 'bounded rationality', is also shaken.

What is wrong with the theoretical construct of full or perfect knowledge as the bench mark against which both sophisticated orthodox economists – and many less-orthodox critics – have constructed 'more realistic' behavioural theories which attempt to capture the way actors act in its absence? There are two parts to the answer. The first has been briefly touched on already and concerns the way actors 'receive' information: facts simply cannot 'speak for themselves' but are inevitably theory-dependent. As Hodgson (1988, p. 119) – one of the rare economists to make what is an uncontroversial point throughout the rest of the social sciences – puts it:

> Whilst living and acting in the world we are continuously in receipt of a vast amount of sense data. The attribution of meaning to this apparently chaotic mass of data requires the use of acquired concepts, symbols, rules and signs. Perception is an act of categorisation, and in general such categories are learned.

An important corollary is that what is learned undoubtedly varies, even within cultures. Between cultures 'cognitive worlds' may vary greatly.[13] The implication is, of course, that the actors' 'knowledge' of the external world cannot be viewed in terms of how many intersubjectively uniform bits of information they have acquired. Since every actor's history is in some sense unique, 'knowledge' of the same external reality has an actor-specific quality, and this itself has a cultural dimension, since the actor's subjectivity has been formed within particular cultural contexts or cognitive worlds. This is important for, and destructive of, claims that we can talk about the rational or optimizing decision for rational maximizing actors facing the 'same' situation and in possession of the 'same' information or knowledge. But note that this statement does not depend on our abandoning the idea of rational maximizing actors completely. What it implies is that even if actors were rational maximizers, this would not imply uniformity of action in what appears from the 'outside' to be an identical situation. The implications for cultural diversity in technical problem-solving are obvious. Recognition of cognitive diversity implies recognition that different decision-makers' perceptions of what are ostensibly 'the same' problems and 'the same' constraints, vary. Furthermore the social and institutional and legal frameworks within which decisions are made themselves vary considerably across cultures. We should not be surprised to see different cultural 'styles' of technical problem solutions.[14]

In international markets, where firms have to make profits in order to survive, there is also, of course, a clear sense in which firms all face the same ultimate constraint on their actions: the need not to make continuous losses. This latter 'sameness' might be described as a relatively objective characteristic of the system, and it can have real effects: those firms whose solutions consistently fail in the marketplace will ultimately go out of business. Thus at any given time the economic system provides an envelope around the set of technological solutions which are economically feasible, although the envelope has fuzzy edges, for reasons we are about to discuss. The discipline of the market decides which firms stay in business independently of whether they make profits or losses by accident or design; that is to say, whether the processes leading to decision-making within them might be deemed in any sense 'rational' or consistent or well-informed, or not. This is simply to emphasize the argument of evolutionary economists such as Nelson and Winter (1982), that the market is a selection mechanism that plays a role in the selection of 'successful' technologies independently of the mechanism that throws up those technologies.

We now turn to the second problem with the theoretical construct of full or perfect knowledge. Unlike the fantasy world of general equilibrium, where everything happens instantaneously, the real social world is a process which takes place in real time. Actions now affect future actions and states of the world, and expectations about future states of the world are part of the conditions for present actions. There is a powerful argument, which has been forcefully stated by Popper, that we cannot in principle reliably predict future states of the world, because the state of human knowledge in the future is part of the future state of the world, and if we knew now what our knowledge would be like in the future we would, in a sense, be there already. The argument is one which can hardly fail to impress students of technical change, for how can one imagine the social and economic consequences of a technology which no one has yet conceived? It is an argument which is extremely destructive of the conventional assumption of rational, maximizing behaviour. To maximize one does not need perfect knowledge so long as one can assign probabilities to risks, weight likelihoods of different possible outcomes, or whatever. This is the kind of route down which many modifiers of the behavioural assumptions of neoclassical theory have gone. But how can we objectively weight the likelihoods of different possible unimaginable outcomes of present actions?[15]

This is a question to which the 'Austrian' and 'subjectivist' tradition in economics draws attention. Subjectivists argue that the unboundedness of the choice-set faced by actors in a real world of time and ignorance makes a formal maximizing model of action senseless and inapplicable. Action is more like a voyage of discovery, and actors as much create as take opportunities by acting. No one can predict the consequences of their actions – though they will no doubt be led by hopes, guesses and intuitions – for by their actions they themselves affect the actions of others, acquire knowledge and help create the future. But these alternative traditions stress that although actors cannot maximize in a world of radical uncertainty or ignorance, this does not license a view of actors as non-rational or irrational. Rather, human action is purposive and directed not to maximizing some pre-existent utility function but towards the attempt to discover and create states of the world which the actor prefers to the present.[16] We find it hard to imagine how an adequate account of the processes by which new technologies arise could omit some role for human purposive action so conceived.

We do not want to argue for a radically individualist subjectivism which denies the power of social forces to shape human imagination and creativity. But we believe there is something valuable in the 'Austrian' account of human action and human knowledge, something which is missed both by the determinism of the neoclassical rational maximization, and by the many critics who reject this view of action in favour of various combinations of watered-down rational maximizing (for example, satisficing), and less-than-rational routine following. Austrian theorists see human actors as 'rational' without meaning by this that in any situation they face there is some externally and 'objectively' definable thing which it would be optimal or 'rational' for any actor to do. By contrast with the neoclassical view and that adopted by many critics, rationality is seen as a characteristic of the actor and not the act. And put rather loosely, we might say that this characteristic of the actor is the tendency to try to bring about subjectively preferred states of affairs, rather than subjectively less-preferred states. In a radically uncertain world this does not mean that action will necessarily look consistent (with some unchanging set of objectives) to an observer, but it does nevertheless imply that there is non-random patterning behind human action, which, after the event, invites detection by the social analyst.[17]

Why should anyone seeking to replace the empty formalism of neoclassical rationality maximizing choose to reject this alternative subjectivist account of rational action? Hodgson (1988, p. 121), who discusses the question explicitly, seems to oppose it because he views it as inextricably connected to radical methodological individualism.

The implication that a position that treats individuals as subjectively rational must reject 'the social dimension' of action is, we believe, a mistake. That most (though not all) Austrian writers see their methodological position as intimately connected with a radical political libertarianism, and seek to minimize (or eliminate) social factors in the construction of the individual's subjectivity, does not mean that this connection is a necessary one. We see no difficulty, for example, in accepting Hayek's powerful case that only individuals have full knowledge of their own valuations of the uses to which society's resources could be put (Hayek, 1945) without having to accept that those valuations have not themselves been influenced by the experience of living in a particular society, culture or cognitive world. The idea that subjectivism is necessarily individualistic has perhaps been reinforced by the (reverse) assumption – made explicitly by Hodgson, and widely found amongst writers of similar persuasion – that sociology, in generally endorsing a view of the individual as socially constructed and/or propelled by 'Durkheimian social forces', must (inevitably?) reject a conception of the individual as a rational actor. This too is mistaken.

There is no space here for a review of the extremely large and heterogeneous range of work in contemporary sociological theory. But it is interesting to note that at the same time as various heterodox and new-institutional economists have been seeking to carve out a far larger explanatory role for routines, customs, habits and social norms in explanations of economic behaviour, the sociological mainstream has been moving in precisely the opposite direction, trying to reintegrate into sociological theory some conception of active human agents who are not simply the dupes of external social forces, norms, pressures or whatever. Whilst Hodgson frequently quotes Anthony Giddens's concept of 'practical consciousness' in support of his view that we should give more recognition to the 'habitual' and non-purposive aspect of human action, this sociologist has also been one of the more powerful voices arguing for a greater recognition of the purposive nature of human agency, as evidenced by the following quotation:[18]

> The most mundane forms of day-to day conduct can quite properly be called intentional. It is important to stress this, since otherwise it might be tempting to suppose that routine or habitual conduct cannot be purposive (as Weber tended to do).   (Giddens, 1976, p. 76)

At this stage in the discussion of agency it is important to stress something that has so far been implicit in our discussion. Individuals and firms are different kinds of actors. This fact has analytical consequences for the behavioural assumptions it is appropriate to make about them. 'Subjective rationality', it has been suggested, is what might be called an emergent tendency in human actors, around which we can frame our explanatory questions about their actions. And if we accept that what human actors do is purposive in the sense employed by subjectivists, this allows us to attempt to tease out answers to questions about what, in particular situations, their purposes were, how they were affected by their perceptions of the constraints on their actions, and so on. 'Human purposes' are not, on this account, goals clearly defined or even perceived, and fixed through time. Rather, they are fuzzy and changing imagined configurations of the actor's future world on which their active interventions in the present are sighted.

It does not, however, make sense to attribute subjectivity to firms or to assume rationality in their actions. Firms, depending, for example, on the properties of their internal organization, can quite possibly fail to pursue their objectives consistently, or indeed even articulate objectives at all. To assume otherwise is to reify them unwarrantedly. It is possible to employ an 'objectivist' conception of rational action (as the characteristic of the action rather than the actor), by forming a behavioural hypothesis about the empirical behaviour of particular firms in a particular environment. For example, we can hypothesize that certain firms do indeed maximize profits. But this is a matter for empirical confirmation or otherwise, not theoretical dogma. And it does not follow that because particular firms have been observed to pursue particular objectives consistently in the past they will necessarily continue to do so. Changes in personnel, organizational form, cultural and market environment can all change the way in which a firm behaves, by accident or by design. The important connection to make here is that the particular organizational forms and objectives which firms display at particular times are in part both product and producers of the – in part, socially constructed – subjectivities of the actors involved in them. The greater our understanding of the cultural and cognitive environments which affect their operation, the less we shall be inclined to treat variations in the behaviour of firms through time, or between cultures, as incomprehensible noise around our tidy behavioural assumptions.

6.   THE SOCIAL CONSTRUCTION OF TECHNOLOGY AND RATIONAL ACTION

Much work by sociologists writing in the 'social construction of technology' tradition reinforces and exemplifies the point we have been trying to make. There is nothing necessarily incompatible between an approach which stresses the way in which social and cultural factors shape technologies, and the treatment of actors as rational, so long as acting 'rationally' is interpreted as meaning 'acting in the way the actor believes (or hopes) will bring about a preferred state of affairs, rather than as making some objectively and aculturally "correct" decision'. Indeed, it is only by interpreting 'acting rationally' in a subjectivist rather than an objectivist way that it is possible to leave open a role for the social shaping of individuals and their cognitive world, and therefore, of course, of the technologies they develop.

Micro-level accounts of the construction of particular technologies, which comprise the bulk of the 'social construction of technology' literature, generally attempt to give a plausible account of the goals and objectives of the relevant actors, in order to reveal how the social environment both shapes these goals and impinges on their achievement. Thomas Hughes's (1985) famous account of Edison's development of his electricity supply system exemplifies this form of argument. Hughes gives due weight to the innovative and creative aspects of Edison's ideas, by recognizing that things could have developed other than the way they did and, indeed, that Edison himself was conscious of this in his concern to create a market for his invention. Nevertheless, Hughes's account stresses the extent to which Edison's development of the technology was also shaped by the cost and incentive structure, and indeed by Edison's formation, within a capitalist culture, as a remarkable example of the economically calculating individual. It is by treating Edison's behaviour as rationally explicable that Hughes is able to illuminate the way in which choices were thus made by a socially constructed individual, within perceived and social and technical constraints.

What advantages are there in viewing actors as 'rational' in this sense, rather than as followers of routines, carriers of habits, and so on? Those, such as Hodgson and Nelson and Winter, who have argued, in various ways, for the importance of habits or routines in analysis, combine this with an evolutionary selection mechanism, in order to account for change within the system. We have no quarrel with this. Systems such as competitive markets, for example, clearly act as selection mechanisms, selecting winners and losers. For Nelson and Winter 'routines' serve the purpose of characterizing 'what the firm is' from a behavioural point of view, for the purpose of constructing formal evolutionary models. They are the 'regular and predictable behavioral patterns' which 'play the role that genes play in biological evolutionary theory' (Nelson and Winter, 1982, p. 14). They are what the selection mechanism selects amongst. But they are no more than a simple, instrumentally useful representation of a much more complex reality in which real decision-makers attempt purposive interventions in the world whilst grappling with orders of complexity well beyond the capacities of theorists' formal models.

Evolutionary models cannot adequately explain the critical junctures when new 'routines' emerge, and indeed Nelson and Winter (1982, p. 410) admit that their formal evolutionary modelling will never be sufficient for this purpose. On the other hand *post hoc* empirical studies of critical periods of technical change, though more modest in scope, do seem able to get 'closer' to an understanding of these processes. This is because they can take on board cultural specificity, the substance of which cannot of course, be represented in general by *a priori* formal models. But it is cultural particularity which must always be at the heart of the explanation of the emergence of new technological problem solutions. For the goals of actors, their perceptions of possibilities and impossibilities, their weightings of design trade-offs and their weightings of costs and incentives, are all aspects of the situation which are intrinsically embedded in a culturally formed, subjective cognitive framework. On the other hand, without an assumption that individuals act in a way which is purposive, in the sense that they try to produce the best outcome they can, given the way they perceive their situation, none of these factors can play the explanatory role they so clearly do in the best examples of the social construction of technology literature.

7.   CONCLUSION

We began with the problem of what methodological framework we should bring to bear on the difficult task of trying to understand and explain national cultural differences in technological problem solutions. We have argued that the orthodox economic theoretical framework, with its usual assumption that actors are global optimizers, has little to offer, despite its apparent concern with choice, but that approaches which stress the routinized, habitual, socially determined aspects of behaviour – the supposed sphere of the sociologist – are equally weak. A more satisfactory solution nevertheless draws both on 'economic' and 'sociological' traditions.

We have stressed that technical change must originate largely, if not wholly, in the making of active and subjectively rational choices by human beings responding to perceived opportunities and constraints. It is difficult to see how any approach which refuses to acknowledge this element of human creative activity in technological change can be adequate to its task. However, we have also emphasized that there is a crucial difference between human actors and collective actors such as firms. Whilst we think it necessary to treat the former as subjectively rational actors there can be no possible ontological justification for assuming rationality of action, in any sense, to be a property of the latter.

Differences between firms and between national cultures in organizational forms and technological choice have often been used to justify an opposition between 'rationality' and 'culture'. If different cultures do things differently it is assumed that their practices cannot all be equally rational. But, we have argued, cultural differences in technological choices made by actors within firms apparently facing the same problems in the same market conditions are no evidence of irrationality. The way in which an individual perceives a technological problem and constructs an appropriate solution is a function of their culturally embedded cognitive framework and consequent subjective expectations about future states of the world. Of course, the extent to which particular subjectively rational technical solutions are or are not adopted will be a function of the organizational forms of firms and indeed of routines and practices. Also, in a (dynamic) market setting the market process will decide which of those which are adopted will succeed. But, if we wish to understand explain and, indeed, model technical change we must surely recognize tha cultural variation is to a large extent a product of the diversity of culturally conditioned understandings of 'technical problems'. We should not look simplistically for 'best practice' technical change, and judge real innovations by supposedly 'objective' criteria.

In a changing world we cannot know with any certainty in advance what technical innovations will be successful. But it is because of this radical uncertainty about our future that evolutionary theory suggests that the existence of a pool of different ways of thinking about and solving problems across different cultures is a valuable resource, not a problem to be assumed away.

NOTES

1. The authors would like to thank the following people for their numerous and helpful comments: Rod Coombs, Geoff Hodgson, Tony Lawson, Brian Loasby, Luigi Marengo, Ian Miles and Andrew Sayer. An earlier version of the chapter was given as a paper at the conference on 'Firm Strategy and Technical Change: Micro Economics or Micro Sociology?', University of Manchester, 27–28 September 1990, as well as at the European Association for Evolutionary Political Economy (EAEPE) 1990 conference in Florence. Mark Matthews would like to thank the UK Economic and Social Research Council's Designated Research Centre on Science and Technology Policy for their financial support in carrying out research upon which this paper draws.
2. We use the terms 'technical change' and 'technological change' interchangeably here to refer to any change in knowledge or artefacts, whether incremental or revolutionary.
3. The characterization of some technical solutions as unequivocally superior to others, judged by performance under current market conditions, is problematic, since changing market conditions are capable of re-ranking their relative economic performance.
4. Discussed by Hodgson (1988, pp. 14–15).
5. An excellent example is the discussion of military technology in section 5 of Mackenzie and Wajcman (1985).
6. See the discussion in Vanberg (1988). This kind of distinction can be found in Becker (1976, ch. 1); Hodgson (1988, ch. 6); Barry (1970). Hodgson, it should be stressed does not accept that neoclassical economics *really* embraces purposeful choice.
7. See Farmer (1982) for an extensive discussion of the confusions which are in fact embedded in this conception. A growing body of literature is attempting to extend 'the economic approach' to explanation into other areas of social science (Radnitzky and Bernholz, 1987). It is striking that this has been happening simultaneously with the growth of a critical literature stressing the failures of this same economic approach to deal satisfactorily with the central traditional concerns of the classical economists, particularly economic growth, change and development. It has been argued elsewhere that, to an extent, it could have been these very fundamental problems with the application of orthodox economic theory to issues in the core of the traditional concerns of economics which made imperialistic ventures into initially 'easier' territories – where even relatively simplistic formal models still had the power to impress – attractive to some theorists over the last two or three decades (Farmer, 1989).
8. The influence of classical mechanics on the development of neoclassical economic theory is discussed at length in Mirowski (1989).
9. That neoclassical economics is at heart instrumentalist, and wedded more to its particular 'technology' of formal theory than to a concern with explanation, is suggested by the unconcerned way in which the same formal model of action is applied both to human

individuals and to firms. This is despite the frequent claim of economists to be methodological individualists! It has been common for neoclassical economists to assume that the firm is maximizing, despite the obvious conceptual problems of defining the utility function or maximand of such a collective actor.

10. See, for example, Ward (1972); Hollis and Nell (1975); Wiseman (1983); Hodgson (1988); Etzioni (1988).

11. It can be hard to draw a line between mere modifiers and full-blown critics. Though distinguished by the extent to which they use hostile rhetoric to attack neoclassical assumptions, there are many parallels between the ways in which both the relatively more sympathetic critics (e.g., Heiner) and more hostile critics (e.g., Hodgson) set about reconstruction via the adoption of 'more realistic' behavioural assumptions which attempt to recognize the real-world complexity of decision makers' environments.

12. Nelson and Winter, in their influential development of an evolutionary theory of economic change, are far more circumspect in their critical discussion of the treatment of rational action theory, acknowledging that 'recent sophisticated versions of the theory back off from' the presumption that 'the actions taken by firms are truly maximizing in the sense that, given the circumstances, there are no better actions' (Nelson and Winter, 1982, p. 66). Some commentators seem to have read Nelson and Winter as proposing the concept of 'routine' as a substitute for the behavioural assumption of rational action. But as they make clear in their concluding discussion, Nelson and Winter (1982, p. 410) hold that no theoretical model of firm behaviour can be imposed: 'The ultimate discipline on the representation of firm behavior is considered to be empirical.' This a position which we endorse.

13. There is a large literature on the problem of cognitive relativism which addresses the question of whether different culturally-embedded world views are potentially mutually 'translatable'. See, for example, Wilson (1970). One does not need to be a cultural relativist, however, in order to recognize the implications of differences in cognitive structures arising in different cultures.

14. See Hughes's discussion of technological style in his contribution to Bijker *et al.* (1987).

15. To argue for the possibility of presently unimaginable events occurring in the future is not, of course, to deny that there may be a considerable degree of predictability in the development of some technologies over extended periods of time, as suggested by the notion of technological trajectories (Dosi, 1982).

16. See O'Driscoll and Rizzo (1985), for an illustration of this position.

17. In the essay on 'The Theory of Complex Phenomena', Hayek (1967) develops the case for this view of social scientific explanation.

18. In stressing the extent to which mainstream sociological theory has been moving away from Parsonian functionalism and postwar Marxist-structuralism and towards theories which give a greater role to human agency, we should also mention the growing interest in 'rational action theory' within sociology. Coleman (1990) is a *tour de force* of this genre.

8. How do National Systems of Innovation Differ?: A Critical Analysis of Porter, Freeman, Lundvall and Nelson

Maureen McKelvey[1]

1. INTRODUCTION

The relations between technological change, the economy and wider society have been the subject of much speculation and research. Some researchers have concentrated on cultural adjustment in the West to rational, linear, technological ways of thinking. Others have focused on technology's importance to the capitalist system – and the importance of capitalism to technological change. Within this wide range of ways to investigate technology and society, some researchers have tried to explain why countries differ in regard to technological development.

An important question arising from our current understanding of the relation between technological development and nations is as follows: Why and how have particular nations succeeded in producing so much scientific invention and market innovation, leading to the diffusion and use of technology, while other countries have had so many difficulties? This chapter is a critical comparison of recent attempts to answer this question.

One approach which is gaining much attention today is that of *national systems of innovation*. Some researchers use national systems of innovation as an interchangeable term for a country's narrow R&D system, where a linear view of innovation – from science to technology and to economic growth – has often been used to justify government R&D subsidies. Important scientific and technological indicators have been developed in the post-Second World War period, but attempts to measure the 'input' of R&D (in a company, industry or country) and to compare it with economic output indicators implicitly accept this basic linear progression from science to growth. In contrast, however, much of the new research on national systems of innovation has involved an attempt to widen the analytical scope, to reach a deeper understanding of the relationship between technological change and economic growth.

117

National systems of innovation is a broad term, which includes the processes of innovation and diffusion in the context of the production system and of social and economic institutions. In general, the term innovation is commonly used with one of three meanings:

(a) to denote a specific stage in the process of technological change – when an invention is introduced into the market;[2]
(b) to denote all kinds of non-technical novelties of an organizational, social, institutional nature; and
(c) to denote the process of creating, diffusing or using these various changes.

Although economic factors and explanations are stressed, cultural, social and historical explanations have to varying degrees also found their way into theoretical work in this area. This is because the process of technological innovation can include many complex determinants and factors, such as key industrial sectors, the national environment, cultural orientations, producer–user interactions and so on.

In the critical evaluations of different approaches in this chapter, a number of fundamental issues are considered. These include: the general adequacy of each theory in addressing real-world national systems of innovation; the adopted definition of technology; the relative emphasis on technology or on the economic processes of innovation; and the perspective taken on the relationship between actor and structure. Such general questions are raised in section 2. The four main researchers discussed in more detail in section 3 are: Michael Porter, Christopher Freeman, Bengt-Åke Lundvall and Richard Nelson, along with other collaborators in each case. They present different definitions of national systems of innovation and divergent theoretical arguments for their existence. Section 4 concludes the essay.

2.   COMMON PROBLEM AREAS

A National or an International World?

A key problem relates to the level at which systems of innovation are to be analysed. To assume the existence of *national* systems of innovation implies some meaningful and systemic integrity at that level. To what extent are such national systems important in an increasingly integrated and international world, and are national boundaries the decisive analytical category?

Clearly, this demarcation is threatened by the existence of regional imbalances in innovation and growth performance – both within countries and among areas of the world. The uneven nature of capitalist development may make it more meaningful to analyse groups of countries (such as developed versus developing, or the triad power of Japan–Europe–USA) or, on the other hand, smaller regions (for example, northern versus southern Sweden) rather than nations.

Furthermore, international pressures may undermine national autonomy. For instance, Peter Katzenstein (1985) argues that flexible industrial policy is sometimes possible in small developed countries due to the existence of corporatist social structures, involving the co-operation of the state, labour and capital. However, as economic internationalization continues apace, national capital becomes international and is no longer dependent on national labour and national government to the same extent.

A related problem with using nations as the unit of analysis is that international trade is not just trade among countries, because there are entities which co-ordinate economic activities across many countries, namely multinational enterprises. At the same time, multinational enterprises now try to have multiple identities, which means 'trying to become local companies in many countries' (*Business Week*, 14 May 1990, p. 56). Multinational enterprises form an important part of actual innovation systems in several countries. This has implications for each national system, while at the same time each multinational enterprise is a relatively coherent actor. In addition, many national policies are affected by, and affect, people and events, well beyond national borders. Further, much activity in science and technology is clearly international.

However, the national systems of innovation approach does not necessarily deny that an international system of innovation can and does exist. Perhaps after identifying national differences – which may prevent the mistake of over-generalizing about the characteristics of capitalism – an understanding of each international system of innovation can emerge. In a more traditional international-relations approach, an international system of innovation could be regarded as the interaction between countries and between (relatively) national firms. It could also provide a map of international systems of innovation within a particular industrial sector. Or it could be company-specific in the sense of mapping one company's strategic alliances, location of research, important interactions with users, demand conditions and company culture. The problem is how much and where economic boundaries coincide with political or national boundaries.

These on-going processes of internationalization obviously spell problems for social science research which is designed to explain national differences in the ability to innovate and diffuse technology. Despite these problems, nations do still constitute an interesting, meaningful and useful level of analysis. Although the processes of internationalization are challenging sovereignty to some extent, governments still make policies which affect many areas of corporate and private life. In addition, the entire system of national political agreements (legal, social welfare, labour market relations, defence and so on) along with the associated customs and institutions, form an integrity and vary significantly from country to country. For these and related reasons, nations still constitute a valid analytical category.

Structure versus Actor Perspective

In the social sciences, 'structure' and 'actor' are often placed at opposite ends of a continuum, where a structural perspective emphasizes supra-individual processes which determine individuals' actions while the actor perspective emphasizes the free will of individuals. As Anders Boglind (1989, p. 32) asks, 'Is society the unpredictable changing result of individuals' interpretations and actions, or is it a pattern which is created and recreated independently of the individual actor's will and knowledge?'

Neoclassical economic theory embodies a version of methodological individualism, while simultaneously denying sufficient diversity of action by assuming fixed preferences and technology, and by assuming one rational response to any fully specified decision problem (Hodgson, 1988; Farmer and Matthews, this volume, ch. 7).

The theory of comparative advantage can be used as an illustration. Under certain assumptions it argues that all participants benefit if they specialize in production and then trade. This gives a predetermined outcome. It would seem that individual actors have thereby to choose rationally in accordance with general principles, to reach an optimal and equilibrium outcome. However, the narrow choice set that is revealed by the theory of comparative advantage is illusory. If the basic assumptions are relaxed, and changes in capital and technology are considered, then a number of 'optimal' outcomes become possible. Thus Friedrich List argues that individual countries can act to protect infant industry from the negative consequences of trade with a more developed country (Senghaas, 1985).

Other research traditions try to combine the two extremes into an understanding of how structure and actor are related. For example, Charles Edquist (1985) recognizes the difference but tries to use both in his study of why certain techniques are chosen instead of others. The term 'social carriers of technique', which lists the conditions necessary for choosing and actualizing the implementation of a technique, explicitly recognizes that actors' 'degree of freedom of action is determined by structural factors' (Edquist, 1985, p. 11). Edquist attempts to combine order and uncertainty, structural limitations and free will. Anthony Giddens (1984) takes another approach and tries to encompass both actor and structure in his structuration theory. Giddens argues that structures are both the medium for and the result of social action. In other words, every action happens in an already structured environment, while at the same time social action has effects on the structure, either to reproduce it or to change it (Brant, 1989, p. 13). The conceptualization of the relationship between actor and structure overshadows the question of how much room for choice or novelty is assumed to exist in the innovation process.

3. FOUR CONCEPTIONS OF NATIONAL SYSTEMS OF INNOVATION

The concept of *national systems of innovation* now has a wide usage. However, definitions of the term vary and it is important to analyse the similarities and differences. In particular, different definitions imply different things about the importance of government policies and about the possibilities of affecting the future. Moreover, these definitions are based on different theories and point to different empirical phenomena.

The four researchers examined here all assume that national differences do exist, such as in terms of markets, institutions, mechanisms for introducing and selecting innovations, and so on. Thus they each legitimate a level of analysis above that of the individual or the firm. Instead of the reductionist imperative to explain all phenomena in terms of the (rational) individual (or firm), these four researchers imply that national systems have their own autonomy. To varying degrees, they each suggest that the national system may represent a level of analysis that is not entirely reducible to its individual components.

Accordingly, aspirations of universal explanation, based on general assumptions about markets and market behaviour, are dropped. The focus of the analysis changes from bland universality to the particularities of nations, with the idea that differences at the national level, in terms of routines and institutions, for instance, will eventually provide a better explanation of the dynamics of capitalist economic systems. Furthermore, conceptions of dynamism and structural change – which can be both destructive and creative as Joseph Schumpeter (1934[1912], 1942) emphasized – are an integral part of all four analyses presented here. This contrasts to the static outcome of neoclassical general equilibrium analysis.

The four authors also share a common understanding of the importance of technical change, although they differ as to what sort of technical change (or wider innovation) is important and why. They also differ as to whether it is technological change, economic growth or societal adjustment which is the problematic factor in economic development.

In orthodox economic theory, technology is generally regarded as codifiable knowledge, which is easily transferable and often without cost. In this orthodox tradition, technology is seen as 'information that is generally applicable, and easy to reproduce and use ... one where firms can produce and use innovations by dipping freely into a general "stock" or "pool" of technological knowledge' (Dosi, 1988, p. 1130).

Instead, however, when technology is seen as tacit or uncodifiable knowledge (Polanyi, 1957, 1967; Nelson, 1981), technological development is dependent on historically determined skills and search routines. Technology itself cannot be easily transferred because of its dependence on the local, specific competences of individuals. With such considerations in mind it will be shown that different definitions of technology are part of crucial differences in the understanding of economic and technological dynamism in national systems.

Several other questions are raised in regard to each of the four researchers' theories of a national system of innovation: To what extent is empirical material used? How general or universally valid is the theory? Is the theory and description mainly a list of necessary elements or a more complex, systematic interaction? How does the theory relate to specific countries? How is technology defined? What is the conceptualization of the relation between technology and society? Is technological change or economic change at the centre of the theory? To what extent are the differences between countries seen to be due to structural factors, or due to the actions of individual actors? What are the implications for agents interested in influencing technical change?

With these and other questions in mind, each of the four researchers will be addressed in turn, before drawing some more general conclusions.

Michael Porter

The foundations of Porter's theory

In *The Competitive Advantage of Nations*, Michael Porter (1990b) compared ten industrialized countries.[3] The question behind this empirical study was: 'Why are certain companies based in certain nations capable of consistent innovation? ... Why do they ruthlessly pursue improvements, seeking an evermore sophisticated source of competitive advantage?' (Porter, 1990a, p. 77). Ultimately, Porter is interested in why a specific country is successful in specific *industries*. Indeed, he sees it as meaningless to compare nations at a more aggregated level – for example, overall performance or balance of trade. However, Porter does identify non-reducible features of a national economy which influence the success of specific industries.

Existing resources and technology are no longer the sources of comparative advantage, as in Ricardo's static theory. Instead, Porter argues for a dynamic process, where companies create competitive advantage through innovation.

Innovation can be technical or organizational, or be 'a new way of doing things' and can be radical or incremental; although innovation in Porter's meaning also includes taking a relatively undramatic new concept (like smaller, cheaper radios), seeing its possibilities, and creatively turning it into a domestically and internationally competitive product. Porter's cornerstone for comparing firms and countries is thus economic change – particularly productivity and growth. 'The only meaningful concept of competitiveness at the national level is *productivity*. The principal goal of a nation is to produce a high and rising standard of living for its citizens' (Porter, 1990a, p. 84).

Porter outlines four reasons why nations are able to support innovative activity in firms:

(a) *Factor conditions* include not only the existing resource endowment but also the factors of production which the nation can help to create. For instance, nations can augment the reserve specialized skills needed by firms and help to develop a scientific base. In addition, apparent national disadvantages, such as a lack of natural resources, can spur government or private policies for dynamic innovation.

(b) *Demand conditions* include both the composition and character of national demand. Clearly, demand conditions, both in quantitative and qualitative senses, can be an important stimulus to innovation if certain conditions are fulfilled: if buyers are sophisticated, if that industry is dominant in the home market, or if values related to consumption in that market are spreading internationally. Porter argues that the home market demand is crucial for international competitiveness.

(c) The third factor in Porter's analysis is the *related and supporting industries*, which must also be internationally competitive. Upstream and downstream linkages as well as related industries provide access to new components or machinery, and to flows of information, leading to the development of close working relations or networks.

(d) Finally, *firm strategy, structure and rivalry*. Porter argues that the national context strongly influences the organization and strategy of firms and the degree of rivalry between them. The ability of companies in a specific industry to innovate successfully is dependent on this contextual, national system of linkages and relations.

Porter stresses that these four factors must be considered together, as elements of an interacting whole. One cannot understand the success of individual firms only by examining that firm's actions; each firm has to be considered as part of the national system. Porter differs from more traditional economic theory in the inclusion of some institutional and contextual factors and in his emphasis on the dynamic nature of competition, where firms play an active and creative role.

Critical analysis of Porter

Porter's implicit definition of technology is similar to the traditional conception of technology as material objects and blueprint knowledge. The problem is that this simple definition can give a rather misleading view of the nature of technological development and transfer, and hence a misleading view of the actions of firms and the nature of economic activities (Dosi, 1988). Porter's notion of innovation, based on Schumpeterian dynamic competition, is better-developed, but all innovation which Porter discusses is directly cost- and demand-related. (See the section below on Freeman for a more extensive discussion of this point.)

In Porter's argument, the goal of innovation is to increase the standard of living, leaving little room for other values (social, environmental, and so on) which may influence the specific characteristics of innovation. The adoption of process technology which pollutes less is one current example. Porter (1990a, p. 87) does argue that 'strict product, safety and environmental standards can promote competitive advantage by stimulating and upgrading domestic demand'. But these social or environmental goals are deemed to be important only because they are also economically profitable. For Porter, costs and demand remain the key analytical tools.

Another problem with Porter's analysis is his over-emphasis on the importance of *national* home markets and *national* firms. His concept of the company does not distinguish clearly between firms operating only nationally and those operating internationally. National markets are important to small and medium enterprises, which, as Porter argues, can create competitive advantage through innovation and become international firms. Multinational enterprises are actors in many markets and in each such country Porter's four considerations apply. Therefore these companies' capacity to innovate may be based on many national systems of innovation and not just one. To solve this problem, Porter (1990a, p. 93) argues that companies 'can have different home bases for distinct businesses or segments'. The choice of home market depends on its ability to support innovation; if the home market is not conducive to creating competitive advantage, then the company should move to a new home market. Companies (rather than countries) may also create their own factor conditions, such as skilled labour through in-house training. However, these questionable solutions to difficult problems undermine the appeal of Porter's research, because he specifically sets out to analyse how a national environment supports industrial innovation.

Another problem with Porter's analysis has to do with the uneven pattern of capitalist development. If a company benefits from one favourable national environment for innovation, it could still expatriate the earnings to another country. Thus the country with a favourable environment for innovation does not automatically benefit from companies' innovation. There is, therefore, a major logical flaw in Porter's argument that creating or supporting innovation in a country will tend to increase its standard of living. The degree of expatriation of earnings and the general distribution of economic benefits between countries is determined by legal, fiscal and other factors. It is partly thus a political question, and Porter's analysis ignores this.

The problems raised above all relate to Porter's reliance on the firm as the main level of analysis, with relative costs and demand in different nations affecting the degree of competitive advantage. It is to his credit that he includes other advantages of the industrial structure such as learning-by-doing and clustered linkages. However, the vague concept of 'national circumstances and context' provides little understanding of why national firm strategy, structure and rivalry differ, for example, in terms of social or institutional factors, or of regulatory regimes (Boyer, 1988).

Porter's explanatory framework can be credited as an attempt to move beyond the strict assumptions of traditional economic theory. His theory no longer takes production functions and technology as given, where the firm simply responds to input prices and demand. Instead, Porter stresses the possibility – indeed, the necessity – of firms and governments taking an active role to shape the general competitive situation.

In so doing, however, he ignores some structural features and some interesting problems about the relationships constituting a national economy. For example, Porter's emphasis on successful industrial sectors bypasses the problem about the relation between successful and less-successful industries in a national economy. Even industries which are less successful at innovating can be strategically important to a nation. These are at a higher level of analysis than the individual firm and cannot be reduced to firms' actions. This higher level of analysis is necessary in order to understand national differences.

Christopher Freeman

The foundations of Freeman's theory
Christopher Freeman's approach to national systems of innovation draws insights from his own and from his joint work with Carlota Perez on long waves of economic activity (Freeman and Perez, 1988; Perez, 1985). In turn, such theories are inspired by Schumpeter's dynamic analysis, with its incorporation of radical technological change, and by Kondratiev's earlier work on long waves. Since the Freeman-Perez theory is based on technological change, their taxonomy of technology is a logical starting-point here:

(a) *Incremental innovations.* These refer to small changes, which result from the production process or from users. Cumulatively, they are an important source of increases in productivity.

(b) *Radical innovations.* These involve novelty and discontinuous development, usually the result of R&D. They are often a springboard for new investments and new markets.

(c) *Changes in technological system.* These combine radical and incremental technical innovation with organizational and managerial innovation. They often involve clusters of technology.

(d) *Changes in techno-economic paradigm.* These refer to changes in the meta-paradigm that affect all sectors of the economy, as well as leading to the creation of new products and new industries.

Like Porter, their implicit definition of technology is based on material objects and information, although categories (c) and (d) also include social and organizational factors. Each category has a different implication for the cost structure and for economic dynamism, and category (d) is the basis of their long-wave theory.

In Freeman and Perez's theory, the basis for upswings in long waves is found in changes in the techno-economic paradigm. The shift in paradigm is based on the creation and diffusion of radical technology containing new productive potential and redefining technical and economic efficiency, thereby affecting production in all sectors of the economy. However, 'not all [countries] have to produce [the new technologies which are the basis of the next Kondratiev wave] but have to use new techno-economic paradigm in their area of specialization' (Freeman and Lundvall, 1988, p. 3). The radical technological change must, however, be accompanied by a new socio-institutional paradigm, which pervades social behaviour, government policy, institutional structures, ways of organizing production, and so on.

The downswing occurs when the innovative and productive potential of the old radical (or base) technology runs out. At the bottom of each cycle there is a mismatch between the existing institutions and the emerging dominant technology and its paradigm. The long-term, structural economic booms and busts of capitalist economies are thus explained in terms of the interaction between radical technological developments and institutional structures. Freeman differentiates and analyses countries in terms of how well they have adapted to the new 'socio-institutional paradigm' brought by waves of radical technology. National systems flexible enough to adjust their socio-institutional paradigms in downswings to the new requirements are seen to be leaders in the new upswings.

Freeman's (1987, p. 1) definition of national systems of innovation is 'the network of institutions in the public and private sectors whose activities and interactions initiate, import, modify and diffuse new technologies'. This is a broad definition, but Freeman concentrates on four features when describing the Japanese national system of innovation:

(a) the role of government policy (particularly MITI, the Ministry of International Trade and Industry);
(b) the role of corporate R&D, especially in relation to imported technology;
(c) the role of education and training; and
(d) the general structure of industry (Freeman, 1987, p. 4).

For Freeman, the other socio-institutional factors which can differ among nations include: whether the business atmosphere is conflictual or consensual; the organization of the market and of the production system; and the role of the government. These represent key institutions and ways of organizing society; they are key because they critically affect whether or not a nation will be able to benefit from the new technologies.

Critical analysis of Freeman

Freeman's underlying theory neither focuses on capitalism as a system nor on nations *per se*. Rather, the analytical starting point is radical technological change as the driving force for change within nations. Freeman stresses that technology spreads internationally and thereby affects existing social and production relations. Although radical technological change is at the heart of the theory, the process and problems of actual development of technology is almost taken for granted. Freeman tries to allow some scope for actors in technological development by saying that we cannot predict the new base technology, the details of the new paradigm or necessary social adjustments, but he does not attempt to elucidate these opaque processes. This indicates a kind of technological determinism, in which technology is regarded both as an asocial process and as the prime mover of economic progress.

Another issue is the emphasis placed on structural necessity rather than autonomous scope for action. Indeed, what exactly are the mechanisms within nations for social innovation and adjustment to radical technology in Freeman's analysis? On the one hand, the combination of each Kondratiev wave with a *radical technology* presents a structural explanation and the picture of a seemingly unalterable historical process. On the other hand, the process of *social innovation* seems to be the result of individual actions. But whether they act with some possibility of novelty or free will, or only as a reaction to costs or technology, is unclear.

The problem is that Freeman and Perez argue that a specific 'socio-institutional framework' is necessary for full exploitation of the innovative possibilities of the dominant technology. They clearly admit that societies differ in their ability to adjust to the requirements of technology. However, the crucial question is whether there is one best way: a structurally determined optimal strategy of innovation and adjustment in each historical period.

A related question is whether this optimal adaptation strategy will arise out of rational evaluation of the circumstances, or out of some more random process of evolutionary selection. According to Freeman and Perez (1988, p. 48), the optimal socio-institutional adjustments arise because the new technological paradigm profoundly changes the cost structure of the economy: 'The organising principle of each successive paradigm ... is to be found ... most of all in the dynamics of the relative *cost* structure of all possible inputs to production' (emphasis in original). Indeed, they put repeated stress on given and presumably unambiguous cost and supply conditions in their description of the circumstances of innovation.

As in the case of Porter, above, Freeman and Perez focus on changes in input cost structure as a primary mechanism for profound changes in production. A major problem with this argument is that they consider costs as an impartial and unambiguous means of evaluation, albeit one that is dependent on technology. Costs and prices are not, however, given and objective measuring tools. Instead, costs reflect demand and distributional conditions, and thus are partly based on cultural values and on social relations and conventions.

Freeman and Perez's theory stops short at this limited 'economic' context of technological change, without consideration that different actors may have different modes of calculation and different means of evaluating or interpreting costs. They ignore the fact that actors take into account not only given but *expected* costs, and that expectations have a subjective and even indeterminate quality. Thus they simultaneously deny significant scope for the autonomy of each actor in this area, and miss out the processes of cultural and social formation of costs.

Bengt-Åke Lundvall

The foundations of Lundvall's theory

As in Porter's and Freeman's analysis, Bengt-Åke Lundvall's theory of national systems of innovation stresses the dynamic nature of economic activity. In other words, Lundvall, again following Schumpeter, views the economic process as both a creative and a destructive process. Whereas Porter asks only how or why companies in a certain industry can successfully innovate, Lundvall wants to move up a level of abstraction and compare truly national differences in innovative capacity and in economic performance. Although his theory stresses the importance of firms and structured interactions among firms, Lundvall (with Charles Edquist) does have a non-reductive level of analysis – the nation – in his empirical work.

As in Nelson's theory, Lundvall (with the Aalborg group) considers technical change to be a complex, dynamic, cumulative and uncertain process. Lundvall places emphasis on the economic process which aids the creation and diffusion of innovation, which includes but is not limited to technical change, rather than technical change alone. Innovation can involve changes in organization of firms, institutions or markets, participation by new actors, and so on.

In capitalist systems, Lundvall argues, innovation occurs within normal economic activities like routine production and marketing, as well as in R&D: 'In all parts of the economy at all times, we expect to find on-going processes of learning, searching and discovering, resulting in new products, new techniques, new forms of organization and new markets' (Lundvall, forthcoming). Innovation is not necessarily a separate activity carried out by the R&D department. Seeing innovation as an inherent part of normal economic activities also means that it is not possible to identify technological change as an independent process.

In Lundvall's theory, user (buyer) and producer (seller) interactions are extremely important for innovation. Through interaction, the user can communicate potential needs (demand-pull innovation) and the producer can communicate potential technical opportunities (technology-push innovation). Such interactions enable the actors to learn and hence innovate. In this process, Lundvall concentrates on the importance of:

(a)   the exchange of qualitative information;
(b)   the necessary networks of communication between actors or firms; and
(c)   the linkages among firms and sectors in a national economy.

In contrast to neoclassical ideas, where the goals or preferences of firms are normally assumed to be fixed or unambiguous with given information, Lundvall argues that contacts among firms condition their future actions, because their conceptualization of the situation changes.

Thus, the key to understanding innovative activities lies in the actions and organization of firms and in interactions between them: 'Interactive learning [is] at the centre of the process of innovation' (Edquist and Lundvall, forthcoming). Although this brief account may give the impression that the micro level of firm interaction is the most important, Lundvall is also interested in the 'structural determinants of innovative activity' (Freeman and Lundvall, 1988, p. 15).

Each country is seen to have its own specific system of innovation, based on existing institutions, historical resources, industrial development and key sectors. In the Edquist and Lundvall (forthcoming) comparison of the Danish and Swedish national systems of innovation, they argue that 'the precise boundaries of such a system must be determined by a combination of theoretical and historical analysis'. In other words, this theory specifies two key universal components of national systems of innovation – institutions and industrial structure – but it does not give clear criteria for identifying the most important ones.

According to Lundvall, the structural determinants of innovation in a country – resulting from interactive learning – are thus institutions and the economic structure. Institutions refer to both formalized rules and organizations and non-formalized rules or norms. Institutions are seen as vital in their role of regulating economic activities, including innovation. Important institutions for the national system of innovation include regulation of the labour market, of the monetary system, problem-solving procedures, the common historical experience of industrialization, and so on. An especially important institutional structure is the formalized system of knowledge search, or R&D activity, within countries, including shared national assumptions about technology and the economy. The institutional basis of such research activities means that each country has its own specific national characteristics and patterns of behaviour.

Concerning the economic structure, Lundvall is here influenced by the French structuralist tradition. Forward and backward linkages – which enable learning-by-doing and -by-using – are essentially based on the micro-foundation of inter-firm relations. But the whole industrial structure adds up to a system of interaction which cannot be reduced to these individual relations. Within the production structure, Edquist and Lundvall stress the importance of key sectors or 'development blocks'. As with Porter (1990b), an underlying thought is that industries successful in international markets are a vital source of innovation in the national economy. Development blocks are also an important source of broader economic change and dynamism, especially when countries can succeed in creating new development blocks and not just rely on traditional products and industrial sectors.

In their discussion of the national systems of innovation in Denmark and Sweden, Edquist and Lundvall show that they do not view existing national systems of innovation as necessarily optimal or superiorly adapted to circumstances. Whilst the existing systems are seen to have historical roots, there is scope for improvement in terms of, for example, the growth rate of product markets, and the degree of adaptability to changing international circumstances.

Lundvall's research represents an important attempt to deal with both actor and structure, and an insightful discussion of the relationship between production and R&D. Edquist and Lundvall provide a sophisticated account of national differences in innovation system, institutions and production structure, involving the interactions between firms. Arguably, these are the richest case studies in this area.

Critical analysis of Lundvall

However, there are many gaps in Lundvall's analysis. Much of the empirical work is *ad hoc* and lacking in clear or adequate theoretical explanation of the mechanisms involved. For example, there are no explicit criteria on how development blocks or key institutions within countries emerge. An explicit analysis of the structured environment within which agents act (Edquist, 1985) would be an initial step towards full integration and development of the theory. In addition, the theory should explain how the changing conceptualization of the situation by agents and changing behaviour (through interactive learning) can influence the higher level of analysis of institutions and industrial structure.

Richard Nelson

The foundations of Nelson's theory

Nelson and Winter (1982) develop the idea of evolutionary processes in capitalist economies, where routines in firms act as relatively durable 'genes'. Economic competition leads to the selection of certain 'successful' routines, and these can be transferred to other firms. In some cases direct imitation is possible, but the transfer of routines can also occur through buy-out, training, labour mobility and such. Their evolutionary theory is Lamarckian in that acquired characteristics can be passed on, rather than in modern Darwinian biology where individual genes can alter only through mutation at birth and the inheritance of acquired characteristics is ruled out. Lamarckian theory applies particularly to society because our cultural evolution is based on learning, whereas our genetic structure has hardly changed (Gould, 1987).

Nelson (1987, p. 7) sets out to identify 'essential characteristics of technical change in capitalist economies'. Three key elements of his theory of technical change are:

(a) a mechanism which 'introduces novelties into the system' thereby giving rise to unpredictable outcomes;
(b) 'some understandable mechanism that "selects on" entities present in the system'. An understanding of the processes behind the selection of technology would allow us to explain why one technical solution is chosen over others;
(c) contingent outcomes: 'At any time, there are feasible entities not present in the prevailing system that have a chance of being introduced' (Nelson, 1987, p. 12).

The continuing existence of feasible alternative developments means that the system never reaches a state of equilibrium or finality. The process remains dynamic, and never reaches an optimum. In contrast, the assumption that the system may reach an enduring optimum means that future options are knowable. According to Nelson (1987, p. 12), diversity itself exists because technological change is an open-ended, multi-path process, where no best solution to a technical problem can be known beforehand or identified *ex post*. As a consequence, technological change is a very wasteful process in capitalist economies, with many duplications and dead-ends.

The selection process and the generation of diversity are both key features of this type of evolutionary theory. In both Darwinian and Lamarckian evolutionary change, the existence of variety, and possibly its enhancement through mutation or recombination, are crucial. Nelson identifies the pluralistic development of technology, of continuous technical innovation and of competition between designs, as key characteristics of the capitalist system.

Evolutionary and institutional economics differ from neoclassical theory both in their definition of technology and in their incorporation of technological change into the centre of economic processes (Dosi, 1988). In Nelson's view, technology exists in different forms such as coded information, public knowledge, privately owned knowledge or artefacts (protected by patents). Finally and importantly, there is uncodifiable or routinized knowledge, specific to individuals, teams, a firm or an industry (Nelson, 1981). Nelson argues that most technology eventually moves from private ownership to become a public good, which allows society as a whole to benefit.[4] However, ownership alone does not identify whether technology is generally available or not. Nelson also argues that technologies can be ranked according to their *latent publicness*. Some are more generic, having to do with abstract rules or problems common to an entire research field or industry while others are more specific, and tied to a particular process or product.

This definition of technology means that technology is embedded in the social relations of the firm (Nelson, 1981). Tacit knowledge, worker and managerial competence and other human-based knowledge are thus crucial for technological change, and especially for firm-specific changes. This is an important contrast with the more mechanical representation of the firm in neoclassical theory, where managers 'control' the production process by making rational decisions based on full and codifiable knowledge. This difference is crucial because Nelson recognizes that although individuals can make decisions and act, they are bound by conceptual habits and routines. Thus social institutions, which can differ between countries, may mould preferences and perceptions and are thus important in the innovation process.

Nelson's (1988, p. 312) discussion of the US innovation system identifies 'three rather obvious characteristics of national innovation systems in capitalist economies'. These are:

(a)   the privatization of much new technology, which brings market selection and the profit motive into the creation of technology;
(b)   the evolutionary nature of technical change, particularly its multiple sources and its inherently wasteful process;
(c)   'the heavy reliance on *ex post* market forces' for selection.[5]

Nelson argues that these three characteristics are present in capitalist economies, as opposed to Soviet-style centrally planned ones. In addition to firms or other parts of the industrial structure, Nelson emphasizes the role of research laboratories and universities, thereby widening the typical compass of economic analysis. However, in his discussion of the US innovation system Nelson (1988) concentrates on the R&D sector.

Nelson has subsequently developed his argument, seeing the innovation system as broader than the traditional R&D system. Elements of this include the 'character and effectiveness of a nation's system of schooling, training, and retraining', work relations such as 'the patterns of labour – management bargaining and negotiation, dispute resolution', characteristics of financial institutions, and the way firms are organized and controlled (Nelson and Rosenberg, forthcoming). These institutions are vital both to producing knowledge and to spreading it widely.

In this analysis, national variations in capitalist systems are important. Thus is partly because 'nations differ in their mix of industries and these [inter-industry] differences strongly influence the shapes of the national innovation systems' (Nelson and Rosenberg, forthcoming). It is also because there are differences between nations in the composition and structure of other institutions. These institutions differ in the role they play, their organization and problem-orientation, how much they help national firms, as well as whether funding is public or private. National characteristics of the R&D system have implications for how well science and technology is integrated into the activities of industry and therefore how easy or difficult it is for innovation to occur in a country. Different balances between public and private technology means that different institutional arrangements for concealing and for sharing technological knowledge evolve over time in varying national patterns.

Critical analysis of Nelson
Typically, evolutionary selection operates on performance outcomes rather than intentions and purposes. Hence evolutionary theory has trouble incorporating the purposefulness of human actors. Although Nelson and Winter embrace Lamarckian rather than Darwinian theory, this difficulty is not resolved (Hodgson, 1991a). The question of intentionality stirs up debate over the

proper level of analysis, and indeed relates to the question of methodological individualism, as economists of the Austrian School have insisted.

The work of Nelson and Winter (1982) shows some of the problems of an evolutionary approach in dealing with truly spontaneous action. In their theory, the energization of specific types of routine depends upon the level of profit. Below a low-profit threshold firms may become extinct. Above a higher profit level, firms continue through inertia with previously successful routines. Only when firms are in the middle profit range do they change their routines and begin searching for new ones. The problem with this is that it portrays firms as passively responding to exogenous circumstances; there is no scope for goal-directed behaviour beyond this response mechanism. Although much behaviour may be routine, many writers stress the spontaneous and indeterminate characteristics of entrepreneurial activity. Arguably, such spontaneity does affect economic development.

It has been noted that Nelson stresses the importance of the pluralistic context of innovation. However, this still leaves unclear the nature, extent and severity of technological competition. Does the United States exhibit a superior variety of pluralistic competition, or are other, more consensus-building ways of innovation (Freeman, 1987) also viable? Notably, there are different types of competition such as among technologies, among firms, and among structures and forms of ownership. Technological diversity may remain while the organizational structure of competition or co-operation between firms differs between countries (Rosenberg, 1976).

Nelson and Winter suggest that the predominant mechanisms to select technology are government procurement and the market. However, other research in the social sciences has emphasized additional selection mechanisms, such as the struggle among groups to define or interpret technology discussed by the 'social construction of technology school' (Bijker *et al.*, 1987). The selection process is more multi-dimensional than the market and government processes that are represented in Nelson's work.

The missing multi-dimensionality of the selection process relates to another problem. Although Nelson specifically argues that the technology which is developed is not optimal in an absolute sense, only superior in a relative sense, his discussion of national systems of innovation essentially argues that the capitalist system is generally an optimal organizational pattern for technological change. Capitalism is seen to embody the key evolutionary forces: encouraging diversity and tending to select technology that reduces costs. It is not clear if Nelson really means that the capitalist system is optimal in an absolute sense or if it is the best existing system. One of the reasons for this opaqueness is that in the discussion of technological change, the capitalist system is considered as a given (i.e. the environment of selection) rather than one of the factors being selected and adapted.

4.   SUMMARY AND CONCLUSIONS

A series of questions has been addressed in connection with each of four researchers' work. Although their definitions of technology differ, the four repeatedly stress the dynamic role of innovation in the economy. This still leaves open the question whether innovation is the result of individual spontaneity or is dominated by structural factors.

Table 8.1 below summarizes the different perceptions of technology and technological change, and thus serves as a basis for understanding the different conceptions of national systems of innovation that have been discussed here.

Table 8.1: Conceptions of technology and technical change

	Conception of technology	Effective use depends on	Criteria to select relevant technology	Nature of technological change
Porter	Blueprint-type information	Skill of entrepreneur or manager	Given market costs and demand	Simple generation by actors
Freeman	Taxonomic ranking involving science and institutions	Socio-institutional adaptation	Given market costs and demand	Long waves
Lundvall	Interactive, knowledge -based and embedded in routines	Technology-push and market-pull. Structure of R&D system	Given market costs and success in the world market	Incremental accumulation plus long waves
Nelson	Different types, from scientific to tacit and routine-based	Adoption by competent and viable routines	Structure of costs, plus routines and culture	Evolutionary selection (competition) and mutation (search)

What, then, is a national system of innovation? For the four researchers, national systems of innovation mean something larger than the quantifiable aspects of national R&D systems. The R&D system, whether corporate- or government-financed, is an important cornerstone in a nation's ability to innovate and diffuse technology, but it does not describe nor account for all the differences among nations. The differing conceptions of national systems of innovation are summarized in Table 8.2.

Innovation, Technology and Economic Evolution

Table 8.2: What are national systems of innovation?

Porter	Not possible to analyse general national differences, only specific, successful industries in a country. The national system refers to the environment supporting innovative activity in companies, i.e., competition in the home market, supporting industrial structure etc. *Empirical focus*: Comparison of industries.
Freeman	A new, radical technology promotes social and institutional innovation on a national scale. Otherwise innovation may be incremental and technological. *Empirical focus*: Comparisons of nations based on their innovations and adjustments in social institutions.
Lundvall	The national system refers to the national economy, but there is stress on the importance of linkages and on interaction within development blocks. The national system of innovation is formed by the relevant institutions and industrial structures. *Empirical focus*: The historical development of institutions and production structures in different countries.
Nelson	The national system refers to the national economy. Differences in industrial structure (such as the needs of industry for science and technology and whether technology is public or private) and differences in organization of institutions (especially the R&D system) explain how national systems of innovation differ. *Empirical focus*: Current institutional differences between nations.

It has been suggested here that the concept of *national systems of innovation* is a useful analytical tool for understanding national differences in the rate and type of innovation. However, more work has to be done at the theoretical level, to address the problems raised here. An adequate theory must relate to entities at various levels and to different but inter-conditioning processes. As several authors have emphasized, the crucial feature underlying the analytical approach is dynamic change – of firms, managerial strategy, products, markets, technology and the economic structure.

With this outlook, it is necessary to examine the nature of technology – in its material manifestations, as systemized knowledge, and as knowledge embedded in social institutions. Technological change depends on the technological potential, market opportunities, institutions, and the structure of the economy. These are all affected by the specific structure of social relations in a nation. Arguably, the social institution emerges as a key concept, affecting both the perceptions and actions of individuals and the structure and context of their interaction.

The multi-dimensional analysis of national differences hinted at here addresses routines and institutions at different levels. The different levels and processes are related but each level is non-reducible. In particular, the concept of national systems of innovation encompasses an idea of systematic interactions, which cannot be reduced simply to the actions of specific firms, or to the existing R&D system, or to competition among firms or institutions. The structured interaction of these and other components constitutes a world techno-economic system, with a non-reducible national level of analysis.

NOTES

1. Thanks to all who gave comments on this paper, especially Charles Edquist, Chris Freeman, Geoff Hodgson, Bengt-Åke Lundvall, Richard Nelson and colleagues at the Department of Technology and Social Change, Linköping, Sweden.
2. Dividing the process of technological change into three stages – invention, innovation and diffusion – illuminates the difference between making an initial idea a technical reality (invention) and commercializing it (innovation) and spreading that technology to potential users or final consumers (diffusion). However, technological development is a process without clear lines between the stages because both producer and user continue to improve the product (Rosenberg, 1982, ch. 6).
3. The countries included in Porter's analysis are: Denmark, Germany, Italy, Japan, Korea, Singapore, Sweden, Switzerland, the United Kingdom and the United States.
4. Compare with the classic argument for market failure in the private provision of technology (Arrow, 1962).
5. A question about Nelson's interpretation arises in that agents do not simply rely on *ex post* market outcomes; they also try to anticipate future market conditions.

9. Economic Evolution, Chaotic Dynamics and the Marx–Keynes–Schumpeter System

Richard M. Goodwin

The analysis of the processes underlying the evolution of modern capitalist economies has preoccupied many leading economic theorists since Adam Smith. Manifestly, economic development combines long-term structural evolution with multiple types of business cycle with varied periodicity. A central theoretical conundrum is to understand how these elements are inter-related. Three leading contributors to our understanding of the cyclical and developmental processes involved are Karl Marx, John Maynard Keynes and Joseph Schumpeter. Partly from the insights provided by these writers, it is possible to assemble a novel approach to the problem.

Particularly with the ideas of these great economists in mind, the attempt is made here to develop a unitary theory of shorter and longer waves of growth, but with ever-changing contours, endogenously generated. With the recent development of the remarkable new theory of chaos, or 'strange attractors', we now know that a single model can succeed in explaining a large part of the generic irregularity of economic time-series.

The intellectual genealogy of my model may be illuminated by the following brief discussion of the ideas of some key economic theorists. In the beginning were the Classical economists who included a concern with the long run behaviour of the economy. Marx fully absorbed this dynamic, placing his 'law of motion' at the centre of his methodology. He greatly admired Darwin's theory of evolution and plainly aspired to be the Darwin of socio-economic evolution. Unfortunately, his economics were faulty, with erroneous projections of falling real wages and rate of profit. Nevertheless, he had an outstanding insight in basing his dynamics on cyclical behaviour.

Marx died in the year that both Keynes and Schumpeter were born. Schumpeter, no Marxian, was none the less deeply impressed by Marx's vision of the nature of economic dynamics in terms of economic change driven by the search for profit. He translated Marx into the more effective conventional form, retaining, however, the cyclical dynamic but inverting the theory of wages into the more realistic form of fluctuating growth of real wages. Schumpeter in turn fell into error by reasoning in neoclassical terms of full employment, thus ensuring a monotonic average rising output and real wage.

The third party to this ill-assorted trilogy is Keynes, who, using Kahn's multiplier, supplied the theory of output controlled by effective demand. Although Keynes paid little attention to Marx's economics, there are parallels between his theory of effective demand and some of Marx's ideas in the second volume of *Capital*, as Michal Kalecki has shown. The idea of effective demand is crucial for realistic output and wage behaviour, but also it is very helpful as an instrument of self-organization. In my view, Keynes's theory complements Schumpeter's insights to portend an extraordinarily powerful theoretical combination. For these reasons I like to think of my model as an MKS system (Marx–Keynes–Schumpeter).

Keynes and Schumpeter knew one another, admired one another, and yet each failed to incorporate the central contribution of the other. Schumpeter, implicitly assuming full employment, aimed to explain how structural change led to cyclical growth. Keynes, by contrast, strove to explain the unemployment of the 1930s and, by implication, how to cure it. He wrote during the Great Depression, and for him the problem of mass unemployment overshadowed the task of reviving economic growth. As a result he had little to say about the latter. Schumpeter, on the other hand, said that the cycle is simply the form growth takes.

The engine of change is the pursuit of private profit. Consequently, the economy not only generates perpetual motion but also continually alters its own structure. It can be considered either as a single species altering its structure (morphogenesis) or as selection of new species through competitive survival or disappearance. It is ideally suited to self-organization in the specific sense that it consists of a great number of parts, all related, directly or indirectly, by virtue of the fact that the expenditure of each is determined by demand, a demand which depends directly on the expenditure of all the other parts.

One of Schumpeter's great insights, putting him a generation ahead of his contemporaries, was to regard the business cycle as simply the form growth takes. His perception of reality was, alas, totally unrelated to his sadly deficient mathematical capability. I tried to teach him how to use linear cycle theory but he never succeeded in being able to deploy it. When he came to make his final statement on economic development, he opted for three cycles: three Kitchins to a Juglar, six Juglars to a Kondratiev. The very short cycle is important, but involves no innovation, so I shall omit it as a detail. The Juglars and Kondratievs cannot be treated in such a fashion; each is bound to be influenced by the other. Even if they were linear cycles, they would be coupled oscillations and hence both would contain both cycles. With a more-complicated, non-linear dynamic, it is possible to fuse them into a unified model.

Whilst Schumpeter admired the earlier work of Keynes, he totally rejected the *General Theory*. He may have had two reasons for this astonishing verdict, one bad and one good. First, he believed in market clearing, including the labour market. The second reason was Keynes's use of the formulations of aggregate demand, output and income. The first seems a grave error, but the second poses a basic difficulty. Schumpeter rightly insisted that innovative technical progress is specific to particular industries. Hence aggregation masks, and can even falsify, the consequences of structural change. Consequently, the analysis should be in large, multidimensional systems.

Alas, however, I am forced to present an aggregative model, since I am not able to deal with large non-linear systems of the kind addressed here. My only defence is that the problem and the model are complicated and that a simple version does effectively illuminate much of the dynamical structure. Also it is relevant that aggregate demand is a potent agent of self-organization. Innovations are many and different, and partly in regard to timing and duration of integration into the economy. Consequently, for Schumpeter's theory, the innovative 'swarms' would be so many, so disparate in timing, amplitude and duration, that his cycle would tend to be nearly invisible. But because the level and growth-rate of demand plays so great a role in productive decisions, especially in the case of new and risky projects, various innovations are rapidly expanded in a rising market. Then the requisite investment further accelerates the already buoyant economy. Hence a lot of unrelated decisions are forced to march in step. Thus the Kahn–Keynes of the multiplier furnishes a crucial missing link in Schumpeter's theory of technological evolution.

The central motive force is the Schumpeterian 'swarm' of innovations. There is considerable agreement that, after a weak beginning, the archetypical innovation gradually proves its worth and becomes better known by potential users, along with improved design and adaptation to diverse functions. Finally, it decelerates gradually as it is completely integrated into the economy. Thus it tends to have a quadratic trajectory, conveniently represented by the logistic.

The model here can only present an overview of the principal features of a complex problem, with no attention to details. Nevertheless, to be sufficiently realistic the model must: exhibit an unstable equilibrium; be globally stable; endogenously generate morphogenesis in the form of structural change; do so in cyclical form, albeit erratically or aperiodically; generate both short and long waves. Notably, such waves must be growth, not stationary, waves.

With this considerations in mind we now turn to the functioning of the model. Initially the economy is at or near equilibrium. Equilibrium is so defined to isolate the role of innovations from the effects of all other exogenous variables such as government, foreign trade, and so on. Underlying the model is a pair of first-order linear differential equations with parameters giving rise to an unstable oscillation. The two variables are ratios, hence independent of scale, thus permitting a growth cycle. To this is added a third, nonlinear differential equation which defines a dynamic control parameter, which determines a bounded region in state space, within which, after a time, all trajectories of the first two variables are contained.

The first variable, v, is the ratio of employment L, to total available labour force, N, taken as constant to emphasize the other relations (though it is not difficult to introduce a constant or slowly varying growth rate of N). The second variable, u, is the share of wages (including salaries, hence average earned income) in gross product, q.

$$u = wL/q = wa$$

where a is employment per unit of output and u is the unit cost of labour as well. Net product consists solely of wages and profits; all wages and no profits are consumed, a simplification which can be removed at the cost of moderate complication.

A logistic 'swarm', k, of 50 years' duration, is the means by which structural change and growth are introduced. Although Schumpeter perceived the basic nature of the problem in terms of cyclical growth, he did not succeed in arriving at a satisfactory formulation, having simply assumed full employment with the higher productivity output. To implement structural change, there must first be investment. Clearly, the investment increases demand and output, including demand for labour. An increase in employment accelerates demand and thereby output in two ways. First, by the demand increase resulting from the growth in employment itself, and secondly, by the rise in the real wage resulting from the decreased unemployment.

One of the aims of the investment is to lower costs, including labour costs. Thus innovation acts in two opposed directions on employment: by raising output it increases employment but by technological change it lowers employment per unit of output (higher productivity). The rate of decrease of labour input (increase of productivity) is taken to be proportional to the rate of increase of innovational capacity, k/k. The real wage (average earnings) is assumed to increase faster than productivity when $v>v^*$ and to increase less rapidly when $v<v^*$ (v^* being taken as 0.90, i.e., 10 per cent unemployment). When $v>(v^* + c)$, with $c = 0.04$ (i.e., 6 per cent unemployment), the dynamical control parameter, z, increasingly decelerates v, and with $v<0.94$, it increasingly accelerates v. Thus the pair v and u are dynamically unstable but in economics this constitutes no problem since full employment is an impenetrable barrier, implemented here as approaching full employment when $v>(v^* + c)$. There is first the existing limit of capacity, but that can, given time, be overcome. What cannot be extended is the maximum available labour force. As v goes above $v^* + c$, it becomes rapidly more difficult to recruit labour and hence increase output.

It is helpful to see the system dynamic here as a simplified variant of the Lotka–Volterra predator–prey model, with wages as the predator and profits the prey. Setting $v^* = 0$, thus reckoning in deviations from equilibrium, the system is a linearized version of a Lotka–Volterra model with zero constants. Also it is independent of scale and hence not limited to a stationary average level. The central dynamic is given by $\dot{v} = -du$ and $\dot{u} = +hv$, d and h positive. To the first equation must be added a term fv, $f>0$, which makes the model more structurally stable and dynamically unstable, thus answering Kolmogorov's criticism of Volterra's structurally unstable formulation. The term can represent the accelerator or any other aspect of the economy deriving from the simple fact that high and expanding demand leads to further increases in demand and output.

Following Poincaré, the usual solution in such an unstable cycle is to assume upper and lower nonlinearities, yielding global stability and at least one closed limit cycle, a single equilibrium motion. Just as Poincaré generalized the concept of equilibrium from a point to a closed curve, Lorenz generalized the closed curve to a closed region, in which an astonishing variety of aperiodic motions can occur in a seemingly erratic fashion. I shall use a variant of the Rössler Band, as the chaotic attractor most comprehensible and applicable to economics. Instead of defining an upper and lower bound to a variable, one posits a control parameter which provides a growing downward pressure beyond a given high (positive) value and a growing upward one for low (negative) values. This control parameter is specified by

$$\dot{z} = b + .gz(v - c).$$

Such a device effectively stabilizes the system globally and leaves it free to perform wildly erratic motion locally around the zero equilibrium. This is illustrated in Figure 9.1 for a wide variety of initial values resulting in a variety of trajectories which establish a perceivable boundary. Trajectories from outside all eventually enter the closed region and no trajectory exits from the bounded region. This is such a breath-taking generalization of the notion of a stable equilibrium as to negate partially the conception of equilibrium, which originally suggested absence of change.

The concept of a system stable to an equilibrium fixed point has thus been generalized from a point to a closed curve, and now to a bounded region. The closed curve defined a limit cycle, the sole way in which to explain the existence of a cycle. All models from Rayleigh and van der Pol onwards have posited upper and lower values to convert local instability into global stability. They did this by having two non-linearities, commonly in the form

Figure 9.1

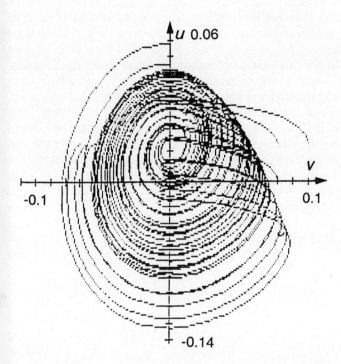

of a cubic. Many years ago I realized that one non-linearity (full employment) would also provide a limit cycle, thus demonstrating that two non-linearities were sufficient but not necessary. It is interesting to note that Rössler found that he needed only one non-linearity to capture the vastly more potent gyrations of chaotic motion.

Within the closed region, endogenously deterministic variables can move in a seemingly arbitrary and unpredictable way. It is for this reason that this recent discovery is so relevant to economics. If one examines the time-series generated by such a model and tries to uncover the mathematical structure which generated it, one would find that to get a correct estimate of the system there is as yet no technique available. Indeed, such problems may remain unsolved. If, however, the model is somehow known, then its contribution can be extracted, leaving the irregularity due to random exogenous shocks in the statistic.

In my view the implications of chaos for economics are serious. Economic statistics are pervasively irregular but this has always been ascribed to exogenous shocks. In the behaviour exhibited in Figure 9.1 there are no exogenous elements; the erratic element is entirely endogenous. Therefore it is necessary to adopt the hypothesis that there are two distinct sources of irregularity in economic statistics, the exogenous and the endogenous. At the very minimum, this seems to me to require a reformulation of some econometric procedures.

These three differential equations, with only one non-linearity, determine the behaviour of the economy in deviations from the exogenous effects and, in particular, from the effects of innovatory technical progress. To this basic transmission mechanism, which is independent of scale, must be added the accumulation of innovative capacity as the mechanism of structural change and growth. Also there must be added an equation for the determination of output, as it is affected by innovative investment and as it in turn affects employment, v, and as that in turn affects the share of labour, with its vital effect on consumption demand.

With a constant labour force,

$v = L/N$, so that

Figure 9.2

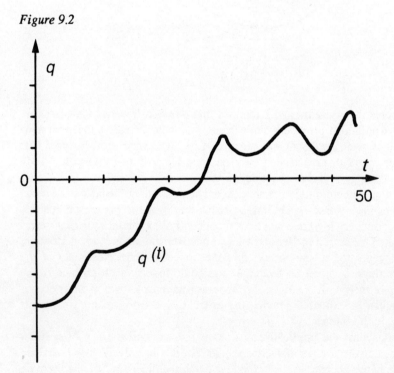

$\dot{v}/v = \dot{L}/L = \dot{q}/q + \dot{a}/a$, with the result that

$\dot{q}/q = \dot{v}/v - \dot{a}/a.$

The rate of change of productivity is taken to be proportional to the accumulation of innovative capacity, thus $m\dot{k}/k = -\dot{a}/a$. Given historically is a 50-year logistic of innovation:

$$\dot{k} = jk(1 - sk)$$

with the investment reaching a peak in 25 years and approaching zero as k -> $1/s$. The complete model then becomes:

$\dot{v} = -du + fv - ez$

$\dot{u} = hv$

$\dot{z} = b + gz(v - c)$

Figure 9.3

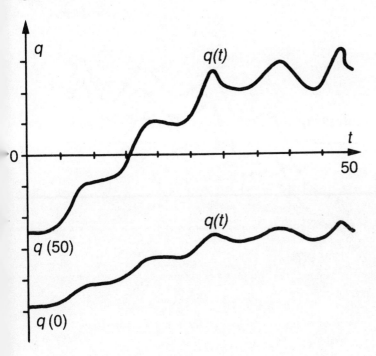

$$\dot{q}/q = (-du + fv - ez)/(v + v^*) + mj(1 - sk)$$

$$\dot{k} = jk(1 - sk).$$

For single parametric changes the model is not very robust, but it is quite robust for economically plausible related parameter variations. A wide variety of generically similar behaviours can be generated. The following set of parameters is chosen solely as a plausible illustration: $d = 0.50$, $e = 0.80$, $h = 0.50$, $f = 0.15$, $b = 0.005$, $g = 85.0$, $c = 0.048$, $m = 0.16$, $j = 0.17$, $s = 0.14$, $v^* = 0.90$.

Notably, initial conditions play a fundamentally different role in non-linear as opposed to linear econometrics. They change type of motion including periodicity, as well as magnitude and phase. Here the chosen initial conditions are respectively: 0.020, 0.030, 0, 5.0, 0.045, with 0<*t*<50 years. The resulting trajectory of output over 50 years is shown in Figure 9.2. In my view it represents the joint insights of Schumpeter and Keynes and represents what the former wanted to say but could not formulate. He maintained that at the end of a Kondratiev there would necessarily be a higher output since

Figure 9.4

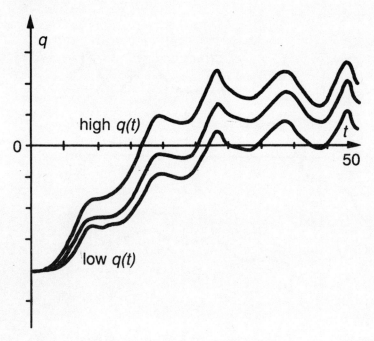

there would always be full employment at a higher productivity. After Keynes one can no longer accept that; there can be those unemployed by labour-saving technology, along with a possibly lower or only moderately higher output and income.

In this model there is no assumption of full employment and yet there is a guarantee of a higher average level of output. The problem is posed by the gradual end of the logistic with investment approaching zero. Without further assumptions, barring arbitrary exogenous investment or public policy (un-employment payments are ignored in the interest of sharpening the issue), there will be a decline of output to its original level or even lower because of labour-saving. Here the problem is solved by the realistic assumption that the competition of producers for given supplies of labour raises the real wage. With the demand-driven Keynesian approach, the investment demand raises output. This increases employment and demand further, and in a twofold way, since it also means higher demand per employee. This more than compensates for the lowered demand for labour.

The Kondratiev peak at a half-century is explained by the uni-modal, quadratic investment function. The rising wave almost completely erases the

Figure 9.5

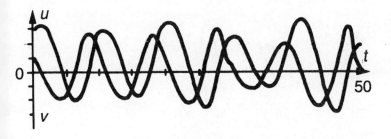

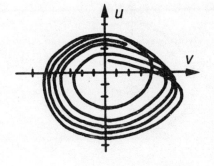

first cycle; then as the Kondratiev levels off at the peak, the cycle slowly re-emerges, and gradually it takes over as the innovations cease. This downside of the Kondratiev is crucial: employment is being cut, though at a decreasing rate, investment demand is rapidly declining. What has happened is that the equilibrium level of output has been shifted upward through the operation of the labour market. In the middle the employment ratio is biased above its equilibrium; this raises demand and the level of wages. Then, as the upward motion decelerates, the equilibrium level of employment remains at 90 per cent (10 per cent unemployment) of a constant labour force with higher productivity and corresponding real wage and hence demand. Thus Schumpeter's vision is confirmed: there are only slightly fewer than five cycles including one large one; average earnings have risen along with output; structural change has been accomplished but in a cyclical form.

What Schumpeter did not say, but no doubt would have agreed with, is that each cycle is individual; is different from all the others, and not only because of innovations. He confidently asserted that once one Kondratiev was completed, a new wave would get under way. If the new wave is the same as the old, the result is shown in Figure 9.3. It recapitulates the process

Figure 9.6

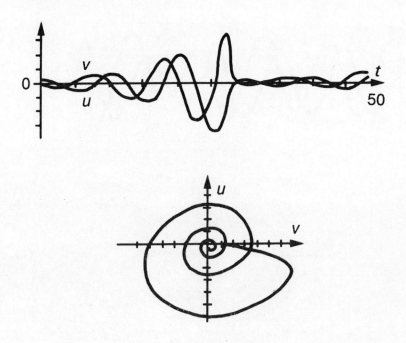

on a larger scale, but close attention will show that each cycle is different between the two half-centuries.

In this form the Kondratiev brings history into economics and it is an attractive feature of the model that each successive long wave can be as different as time and technology choose to make it. By varying the parameter, s, one makes the innovative output capacity greater or smaller; by varying j correspondingly one determines the rate of growth of productivity; by altering m one makes the economic effect (through the capacity/output ratio) greater or smaller. A related fact is that, for historical reasons, some economies grow fast (for example, Japan) and others grow slowly (for example, Great Britain). By altering the parameter j from 0.17 to 0.22 and s from 0.14 to 0.10 one gets the high-growth, Japanese case, and by altering j to 0.15 and s to 0.25, one gets the low-growth possibility, with a middle result given by the unaltered values, as shown in Figure 9.4.

The degree of irregularity in these examples is small, whereas the virtue of the model is that it can produce any degree of irregularity. The regularity is more evident in the time-series and phase portrait of the variables u and v, shown in Figure 9.5. By the modest change of initial values of v and u from

Figure 9.7

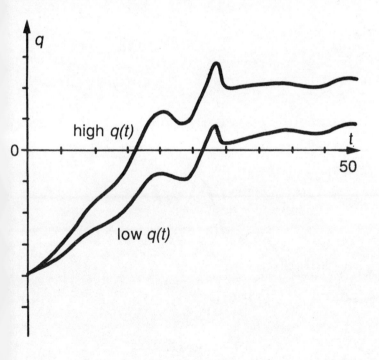

0.02 and 0.03 to 0 and 0.005 and f to 0.18 one arrives at the strikingly irregular resulting time-series and phase portrait of Figure 9.6. These produce
the rather more irregular output growths exhibited in Figure 9.7. These two
examples appear to exhibit the generic character of the non-repeating figures
which one sees in economic time-series. The very short-run wiggles can
happily be ascribed to random shocks, whereas these irregularities represent
a type of dynamic functioning of a simplified economic structure.

This model can be elaborated in varying ways, but one particular change
is especially important. The logistic innovative function should be bilaterally,
not unilaterally, coupled with output, that is, investment heavily influences
demand and output, but is in turn made subject to their influence. Therefore
instead of assuming a constant growth rate, j, of new innovative capacity, we
may assume a linear dependence on the employment ratio (the state of
demand), thus

$$\dot{k} = (j + nv)k(1 - sk), \quad \text{and}$$

$$\dot{q}/q = (-du + fv - ev)/(v + v^*) + m(j + nv)(1 - sk).$$

Figure 9.8

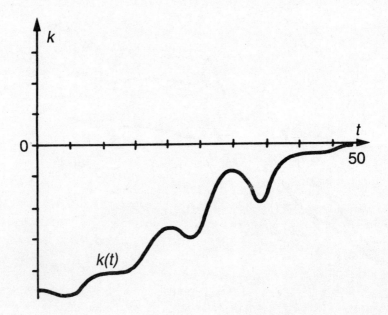

In this form we have a truly unified, single theory of growth with fluctuation. The degree of irregularity can be indicated by growth rates: they were, peak to peak, roughly 26 per cent, 33 per cent, 6 per cent, 5 per cent, and trough to trough, 19 per cent, 28 per cent, 22 per cent, 23 per cent; or averaging peak and trough, 22.4 per cent, 30.7 per cent, 13.8 per cent, 14.1 per cent. The length of each fluctuation trough to trough, as illustrated in Figures 9.8 and 9.9, was roughly 8 years, 15 years, 7 years, 10 years. Perhaps an even clearer indication of the erratic quality is given by employment $v(t)$ and $u(t)$ in Figure 9.10.

The foregoing model is a chaotic attractor and is obviously dynamically stable; but is it structurally stable? This is a difficult question and one beyond the scope of this chapter. To give a simple answer to an unsimple question, I would say it is structurally unstable, which is why it is so fascinating. The interested reader is referred to Guckenheimer and Holmes (1983) for further discussion of this topic.

We have explored here not a solution of a given system subject to exogenous shocks but a non-linear system which generates irregular or erratic behaviour endogenously. Of course, the importance of exogenous

Figure 9.9

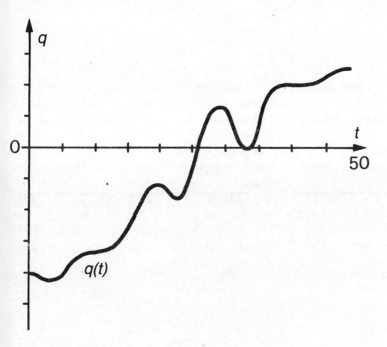

Figure 9.10

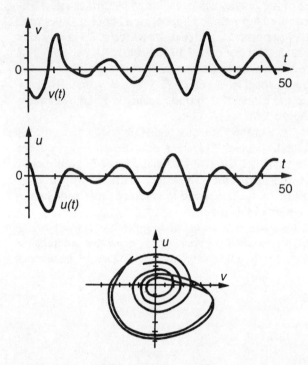

shocks cannot be denied but I think that Ragnar Frisch really misled a generation of economists by saying that you must have a stable system dynamically disturbed by exogenous shocks. We now know that that is only half the story. If you have the right kind of non-linear theory you get irregular behaviour of the kind that he thought only exogenous.

This chapter has been concerned with chaotic growth through structural change. Schumpeter's semi-Marxian vision of growth driven by ever-renewed profit through technical change has been linked to the insights of Keynes regarding the role of the multiplier and effective demand. The perspective offered by chaos theory offers an entirely new interpretation of such phenomena, and one which we have only just begun to develop and understand.

10. Socio-political Disruption and Economic Development

Geoffrey M. Hodgson[1]

For orthodox economic theory, the explanation of economic growth in general and productivity growth in particular is still a great mystery. Orthodox economics approaches the issue via one of its scientifically unsubstantiated articles of faith: the 'well-behaved' production function. Any output or change in output is supposedly explained by a change in inputs or a mysterious shift in the function itself. Using this approach, even the most detailed and comprehensive studies have had limited success.

The first section of this chapter addresses orthodox attempts to explain productivity growth and the limitations of the underlying theory. The second section sketches an institutional and evolutionary approach to the problem. This is used to interpret some econometric results which are presented in the third section, and therein the chapter is concluded.

1. EMPIRICAL AND THEORETICAL LIMITATIONS OF ORTHODOX ANALYSES

Despite much empirical effort, the orthodox 'production function' model still faces a problem in explaining considerable inter-plant and international differences in productivity. Much of this evidence has been reviewed elsewhere (Hodgson, 1982; Nichols, 1986). As well as evidence of overall productivity differences between developed economies, even more striking is the evidence for single industries, showing big sectoral productivity gaps between different countries (Prais, 1981).

A typical orthodox response is to suggest that such differences in productivity must be due, in the main, to differences in the inputs of the production function. In fact, there is considerable evidence portraying relatively low levels of capital investment in the UK (Blackaby, 1978; Caves and Krause, 1980). However, there are serious problems in isolating these as the main causes of low productivity. For instance, studies show that the average increase in output resulting from a unit of investment expenditure has been much lower in Britain and Japan than in France, Italy, West Germany and the USA (Brown and Sheriff, 1978; Blume, 1980). Pratten (1976) found that differences in the amounts of machinery appeared to be responsible for no more than one-fifth of the average difference in productivity found in comparable plants in Britain, the USA, West Germany and France. Prais (1981, p. 269) argued that low UK productivity could not be attributed to low investment in machinery but to inadequate 'knowledge of how to create and operate modern machinery efficiently'. We are led to the conclusion that varied amounts of capital equipment per employee are not the main factor explaining internationally diverse levels of productivity.

Of course, an inferior labour input could be blamed, but the 'production function' model is still in some difficulty in explaining the lack of a clear relation between outputs and capital inputs. Witness the limitations of the 'growth accounting' approach. For instance, Edward Denison (1979) finds that 'factor inputs', including capital stock, the educational level of the workforce and the amount of expenditure on research and development, explain no more than a small fraction of the US productivity slowdown in the 1970s.

Angus Maddison (1987) gets better overall estimates for growth in total factor productivity in a study using three historical time periods and covering six major countries. However, his approach is more eclectic and 'speculative' including 'structural' and 'catch-up' effects. Arbitrary and 'illustrative' features of this analysis include the assumption that capital always has a contribution weighted at 30 per cent of the total. Consequently, a large proportion of 'explained' productivity growth in Maddison's analysis – as high as 78 per cent in one case – is made up of a universal and arbitrarily assumed growth rate of 'capital quality' of 1.5 per cent.

Clearly, orthodox economists have empirical as well as theoretical difficulties in this area. Although great strides have been made in improving the quality of the data – both Denison's and Maddison's own contributions to this should be noted – the measures of such factors as the 'quantity' and 'quality' of growth are patchy and speculative, to say the least.

The response of most orthodox economists will be to put further effort into gathering and refining the data and making additional econometric estimations. Such efforts have some value. However, the underlying theoretical problems with the orthodox approach should not be ignored. It would be wise to invest a fraction of the available effort on alternative approaches.

Underlying Problems with Orthodox Theory

We should remind ourselves of the shaky foundations of orthodox theory in this area. Although some aggregation is inevitable with such empirical work, the capital debates of the 1960s and 1970s show that concept and measurability of 'capital' is highly problematic.[2] Furthermore, even if capital was meaningful and measurable, the arbitrary assumption of a 'well-behaved' production function remains a great fabrication, supported by the most slender and dubious of evidence. For instance, economic historians such as Avi Cohen (1984), Paul David (1975) and Nathan Rosenberg (1982) have found no clear evidence of neoclassical factor substitution in the evolution of technology. Generally, such changes are qualitative, involving different outputs as well as different types and quantities of input.

In addressing production, the problems with orthodoxy emanate from the deepest conceptual level, as Nicholas Georgescu-Roegen (1971, ch. 9) and Philip Mirowski (1989, ch. 6) have elaborated. In particular, the social and organizational aspects of production are ignored. Orthodox theory regards output as mechanically dependent on the number of hours of work that is agreed between employer and employee. However, due to uncertainty and imperfect knowledge, the amount and efficiency of work has to be imperfectly specified in the contract; it depends not only on the given technology but also upon both the motivation and skill of the workforce and the organization and supervision of management. These, in turn, depend on complex institutional structures and routines and on cultural norms that are inherited from the past. This is not, however, a deterministic view; the fact that the employment contract cannot be fully specified in advance means that outputs are not completely nor mechanically determined by inputs.

In orthodox theory there is no substantial distinction between production and exchange, as the former is seen as being animated by (and even taking the form of) the latter. Once the deal is struck the wheels of production are essentially predetermined. The law of contract, through appropriate penalties, ensures that the goods will appear at the appointed time and in good order. Production is merely an annex of the market; a place where agents act in accordance with the relevant clauses of the deal. It is no wonder that orthodox theory regards outputs as a determinate mechanical result of contracted inputs; to embrace a degree of indeterminacy in the sphere of production would be to relegate the sphere of the market from its dominating and determinate role.

Instead of further attempts to fit evidence into the 'meat grinder' model, where production results from the automatic or mechanical transformation of given inputs, the process of production should be conceived in a different manner. Production should be regarded as a social process involving people with aspirations of their own, in structured social interaction with each other.

Instead of the orthodox symmetry of 'factors of production', labour should be seen as an active agency with capital goods as passive instruments. This would follow a number of unorthodox writers, including both Karl Marx

(1976, ch. 7) and John Maynard Keynes (1936, pp. 213–14), who have proposed the view that human agents are capable of purposeful behaviour but capital goods are not. The owners of labour power and the owners of capital goods are both active and purposeful decision-making agents in the sphere of exchange. But during the process of production, capital goods themselves are passive instruments, subject to the purposeful activity of the workers and managers.

2. OUTLINES OF AN INSTITUTIONAL AND EVOLUTIONARY APPROACH

Of course, orthodox theory will retain an appeal as long as no well-developed alternative exists. It has to be admitted that at present there exists no more than a rough outline of an alternative approach, and this is discussed in this section. Nevertheless, econometric work based on various unorthodox approaches has already notched up some creditable regression results.[3]

The alternative approach sketched here is unashamedly eclectic. We start with some of Thorstein Veblen's insights into the economic process, connecting these with some ideas from modern evolutionary theory.

Production: Routines, Institutions and Knowledge

As Veblen (1964) has elaborated, labour is made up of congealed habits or skills, which may take some time to acquire and which depend upon their institutional integument. Later writers have stressed that it is difficult to codify or readily communicate such skills, hence the references of Edith Penrose (1959) to 'unteachable' and Michael Polanyi (1957, 1967) to 'tacit' knowledge. The general social importance of routinized behaviour has been more recently emphasized by Anthony Giddens (1984) and Richard Nelson and Sidney Winter (1982). Contrary to the treatment of 'information problems' by neo-classical theorists, 'tacit' or 'unteachable' knowledge cannot be reduced simply to 'information' because it is partly embodied in routines or unconscious reflexes, and it cannot be reduced to, or transmitted in, a codified form.

Veblen drew a number of implications from his conception of habit and routine. For instance, he saw production not primarily as a matter of 'inputs' into some mechanical function but as an outcome of an institutional ensemble of habits and routines: 'the accumulated, habitual knowledge of the ways and means involved ... the outcome of long experience and experimentation' (Veblen, 1919, pp. 185–6). Furthermore, they do not relate to single individuals because the 'great body of commonplace knowledge made use of in an industry is the product and heritage of the group' (ibid., p. 186). 'These immaterial industrial expedients are necessarily a product of the community, the immaterial residue of the community's experience, past and present; which has no existence apart from the community's life, and can be transmitted only in the keeping of the community at large' (ibid., p. 348).

The group-based nature of the immaterial assets of production means that they are not part of the labour contract between employer and employee; they reside in the interstices of the social organization of the firm and its associated community. The 'continuity, congruity, or coherence of the group, is of an immaterial character. It is a matter of knowledge, usage, habits of life and habits of thought, not a matter of mechanical continuity or contact' (ibid., p. 325).

Veblen (ibid., p. 344) points out that 'the capitalist employer is ... not possessed of any appreciable fraction of the immaterial equipment necessarily drawn on in the construction and subsequent use of the material equipment owned (controlled) by him'. Veblen thus argues that 'the substantial core of all capital is immaterial wealth, and that the material objects which are formally the subject of the capitalist's ownership are, by comparison, a transient and adventitious matter' (ibid., p. 200).

In sum, Veblen points out that orthodox capital theory over-estimates the tangible assets to the detriment of the intangible. The individualistic and reductionist tendencies in neoclassical theory remove from view the intangible assets of the group. Veblen thus abandons the capital–labour, 'factors of production' approach, to propose a conception of production based on the organic interaction of the human workforce with capital goods.

More recently, the deficiencies of the orthodox approach have led Maurice Scott (1981, 1989) to question the standard definition of investment in terms of tangible assets. He argues that investment should include research and development, the creation of new production-related institutional structures, and the formation of new management teams. Economic growth is predominantly a cognitive, learning process in which the scope for learning is progressively extended by gross investment. In many respects, Scott's arguments are compatible with and develop the Veblenian approach.

Given that the productivity of an economy is crucially related to the transmission and interpretation of information, and the growth of different kinds of collective knowledge, there are clearly important consequences for the theory of economic growth. For instance, improvements in work organization are often designed to facilitate both the communication of information and the enhancement of collective skills within the plant. Significant increases in productivity can result from better deployment of tasks, a reduction of waste, and improved organizational or other skills. Notably, and contrary to both Taylorism and Marxian exploitation theory, these developments are not necessarily associated with an increase in the intensity of work.

Furthermore, the behaviour of the firm is not, within the given constraints, entirely determined by, or entirely subject to, the decisions of its managers. Because much of the 'expertise' of the firm is embedded in the firm's routines and the habitual skills of its workforce, it is neither completely codifiable and communicable nor completely manageable from the apex of the organization.

Thus any model of productivity growth which is centred on the application of, and resistance to, 'employer leverage' will give us only part of the picture. Because behaviour within the firm and other economic institutions is largely routinized, economic development can appear, for significant periods of time and with exceptions discussed below, to be subject to inertia. An adequate theory of the development of productive capabilities must take into account both the social culture and institutions within which habits and routines are reproduced, and the conditions which lead to their disruption or mutation.

The Relative Stability of Systems and Institutions

One thing that is remarkable about modern, complex economic systems is their enduring stability and resilience over long periods of time, despite the multitude of decisions and actions and the plethora of variety at the microeconomic level. We may conjecture that for years or sometimes even decades, socio-economic systems become locked-in to a fixed overall pattern of dynamic development. Whilst there will be *parametric* change in economic variables such as output and employment, there may be years or decades of overall and relative *structural* stability, punctuated by rapid transitions from one structural regime to another (Dardi and Screpanti, 1987).

Support for such a notion can be found in the modern theory of non-linear systems. As Jay Forrester (1987, p. 108) argues:

> A rich representation of nonlinearities leads to a model that is relatively insensitive to parameter values. Being insensitive to parameter values is also a characteristic of most social systems. ... In fact, the operating point of a system tends to move along the changing slopes of its nonlinearities until it finds an operating region that is determined more by the structure of the system than by plausible differences in parameter values. In a high-order nonlinear system, one can move many parameters within a plausible range with little effect on essential behavior.

The modern theory of complex systems has led to the idea of *autopoiesis* (Varela *et al.*, 1974; Maturana, 1975; Benseler *et al.*, 1980; Zeleny, 1980, 1981, 1987), involving renewal, self-replication and growth. An autopoietic system is not in a state of equilibrium, at least in the normal senses of that term. Precisely because it is far from a thermodynamic or mechanical equilibrium such an open system must absorb energy from its environment. Autopoietic systems 'can maintain themselves in time only if they evolve the capacity to replicate or reproduce their structure' (Laszlo, 1987, p. 38). Like living animals and plants, such systems maintain an autonomy and continuity of pattern 'despite the endless turnover of their constituents' (Zeleny, 1987, p. 393). Clearly, economic systems may well exhibit autopoietic self-replication and growth.

It is important to note that, just as the botanic features of a plant may change during its growth, autopoietic development in economic systems does not, within limits, exclude changes in technology and tastes. The structural stability implied is not rigid; it is simply sufficient to provide coherence and a consistent mode of self-organization. A socio-economic system in an autopoietic phase will be one that is exhibiting particular patterns of growth and development. The growth rate and economic fluctuations will be within a broad range. Socio-economic structures and institutions will be generally subject to piecemeal rather than fundamental change.

In contrast, there may be apparent randomness at the micro level, with substantial variety in the structure and behaviour of individual units. However, the interactions between these elements help to generate a degree of (impermanent) stability and coherence at the macro level. Such an argument is reminiscent of the 'principle of *stratified determinism*' adduced by Paul Weiss (1969), that is, the 'principle of *determinacy in the gross despite demonstrable indeterminacy in the small*'.

Today, however, with the insights of chaos theory (Gleick, 1988; Stewart, 1989), it has to be accepted that even apparent indeterminacy may have deterministic roots. However, rather than the victory of determinism: 'The chaos literature instead reveals the curious symbiosis of randomness and determinism, the blurring of the boundaries between order and chaos' (Mirowski, 1990b, p. 305).

Thus, to paraphrase and modify Weiss, an autopoietic system exhibits a high degree of order at the macro level, in contrast to apparent chaos at the micro level. At the higher and more complex level, spanning many territories and units, the behaviour of institutions is more stable, and more determined or weighed down by cumulative interactions in the system and the constraints of its past. Variations are buffered out and rendered inconsequential.

Through this feature of 'self-organization', as the work of Ilya Prigogine and his collaborators shows (Nicolis and Prigogine, 1977; Prigogine and Stengers, 1984), order can result from chaos. Indeed, although individual variations are rendered inconsequential in systems in this state, the degree of homoeostatic self-regulation vitally *depends upon* extensive diversity and chaos at the micro level. Without the latter, the system as a whole would be more vulnerable to aggregative and cumulative feedback effects and prone to instability itself.[4]

Elements of these modern arguments for self-organization and periods of relative stability can be found in the work of Veblen. He observed that routines and institutions have a stable and inert quality, and tend to sustain and thus 'pass on' their important characteristics through time: 'The situation of today shapes the institutions of tomorrow through a selective, coercive process, by acting upon men's habitual view of things, and so altering or fortifying a point of view or a mental attitude handed down from the past' (Veblen, 1899, pp. 190–1).

On this basis Veblen argued that economic development is best regarded as an evolutionary process; he was groping towards an understanding of mechanisms which play a similar evolutionary role to that of the gene in the natural world. Such mechanisms involve habits, routines and institutions. Whilst these are more malleable and do not mutate in the same way as their analogue in biology, institutions and routines do have a sufficient degree of durability to regard them as having quasi-genetic qualities. The idea that routines within the firm act as 'genes' to pass on skills and information is adopted by Nelson and Winter (1982, pp. 134–6) and forms a crucial part of their theoretical model of the modern corporation.

The power and durability of institutions and routines are manifest in a number of ways. With the benefit of modern developments in modern anthropology and psychology it can be seen that institutions play an essential role in providing a cognitive framework for interpreting sense data and in providing intellectual habits or routines for transforming information into useful knowledge (Hodgson, 1988). These cultural and cognitive functions have been investigated by anthropologists such as Mary Douglas (1973, 1987) and Barbara Lloyd (1972). Reference to the cognitive functions of institutions and routines is important in understanding their relative stability and capacity to replicate. Indeed, the strong, reinforcing interaction between social institutions and individual cognition provides some significant stability in socio-economic systems in their autopoeitic phase, partly by buffering the diverse and variable actions of many agents.

Bifurcations and Socio-economic Instability

As Veblen recognized, the 'selective, coercive process' of institutional replication is not, however, confined to a fixed groove. Institutions change, and even gradual change can eventually put such a strain on a system that there can be outbreaks of conflict or crisis, leading to a change in actions and attitudes. Thus there is always the possibility of the breakdown of regularity: 'there will be moments of crisis situations or structural breaks when existing conventions or social practices are disrupted' (Lawson, 1985, p. 920). In any social system there is an interplay between routinized behaviour and the variable or volatile decisions of other agents.

Whilst for long periods the reigning habits of thought and action can be cumulatively reinforced, sometimes this very process can lead to sudden and disruptive change. Because of the momentum of technological and social change in modern industrial society, and the clashing new conceptions and traditions thrown up with each innovation in management and technique, the cumulative character of economic development can mean crisis on occasions rather than continuous change or advance.

This Veblenian conception of socio-economic evolution is more like the idea of 'punctuated equilibria' advanced by biologists Niles Eldredge and Stephen Jay Gould (1972, 1977) than orthodox Darwinian gradualism.[5] Recently, Joel Mokyr (1990, forthcoming) has argued that technological change is not as gradual or continuous as sometimes suggested, and exhibits patterns of development akin to the idea of punctuated equilibria advanced in biology.

The modern theory of complex systems – much pioneered by biologists – has embraced similar phenomena. Laszlo (1987, p. 46) argues, 'as no autopoietic reaction cycle is entirely immune to disruption, constant changes in the environment sooner or later produce conditions under which certain cycles can no longer operate. The systems encounter a point known in dynamic systems theory as bifurcation.' Unlike the intervening periods of relative macro-stability, at the point of bifurcation the system is highly sensitive to minute changes. Small variations can affect the entire course and trajectory of development (Prigogine and Stengers, 1984).

Major military, political, social and economic disruptions can be regarded as bifurcations in the above sense. As Laszlo (1987, p. 105) puts it: 'When destabilized by uncontrollable fluctuations, a society does not suffer extinction but is absorbed in other societies – or it transforms and renews itself. In any event, it undergoes a major phase change equivalent to a bifurcation.' Depending on the outcome of this critical phase, the system will then progress to another period of autopoiesis, the nature of which will be affected by a number of critical influences at the preceding point of bifurcation.

Growth Trajectories, Disruption and Democracy

As Arthur Stinchcombe (1965) has argued, social institutions tend to be imprinted with the social, cultural and technological features which prevail at the time of their emergence. Because such imprinted characteristics are resistant to change, social institutions still largely reflect the historical conditions at the date of their foundation, rather than later adaptations. Similar issues of structural inertia and self-reproducibility in organizations are discussed by Michael Hannan and John Freeman (1989).

A number of economic and social historians have noted the enduring effects of the social institutions laid down in the past. Consider, for instance, the varied accounts of Britain's relative decline. Many of these have a common theme. Thus Perry Anderson (1964, p. 50) sees Britain as 'a sclerosed, archaic society, trapped and burdened by its past successes'. Similarly, Eric Hobsbawm (1969, p. 188) argues that Britain's early industrialization 'created a pattern of both production and markets which would not necessarily remain the one best fitted to sustain economic growth and technological change'. Ronald Dore (1973, p. 419) argues that: 'The way a country comes to industrialization can have a lasting effect on the kind of industrial society it becomes. It will be a long time before Britain loses the marks of the pioneer, the scars and stiffnesses that come from the searing experience of having made the first, most long-drawn-out industrial revolution.' Sir Henry Phelps Brown (1977, pp. 25–6) writes of practical minds that 'became bounded by the processes and products that they mastered in long apprenticeships'. Bernard Elbaum and William Lazonick (1986, p. 2) attribute the relative decline of the British economy in the twentieth century to 'rigidities in the economic and social institutions that developed during the nineteenth century, a period when Britain was the world's leading economic power and British industry was highly atomistic and competitive in organization'. These institutional rigidities, they argue, obstructed efforts at economic renovation. These arguments suggest that Britain's relative decline results in part from the relative ossification of its institutions.

Such matters relate to the notion of path-dependency, now receiving considerable attention by economic theorists.[6] In the historical context this suggests that events occurring during a crucial and formative period of change may greatly influence later socio-economic outcomes.

To take an example from a quite different country, as Gérard Roland (1990, p. 403) observes, it is 'extraordinary to note how the first years after the Russian Revolution, and in particular the experience of war communism, have moulded much of the later developments in Soviet history'. Roland's general point about path-dependency seems to have a wider validity: to apply to industrial transformations in the West as well.

Given that earlier industrial transformations are generally associated with less-efficient structures and institutions, significant differences in rates of productivity growth may stem from the timing of the industrial revolution. An early industrialization will project the country concerned on to a future trajectory of relatively low growth rates, whereas a latecomer will experience faster growth after industrialization.[7]

This idea is compatible with the Law of Evolutionary Potential as promoted by Elman Service (1960, p. 97): 'The more specialized and adapted a form in a given evolutionary stage, the smaller is its potential for passing on to the next stage.' Service sees precursors to this in Veblen's (1915) idea of 'the penalty of taking the lead', and in Leon Trotsky's (1934) analysis of revolutionary Russia skipping stages of history, from a backward tsarism dominated by agriculture to a planned industrial economy. However, we must amend this 'Law' by noting that (largely exogenous) disruptions may break down ossified patterns of specialization and permit transition to a more developed stage. The function of such disruptions is discussed further below.

Whilst the trajectory of growth may be dependent on the timing of industrialization, there is the additional question of whether or not institutional sclerosis tends to increase through time. This would imply, *ceteris paribus*, a secular slowdown in growth rates. An assumption that institutions become more ossified with age is present in the attempts to explain economic growth by Mancur Olson (1982) and his student Kwang Choi (1983). They are also incorporated in an analysis of postwar productivity data which I have developed elsewhere (Hodgson, 1989). It shall be shown below, however, that a long-term analysis of productivity data stretching back to the early 1900s questions the validity of the secular ossification idea. Similar doubts about the supposed onset of economic sclerosis with age are raised by John Wallis and Wallace Oates (1988).[8]

Consequently, greater proportionate weight is put here on the effects of disruption and systemic bifurcation. This theme is also found in historical studies of the reasons for Britain's relative economic decline. For instance, Anderson (1964, p. 37) notes that: 'Alone of major European nations, England emerged undefeated and unoccupied from two World Wars, its social structure uniquely untouched by external shocks or discontinuities.' Similarly, Phelps Brown (1977, p. 20) sees British institutions, such as trade unions, suffering from 'the extraordinary continuity of their history: they have had no revolution, no defeat in war and no foreign occupation to give them a fresh start'. Olson (1982) and Choi (1983) also highlight disruptive effects. Many other authors argue that sweeping radical changes, particularly resulting from internal revolution or defeat in war, can provide opportunities for economic restructuring and faster economic growth.

For instance, Randall Collins (1988, p. 34) has argued for the application of a model of punctuated equilibria to socio-economic evolution, along the following lines: 'Historically, major changes in societies have often occurred "catastrophically" rather than gradually. Not only revolutions but even more importantly, wars and conflict in general have played a major part in affecting the form of the state, the economy, religion and culture, the family, and other social institutions.' Similarly, W. McKelvey (1982, p. 271) sees revolutions and wars as 'political disruptions that may change the internal social structure of a nation enough to allow faster development of new ideas and organizations'.

In modern times, the absence of major disruption is observed most graphically in Britain, thus providing a partial explanation of relative economic decline. The US faces the problems of the slowdown in its productivity growth and the erosion of its share of world trade. In this case the relative absence of disruption again seems relevant. The American Revolution was two centuries ago, followed later by the Civil War. In sum, there have been few periods of major disruption to help increase flexibility.

In contrast, countries such as Belgium, France, Germany and Italy have been disrupted both by several revolutions in the past two centuries and by extensive invasion and occupation. Japan's social and economic transformation was greatly accelerated after the foreign occupation of 1945.

In addition to the disruptions promoted by revolutions, occupations and other major socio-political events, it is suggested here that the existence of pluralistic democracy may play a significant part in promoting economic growth. The basis for such an argument is found in a study of the rise of the western economies by Nathan Rosenberg and Luther Birdzell (1986) amongst others. They argue that the flexibility of capitalist institutions under conditions of political pluralism have created the conditions for economic growth. There are strong reasons to suggest that the existence of a pluralistic democracy places checks on the concentration and ossification of political and economic power, and thereby promotes a more dispersed and diversified economy.[9]

3.   A STATISTICAL TEST AND SOME CONCLUSIONS

It is with some hesitation that the above ideas are given a statistical test. The author does not share the widespread belief that econometrics is the salvation of economics. Many of the standard presuppositions of econometric theory are open to question and the idea that the predictions derived from econometric models are the test of theory is naïve, to say the least. The following regressions are used simply to help identify 'stylized facts', and trends of development, rather than the basis of a fully-fledged macroeconomic model. As we peruse the data and confirm, for instance, that the British economy has been on a low-growth track for over a century, we are taking on board all sorts of implicit assumptions about the nature and specification of the quantities observed. There should be no objection to a slightly more involved 'perusal', with the sceptically employed spectacles of econometric technique.

For two reasons, the statistical test here is applied to capitalist economies only. First, the quality of the data is better for the major OECD countries. Secondly, it is likely that the structural differences between Eastern Bloc and capitalist countries will affect growth trajectories to a significant extent. Available OECD data reduced the sample to 16 major capitalist countries (namely Australia, Austria, Belgium, Canada, Denmark, Finland, France,

Germany, Italy, Japan, The Netherlands, Norway, Sweden, Switzerland, the United Kingdom, the United States).

Unlike my earlier (Hodgson, 1989) study, the analysis is not confined to the postwar period. For each of the 16 countries, the data relate to the years 1913, 1929, 1938, 1950, 1960, 1970, 1973 and 1978, giving a pooled sample of 128 observations in all. The annual rate of growth of real GDP per worker-hour is used as the index of productivity growth.

Three types of hypothesis were tested:

(a) Productivity growth is dependent on the timing of the industrial revolution in the country concerned. This timing is taken from the date of the beginning of 'economic and social transformation' (EST) in Black (1966, pp. 90–2).

(b) Productivity growth is dependent on an index of institutional flexibility (FLX). FLX is taken from Hodgson (1989) and its value declines after the time of rapid industrialization given by EST.

(c) Productivity growth is dependent on DIS, the degree of institutional disruption (discussed below).

(d) According to the 'diffusion hypothesis' (Gomulka, 1971, 1979), productivity growth is dependent on the 'technological gap' between each country and the lead country – taken as the United States – measured by the relative productivity levels involved. Maddison's (1982, p. 212) productivity levels were used and converted into a percentage of the US level to give the variable REL.

(e) Productivity growth is greater in periods when the country concerned has an established, pluralistic democracy, denoted by the variable DEM.

(f) The general trajectory of productivity growth for all countries is different in different time periods, reflecting the influence of the level of world trade, world effective demand, and the international supervision of world financial and political arrangements.

The Data on Industrialization, Disruption and Democracy

The conditions here chosen to represent periods of major disruption are broadly consistent with Hodgson (1989) but more restrictive than those in Choi (1983). To qualify, a period of major disruption (PMD) must be:[10]

(i)   an extensive foreign occupation of home soil, or revolution, or civil war, or year of national independence, or national unification, in either case leading to significant social changes;

(ii) at least 10 years from any other PMD;

(iii) in the modern period. This is defined as after the beginning of the period of 'consolidation of modernizing leadership' (CML) marking the time of transition into modernity (Black, 1966, pp. 90–2).

The second criterion prevents over-weighting of single major disruptions which span more than one year. The third excludes disruptions which precede the inauguration of the modern socio-economic system, which are too early to affect modern institutions and structures.

Of course, these strict criteria exclude many other disruptions which have had significant effects.[11] However, their inclusion would involve difficult problems of relative weighting. This statistical study is mainly designed to indicate the general value of the approach, so only the most important disruptions have been included here.

It is argued above that a large-scale disruptive event will generally create the opportunity to recast social relationships and routines and lay down more modern and progressive habits and routines. Disruption on this scale gives the opportunity of ridding the system of many old methods and arrangements and of adopting new ones. The relevant years (PMDs) are shown in Table 10.1.[12]

Table 10.1: Periods of major disruption (PMDs)

	EST	CML	PMDs					
Australia	1901	1801	1901					
Austria	1918	1848	1848	1918	1945			
Belgium	1848	1795	1813	1830	1848	1918	1945	
Canada	1867	1791	1867					
Denmark	1866	1807	1945					
Finland	1919	1863	1918					
France'	1848	1789	1789	1814	1830	1848	1871	1945
Germany	1871	1803	1805	1848	1870	1918	1933	1945
Italy	1871	1805	1805	1848	1860	1922	1945	
Japan	1945	1868	1868	1945				
Netherlands	1848	1795	1795	1810	1945			
Norway	1905	1809	1905	1945				
Sweden	1905	1809	–					
Switzerland	1848	1798	1803	1847				
United Kingdom	1832	1649	1688					
United States	1865	1776	1783	1865				

EST: Beginning year of 'economic and social transformation'. SOURCE: Black (1966, pp. 90–2).

CML: Beginning year of 'consolidation of modernizing leadership'. SOURCE: Black (1966, pp. 90–2).

PMD: Period of major disruption, denoted by the last or most crucial year.

The index of total institutional disruption for each year (DIS) is simply the sum of preceding PMDS for each country. These are shown in Table 10.2.

Table 10.2: Index of disruption (DIS)

Year	1913	1929	1938	1950	1960	1970	1973	1978
Australia	1	1	1	1	1	1	1	1
Austria	1	2	2	3	3	3	3	3
Belgium	3	4	4	5	5	5	5	5
Canada	1	1	1	1	1	1	1	1
Denmark	0	0	0	1	1	1	1	1
Finland	0	1	1	1	1	1	1	1
France	5	5	5	6	6	6	6	6
Germany	3	4	5	6	6	6	6	6
Italy	3	4	4	5	5	5	5	5
Japan	1	1	1	2	2	2	2	2
Netherlands	2	2	2	3	3	3	3	3
Norway	1	1	1	2	2	2	2	2
Sweden	0	0	0	0	0	0	0	0
Switzerland	2	2	2	2	2	2	2	2
United Kingdom	1	1	1	1	1	1	1	1
United States	2	2	2	2	2	2	2	2

SOURCE: Table 10.1

Table 10.3: The existence of pluralistic democracy (DEM)

Year	1913	1929	1938	1950	1960	1970	1973	1978
Australia	1	1	1	1	1	1	1	1
Austria	0	1	0	1	1	1	1	1
Belgium	0	1	1	1	1	1	1	1
Canada	1	1	1	1	1	1	1	1
Denmark	1	1	1	1	1	1	1	1
Finland	0	1	1	1	1	1	1	1
France	1	1	1	1	1	1	1	1
Germany	0	1	0	1	1	1	1	1
Italy	1	0	0	1	1	1	1	1
Japan	0	1	0	1	1	1	1	1
Netherlands	0	1	1	1	1	1	1	1
Norway	1	1	1	1	1	1	1	1
Sweden	1	1	1	1	1	1	1	1
Switzerland	1	1	1	1	1	1	1	1
United Kingdom	1	1	1	1	1	1	1	1
United States	1	1	1	1	1	1	1	1

It is possible to develop criteria to denote the existence or non-existence of a pluralistic democracy.[13] DEM is assumed to be unity if there is a constitutional democracy, with several viable and legal political parties, and roughly equal suffrage covering at least a majority of the male population. The values of DEM are laid out in Table 10.3.

A number of dummy variables were used to test the hypothesis that different periods and states of the world economy affected individual countries. Five dummy variables were contrived:

P1 valued at 1 in 1913 and 0 elsewhere;
P2 valued at 1 in 1929 and 0 elsewhere;
P3 valued at 1 in 1938 and 0 elsewhere;
P4 valued at 1 in 1950, 1960, 1970 and 1973, and 0 elsewhere;
P5 valued at 1 in 1978 and 0 elsewhere.

The level of productivity growth for each country (percentage increase GDP per worker-hour) in each year is denoted by PROD. It is measured by taking absolute productivity levels for the year in question, along with levels for the preceding and succeeding observation in Maddison's (1982, p. 212) data, and estimating the growth rate by quadratic interpolation.

A Regression and Projections

A series of nested testing procedures was chosen, to eliminate variables significant at less than the 10 per cent level one by one. On this basis the variables FLX, REL, P2, P3 and P5 were eliminated. The result for the final regression performed on PROD, DIS, EST, DEM, P1 and P4 alone is shown in Table 10.4.

Table 10.4: Regression

PROD =
−30.66 + 0.3548DIS + 0.01644EST + 0.9063DEM + 0.5662P1 + 1.992P4
 (6.47)   (0.0609)   (0.00337)   (0.395)   (0.340)   (0.217)
 ****   ****   ****   **   *   ****

$R^2 = 0.582$ Adjusted $R^2 = 0.565$

NOTES
128 observations. Method of estimate: ordinary least squares.
Standard errors in brackets.
Levels of significance (two-tailed test): **** 0.1%   ** 5%   * 10%

The regression result shown in Table 10.4 undermines hypotheses (b) and (d) above. No evidence is found to support the idea that growth is retarded by institutional sclerosis acquired with age, and no sustenance is found for the technological diffusion hypothesis of Stanislaw Gomulka (1971, 1979).

In contrast, some degree of confirmation is obtained for the main hypotheses in this essay. The R^2 values are respectable, given the nature of the sample and the timespan involved. First, institutional disruptions seem to be significant in determining and eventually advancing productivity growth. Secondly, there is evidence that the growth trajectory is determined by the timing of industrialization: late industrializers performing better. This gives support to the path-dependency thesis discussed above. Thirdly, the existence of pluralistic democracy is also found to be significant in aiding growth.

Finally, the two periods where there was a relatively stable international order (P1 and P4), are found to be significant and positively related to growth. This is in accord with the arguments of Charles Kindleberger (1973, 1988). He suggests that the pre-First World War period, based on British world hegemony, and the postwar settlement from 1945 to 1973, based on US hegemony, stimulated economic growth in the periods concerned, partly through the ability of the hegemon to act as lender of last resort.[14] The regression here suggests that the overall effect of these factors in the pre-1914 period was to enhance productivity growth by about 0.6 per cent per annum. In the 1945–73 period the growth rate of productivity was increased by about 2 per cent per year.

It is interesting to project the regression-generated equation into the future; although we should not, of course, regard these projections as 'predictions', at least in the standard sense. We shall assume that the effects of recent German unification add another unit to its disruption index in 1990, putting this now ahead of the value for France. For simplicity it shall be assumed that the West German productivity data apply to Germany as a whole after 1990. The projection suggests that Germany and France will overtake the United States in terms of overall levels of productivity in the early 1990s.[15] At about that time, Germany's productivity level moves into the overall lead. After its steep climb, Japan's relative productivity level reaches a peak of about 60 per cent of the German level in about 1995, and then begins to decline. British relative productivity does not advance after 1990. Germany and France are well-established as lead nations in the first quarter of the twenty-first century, followed by Austria, Belgium, Italy, Norway and The Netherlands, in that order. Alarmingly, the projection suggests a strong cumulative divergence of productivity levels within Europe as well as elsewhere, but in the European case this is likely to be redressed to some extent by the policy outcomes of European politico-economic integration.

Of course, these projections ignore variations in performance that may result from changes in effective demand and from the transformation of the socio-economic institutions themselves, as well as the degree of statistical variability that is suggested by the regression. However, what they do indicate is a process which is similar to the idea of cumulative causation developed by Allyn Young (1928), Gunnar Myrdal (1939, 1944, 1957), Nicholas Kaldor (1972) and K. William Kapp (1976).

Regarding policy conclusions, the argument points to an eclectic stance. First, at the international level, consideration should be given to proposals for a new international economic order. Whilst war and revolution may have the effect of increasing institutional flexibility, the first, at least, is not to be recommended. In addition, whilst New Right regimes, such as that experienced in the USA and Britain, may promote some restructuring, including work practices and the ownership of industry, key areas remain untouched and are protected by a strong residual conservatism. Furthermore, New Right restructuring fails to promote long-term initiatives, in contrast with a more interventionist policy. Instead, the emphasis must be the kind of 'deep' institutional transformation that is implied by a radical industrial policy, but its outlines will have to await the results of further study. Furthermore, and again in contrast to the New Right stance, consideration should be given to a strong regional policy within Europe to counter the phenomenon of cumulative divergence.

No doubt there will be additional disruption effects for the countries involved from the future creation of a federal European state. The disruption within Eastern Europe during the momentous events of 1989, and the subsequent establishment of democracy should also be noted. All this reinforces the conclusion that the locus of world economic dynamism is not about to move to Japan, as sometimes presumed, but is returning to Europe from the United States. It is now all the more likely that the most dynamic core of capitalism in the opening decades of the twenty first century will be located in Western Central Europe, in an area uncannily similar to that of the old Holy Roman Empire.

NOTES

1. The author is grateful to Alasdair Dow and participants at the EAEPE 1990 Conference, especially Ernesto Screpanti, for helpful comments on an earlier draft of this paper.
2. See Sraffa (1960); Harcourt (1972); Harcourt and Laing (1971); Hunt and Schwartz (1972); Nell (1980). Note in contrast Maddison's (1987, p. 677) rather prejudiced dismissal of this issue. What he forgets is that the capital debates were actually won by Piero Sraffa, Joan Robinson, Piero Garegnani and their 'Cambridge' followers, to the extent that leading protagonists on the other side, such as Paul Samuelson, essentially

admitted defeat. This is one of the very few debates in the history of economic theory leading to such a clear resolution.

3. Examine the regression results with unorthodox models in Bowles, Gordon and Weisskopf (1984); Hodgson (1989); and Olson (1982). Choi (1983) applies statistical tests to the residuals in Denison's (1979) work.

4. A good illustrative example is James Lovelock's (1979) *Gaia hypothesis*. Simulations based on this idea show that the self-regulating features of the biosphere depend precisely on the degree of biological diversity within the system (Watson and Lovelock, 1983).

5. See also Gould (1982) and Stanley (1980). Note that the use of the term 'equilibrium' by these biologists is different from that found in mechanics in that to some degree it encompasses mutation and change within the same evolutionary track. Overall development is directed by some 'higher order sorting' (Stanley, 1975) of species in parallel evolutionary lineages. Notably, the punctuations refer to abrupt speciation and are thus just as important as the equilibrium.

6. See Kaldor (1934) for an early and implicit discussion of path-dependency. It is raised explicitly in the context of general equilibrium theory by Fisher (1983, pp. 14–16), in regard to technical change in Arthur (1989) and likewise by various authors in Dosi *et al.* (1988).

7. The deductions drawn here are slightly different from those in Hodgson (1989).

8. The analysis herein is thus distanced even further from that of Olson (1982) and Choi (1983). Earlier (Hodgson, 1989), I criticized Olson (1982) for his reliance on Hobbesian and liberal assumptions, for assuming in effect that a mythical institution-free market was the original state of nature, and for proposing that the very presence of Fascism or totalitarianism is an antidote to the growth of interest groups and to institutional sclerosis. For a sample of other recent evaluations of Olson's work, see McCallum and Blais (1987); and Nardinelli *et al.* (1987).

9. Some further arguments along these lines are reviewed in Hodgson (1984).

10. Regrettably, my earlier computations for the value of DIS overlooked the short civil war in Switzerland in 1847. Although this event lasted only 25 days it is generally judged by historians to have had major political and social effects. Furthermore, on reflection, there is a strong case for adding national unification to the list of criteria, so that in particular the German unification of 1870 should be included, placing the postwar degree of disruption in Germany on a par with that in France. Notably, however, these slight alterations to the values of DIS do not decisively alter the present or the preceding regressions.

11. For instance, the effects of demographic changes, such as migrations, are excluded. There may also be regional 'leader' effects, where dynamic development in one country has strong spillover reverberations on adjacent nations.

12. Unlike the preceding model, it is not assumed here that major disruptions would have greater effect the more that economic and social transformation has advanced. Although plausible, on reflection this is an unnecessary complication.

13. See the data and discussion in Therborn (1977).

14. Examining the post-1945 experience, some of the contributions on Marglin and Schor (1990) give a limited endorsement of this view, but they also offer other reasons for the end of capitalism's 'golden age'.

15. Data in Maddison (1987, p. 651) suggest that the French productivity level was 97.5 per cent of the US as early as 1984. In that same year, the level in Germany was 90.5 per cent, Japan 55.6 per cent, the Netherlands 97.2 per cent, and the UK 80.6 per cent.

Bibliography

Adams, Walter, and Lanzillotti, Robert F. (1963), 'The reality of administered prices', in Subcommittee on Antitrust and Monopoly of the Committee on the Judiciary, United States Senate, Eighty-Eight Congress,
First Session, *Administered Prices; A Compendium on Public Policy*,
Washington, DC: US Government Printing Office.

Alchian, Armen A., and Demsetz, Harold (1972), 'Production, information
costs, and economic organization', *American Economic Review*, **62**(4),
December, 772–95. Reprinted in Putterman (1986).

Alchian, Armen A., and Woodward, Susan (1988), 'The firm is dead; long
live the firm', *Journal of Economic Literature*, **26**, 65–79.

Allen, Peter M. (1988), 'Evolution, innovation and economics', in Dosi *et al.*
(1988, pp. 95–119).

Amendola, Mario, and Bruno, S. (1990), 'The behaviour of the innovative
firm: relations to the environment', *Research Policy*, **19**, 419–33.

Amendola, Mario, Ingrao, Bruno, Piacentini, Paolo, and Poti', Bianca (1990),
*L'automazione flessibile: Analisi e interpretazioni delle tendenze a livello
internazionale*, Milan: F. Angeli.

Amin, Ash (1989a), 'Flexible specialisation and small firms in Italy: myths
and realities', *Antipode*, **21**(1), 13–34.

Amin, Ash (1989b), 'A model of a small firm in Italy', in Goodman *et al.*
(eds) (1989, pp. 111–22).

Andersen, Esben Sloth (forthcoming), 'Approaching national systems of
innovation from the production structure', in Lundvall (forthcoming).

Anderson, Perry (1964), 'Origins of the present crisis', *New Left Review*, no.
23, January/February, 26–53; reprinted in Perry Anderson and Robin
Blackburn (eds) (1966), *Towards Socialism*, London: Collins.

Andersson, A. E. (1987), 'Creativity and economic dynamics modelling', in
Batten *et al.* (1987, pp. 27–45).

Archibugi, Daniele (1988), 'Uso e abuso della specializzazione flessibile',
Politica ed Economia, **9**, 86–7.

Arndt, H. W. (1984), 'Political economy', *Economic Record*, **60**(3), September, 266–73.

Arrow, Kenneth J. (1962), 'Economic welfare and the allocation of resources for invention', in National Bureau for Economic Research (1962),

The Rate and Direction of Inventive Activity: Economic and Social Factors, Princeton, N.J.: Princeton University Press, 609–25.

Arrow, Kenneth J. (1986), 'Rationality of self and others in an economic system', *Journal of Business*, **59**(4.2), October, S385–S399; reprinted in Robin M. Hogarth and Melvin W. Reder (eds) (1987), *Rational Choice: The Contrast between Economics and Psychology*, Chicago, Ill.: University of Chicago Press.

Arthur, W. Brian (1988a), 'Self-reinforcing mechanisms in economics', in Philip W. Anderson, Kenneth J. Arrow and David Pines (eds) (1988), *The Economy as an Evolving Complex System*, Redwood City, Cal.: Addison-Wesley, pp. 9–31.

Arthur, W. Brian (1988b), 'Competing technologies: an overview', in Dosi *et al.* (1988, pp. 590–607).

Arthur, W. Brian (1989), 'Competing technologies, increasing returns, and lock-in by historical events', *Economic Journal*, **99**(1), March, 116–31; reprinted in Freeman (1990).

Arthur, W. Brian, Ermoliev, Yu. M., and Kaniovski, Yu. M. (1987), 'Path-dependent processes and the emergence of macro-structure', *European Journal of Operational Research*, **30**(2), June, 294–303.

Auerbach, Paul (1988), *Competition: The Economics of Industrial Change*, Oxford: Basil Blackwell.

Ayres, Clarence E. (1944), *The Theory of Economic Progress*, Chapel Hill, N.C.: University of North Carolina Press.

Bailey, Elizabeth E., and Friedlaender, Ann F. (1982), 'Market structure and multiproduct industries', *Journal of Economic Literature*, **20**, 1024–48.

Barca, Fabrizio, and Magnani, Marco (1989), *L'industria fra capitale e lavoro*, Bologna: Il Mulino.

Barry, Brian M. (1970), *Sociologists, Economists and Democracy*, London: Collier Macmillan.

Batten, David, Casti, John L., and Johansson, Börje (eds) (1987), *Economic Evolution and Structural Adjustment*, Berlin: Springer-Verlag.

Becattini, Giacomo (1989), 'Sectors and/or districts: some remarks on the conceptual foundations of industrial economics', in Goodman *et al.* (1989, pp. 123–35); revised version of (1979), 'Dal "settore" industriale al "distretto" industriale. Alcune considerazioni sull'unità d'indagine dell'economia industriale', *Rivista di Economia e Politica Industriale*, **5**, 7–22.

Becker, Gary S. (1976), *The Economic Approach to Human Behavior*, Chicago, Ill.: University of Chicago Press.

Bell, Daniel, and Kristol, Irving (eds) (1981), *The Crisis in Economic Theory*, New York: Basic Books.

Bellandi, Marco (1989), 'The industrial district in Marshall', in Goodman *et al.* (1989, pp. 136–52); revised version of (1982), 'Il distretto industriale in Alfred Marshall', *L'Industria*.

Benseler, F., Hejl, P. M., and Koeck, W. K. (eds) (1980), *Autopoiesis, Communication and Society*, Frankfurt: Campus.

Berle, Adolf A., and Means, Gardiner C. (1932), *The Modern Corporation and Private Property*, New York: Macmillan.

Bertrand, Joseph (1883), 'Théorie mathématique de la richesse sociale, par L. Walras', *Journal des savants*, 499–508.

Bijker, W. E., Hughes, Thomas, and Pinch, T. (eds) (1987), *The Social Construction of Technological Systems*, Cambridge, Mass.: MIT Press.

Binswanger, H. P., and Ruttan, V. W. (1978), *Induced Innovation: Technology, Institutions and Development*, Baltimore, Md: Johns Hopkins University Press.

Black, Cyril E. (1966), *The Dynamics of Modernization: A Study in Comparative History*, New York: Harper & Row.

Blackaby, Frank (ed.) (1978), *De-Industrialisation*, London: Heinemann.

Blair, John M. (1972), *Economic Concentration: Structure, Behavior, and Public Policy*, New York: Harcourt Brace Jovanovich.

Blair, John M. (1975), 'Inflation in the United States: a short-run target return model', in Means *et al.* (1975b).

Blair, John M. (1976), *The Control of Oil*, New York: Pantheon.

Blattern, Niklaus (1981), 'Labour displacement by technological change? A preliminary survey of the case of microelectronics', *Rivista Internazionale di Scienze Economiche e Commerciali*, **5**, 422–48.

Blume, M. E. (1980), 'The financial markets', in Richard E. Caves and Lawrence B. Krause (eds) (1980), *Britain's Economic Performance*, Washington, DC: Brookings Institution, 261–329.

Boglind, Anders (1989), 'Strukturalism och funktionalism', in Per Månson, (ed.) (1989), *Moderna samhällsteorier: Traditioner, riktningar, teoretiker*, Stockholm: Bokförlaget Prisma.

Bosworth, Derek L. (ed.) (1983), *The Employment Consequences of Technological Change*, London: Macmillan.

Boulding, Kenneth E. (1981), *Evolutionary Economics*, Beverly Hills, Cal.: Sage.

Bowles, Samuel, Gordon, David M., and Weisskopf, Thomas E. (1984), *Beyond the Waste Land: A Democratic Alternative to Economic Decline*, New York: Anchor.

Boyer, Robert (1988), 'Technical change and the theory of "régulation"', in Dosi *et al.* (1988, pp. 67–94).

Brant, Thomas (1989), *Anthony Giddens och samhällsvetenskapen*, Stockholm/Stehag: Symposion Bokförlag.

Brown, C. J. F., and Sheriff, T. D. (1978), 'De-industrialisation in the UK: background statistics', National Institute of Economic and Social Research (NIESR) Discussion Paper.

Brusco, Salvatore (1982), 'The Emilian model: productive decentralisation and social integration', *Cambridge Journal of Economics*, **6**, 167–84.

Brusco, Salvatore (1986), 'Small firms and industrial districts: the experience of Italy', in D. Keeble and E. Wever (eds), *New Firms and Regional Development*, London: Croom Helm.

Bush, Paul Dale (1987), 'The theory of institutional change', *Journal of Economic Issues*, **21**(3), September, 1075–1116; reprinted in Marc R. Tool (ed.) (1988), *Evolutionary Economics*, vol. I: *Foundations of Institutional Thought*, Armonk, NY: M. E. Sharpe.

Bush, Vannevar (1945), *Science the Endless Frontier: A Report to the President on a Program for Postwar Scientific Research*, Washington, DC: National Science Foundation.

Campbell, Donald T. (1987), 'Blind variation and selective retention in creative thought as in other knowledge processes', in G. Radnitzky and William W. Bartley III (eds) (1987), *Evolutionary Epistemology, Theory of Rationality, and the Sociology of Knowledge*, La Salle, Ill.: Open Court, 91–114.

Capecchi, Vittorio (1989), 'The informal economy and the development of flexible specialization', in A. Portes, M. Castells, and L. A. Benton, (eds) (1989), *The Informal Economy*, Baltimore, Md: Johns Hopkins University Press.

Carabelli, Anna M. (1988), *On Keynes's Method*, London: Macmillan.

Carlsson, B. (1987), 'Reflections on industrial dynamics: the challenge ahead', *International Journal of Industrial Organization*, **5**, 135–48.

Caves, Richard E. and Krause, Lawrence B. (eds) (1980), *Britain's Economic Performance*, Washington: Brookings Institution.

Chamberlin, Edward H. (1948[1933]), *The Theory of Monopolistic Competition*, Cambridge, Mass.: Harvard University Press.

Choi, Kwang (1983), 'A statistical test of Olson's model', in D. C. Mueller (ed.) (1983), *The Political Economy of Growth*, New Haven, Conn.: Yale University Press, 57–78.

Clark, Norman G., and Juma, Calestous (1987), *Long-Run Economics: An Evolutionary Approach to Economic Growth*, London: Frances Pinter.

Cohen, Avi (1984), 'Technological change as historical process', *Journal of Economic History*, **44**, 775–99.

Cohendet, Patrick, and Llerena, Patrick (1988), 'Flexibilities, complexity and integrations in production processes', in Ergas *et al.* (1988, pp. 239–68).

Coleman, James S. (1990), *Foundations of Social Theory*, Cambridge, Mass.: Harvard University Press.

Collins, R. (1988), *Theoretical Sociology*, San Diego, Cal.: Harcourt Brace Jovanovich.

Cooper, C. M., and Clark, John A. (1982), *Employment, Economics and Technology*, Brighton, Sussex: Wheatsheaf.

Cyert, Richard M., and Mowery, David C. (eds) (1988), *The Impact of Technological Change on Employment and Economic Growth*, Cambridge, Mass.: Ballinger.

Dardi, Marco, and Screpanti, Ernesto (1987), 'Chi ha paura dell'onda lunga?', *Note Economiche*, no. 3, 75–86.

David, Paul A. (1975), *Technical Choice, Innovation, and Economic Growth*, Cambridge: Cambridge University Press.

David, Paul A. (1987), 'Some new standards for the economics of standardization in the information age', in Partha Dasgupta and Paul L. Stoneman (eds) (1987), *Economic Policy and Technological Performance*, Cambridge: Cambridge University Press.

David, Paul A. (1989), 'A paradigm for historical economics: path dependence and predictability in dynamic systems with local network externalities', Stanford, Cal.: Center for Economic Policy Research, Stanford University, mimeo..

Day, Richard H. (1987), 'The general theory of disequilibrium economics and of economic evolution', in Batten *et al.* (1987, pp. 46–63).

Day, Richard H., and Eliasson, Gunnar (eds) (1986), *The Dynamics of Market Economies*, Amsterdam: North-Holland.

De Bresson, Chris (1987), 'The evolutionary paradigm and the economics of technological change', *Journal of Economic Issues*, 21(2), June, 751–61.

Del Monte, Alfredo, and Esposito, Fabio M. (1989), 'Flessibilità e teoria della organizzazione industriale', Naples: Università di Napoli, mimeo.

Denison, Edward F. (1979), *Accounting for Slower Economic Growth*, Washington, DC: Brookings Institution.

Dopfer, Kurt (1986), 'Causality and consciousness in economics: concepts of change in orthodox and heterodox economics', *Journal of Economic Issues*, 20(2), June, 509–23.

Dore, Ronald (1973), *British Factory–Japanese Factory: The Origins of National Diversity in Industrial Relations*, London: George Allen & Unwin.

Dosi, Giovanni (1982), 'Technological paradigms and technological trajectories', *Research Policy*, 11, 147–62.

Dosi, Giovanni (1984), *Technical Change and Industrial Transformation*, London: Macmillan.

Dosi, Giovanni (1988), 'Sources, procedures, and microeconomic effects of innovation', *Journal of Economic Literature*, 26(3), September, 1120–71; reprinted in Freeman (1990).

Dosi, Giovanni, Freeman, Christopher, Nelson, Richard R., Silverberg, Gerald, and Soete, Luc (eds) (1988), *Technical Change and Economic Theory*, London: Frances Pinter.

Douglas, Mary (ed.) (1973), *Rules and Meanings*, Harmondsworth, Middx: Penguin.

Douglas, Mary (1987), *How Institutions Think*, London: Routledge & Kegan Paul.

Dow, Sheila C. (1985), *Macroeconomic Thought: A Methodological Approach*, Oxford: Basil Blackwell.

Dragan, Joseph C., and Demetrescu, Mihai C. (1986), *Entropy and Bioeconomics: The New Paradigm of Nicholas Georgescu-Roegen*, Milan: Nagard.

Dugger, William M. (1989), *Corporate Hegemony*, New York: Greenwood.

Duijn, Jacob J. van (1983), *The Long Wave in Economic Life*, London: Allen & Unwin.

ECE (Economic Commission for Europe) (1986), *Recent Trends in Flexible Manufacturing*, New York: United Nations.

Edquist, Charles (1985), *Capitalism, Socialism and Technology: A Comparative Study of Cuba and Jamaica*, London: Zed Books.

Edquist, Charles, and Jacobsson, Staffan (1988), *Flexible Automation*, Oxford: Basil Blackwell.

Edquist, Charles, and Lundvall, Bengt-Åke (forthcoming), 'Comparing the Danish and Swedish systems of innovation', in Nelson (forthcoming); previously published (1991) as Tema-T Working Paper no. 77, University of Linköping, Sweden, February.

Eichner, Alfred S. (1976), *The Megacorp and Oligopoly: Micro Foundations of Macro Dynamics*, White Plains, NY: M. E. Sharpe.

Eichner, Alfred S. (1983), 'Why economics is not yet a science', in A. E. Eichner (ed.) (1983), *Why Economics is not yet a Science*, Armonk, NY: M. E. Sharpe, 205–41.

Eichner, Alfred S. (1987), 'Prices and pricing', *Journal of Economic Issues*, 21(4), December, 1555–84; reprinted in Marc R. Tool (ed.) (1988), *Evolutionary Economics*, vol. II: *Institutional Theory and Policy*, Armonk, NY: M. E. Sharpe.

Elbaum, Bernard, and Lazonick, William (eds) (1986), *The Decline of the British Economy*, Oxford: Clarendon Press.

Eldredge, Niles, and Gould, Stephen Jay (1972), 'Punctuated equilibria: an alternative to phyletic gradualism', in T. J. M. Schopf (ed.) (1972), *Models in Paleobiology*, San Francisco, Cal.: Freeman, Cooper, 82–115.

Eldredge, Niles, and Gould, Stephen Jay (1977), 'Punctuated equilibria: the tempo and mode of evolution reconsidered', *Paleobiology*, 3, 115–51.

Ergas, Henry *et al.* (1988), *Firm–Environment Interaction in a Changing Productive System*, Milan: F. Angeli.

Etzioni, Amitai (1988), *The Moral Dimension: Toward a New Economics*, New York: Free Press.

Faber, Malte (ed.) (1986), *Studies in Austrian Capital Theory, Investment and Time*, Berlin: Springer.

Faber, Malte, and Proops, John L. R. (1990), *Evolution, Time, Production and the Environment*, Berlin: Springer.

Farmer, Mary K. (1982), 'Rational action in economic and social theory: some misunderstandings', *Archives européennes de sociologie*, 23, 179–97.

Farmer, Mary K. (1989), 'There is only one social science: economic imperialism in the social sciences', papers of 1989 History of Economic Thought Conference, University of Gröningen.

Fehl, U. (1986), 'Spontaneous order and the subjectivity of expectations: a contribution to the Lachmann-O'Driscoll problem', in Israel M. Kirzner (ed.) (1986), *Subjectivism, Intelligibility, and Economic Understanding*, New York: New York University Press, 72–86.

Fisher, Franklin M. (1983), *Disequilibrium Foundations of Equilibrium Economics*, Cambridge: Cambridge University Press.

Fitzgibbons, Athol (1988), *Keynes's Vision: A New Political Economy*, Oxford: Clarendon Press.

Flash, Edward S. Jr (1965), *Economic Advice and Presidential Leadership*, New York: Columbia University Press.

Foray, Dominique (1985), 'Innovation majeure et transformation des structures productives', *Revue economique*, 5, 1081–116.

Foray, Dominique, and Garrouste, Pierre (1991), 'Changements technologiques et stabilité des formes productives', *Economie appliquée*, forthcoming.

Forrester, Jay W. (1987), 'Nonlinearity in high-order models of social systems', *European Journal of Operational Research*, 30(2), June, 104–9.

Foster, John (1987), *Evolutionary Macroeconomics*, London: George Allen & Unwin.

Fourie, Frederick C. v. N. (1989a), 'The nature of firms and markets: do transactions approaches help?', *South African Journal of Economics*, 57(2), 142–60.

Fourie, Frederick C. v. N. (1989b), 'Government in the economy: the issue that won't go away', paper presented at the Colloquium on the potential of a post-apartheid South African economy, Institut de Hautes Études en Administration Publique, Université de Lausanne.

Freeman, Christopher (1974), *The Economics of Industrial Innovation*, London: Frances Pinter.

Freeman, Christopher (1987), *Technology Policy and Economic Perform-* ✗
ance: Lessons from Japan, London: Frances Pinter.

Freeman, Christopher (1988), 'Japan: a new national system of innovation?', in Dosi *et al.* (1988, pp. 330–48).

Freeman, Christopher (ed.) (1990), *The Economics of Innovation*, Aldershot:
Edward Elgar.

Freeman, Christopher, and Lundvall, Bengt-Åke (eds) (1988), *Small Countries Facing the Technological Revolution*, London: Frances Pinter.

Freeman, Christopher, and Perez, Carlota (1988), 'Structural crises of adjustment: business cycles and investment behaviour', in Dosi *et al.* (1988,
pp. 38–66).

Freeman, Christopher, and Soete, Luc L. (1985), 'Information technology
and employment, Brighton, Sussex: SPRU, University of Sussex, mimeo.

Freeman, Christopher, and Soete, Luc L. (eds) (1987), *Technological Change
and Full Employment*, Oxford: Basil Blackwell.

Friedman, Milton (1953), 'The methodology of positive economics', in M.
Friedman, *Essays in Positive Economics*, Chicago, Ill.: University of
Chicago Press, 3–43; reprinted in Bruce J. Caldwell (ed.) (1984), *Appraisal
and Criticism in Economics: A Book of Readings*, London: Allen & Unwin.

Gaffard, J. L. (1990), *Economie industrielle et de l'innovation*, Paris: Dalloz.

Gaibisso, Ann M., Gros-Pietro, Gian M., Leone, Giovanni, Rolfo, Secondo,
and Trentin, Ilva (1987), 'Gli FMS nel mondo alla fine del 1986', *Bollettino
CERIS*, **21**, 145–72.

Galbraith, John Kenneth (1967), *The New Industrial State*, Boston, Mass.:
Houghton Mifflin.

Galbraith, John Kenneth (1973), *Economics and the Public Purpose*, Boston, Mass.: Houghton Mifflin.

Galbraith, John Kenneth (1980[1952]), *A Theory of Price Control: The
Classic Account*, Cambridge, Mass.: Harvard University Press.

Galbraith, John Kenneth (1981), *A Life in Our Times*, Boston, Mass.:
Houghton Mifflin.

Georgescu-Roegen, Nicholas (1966), *Analytical Economics*, Cambridge,
Mass.: Harvard University Press.

Georgescu-Roegen, Nicholas (1971), *The Entropy Law and the Economic
Process*, Cambridge, Mass.: Harvard University Press.

Georgescu-Roegen, Nicholas (1976), *Energy and Economic Myths*, New York:
Pergamon Press.

Georghiou, Luke, Metcalfe, J. Stanley, Evans, Janet, Ray, Timothy, and
Gibbons, Michael (1986), *Post-Innovation Performance*, London:
Macmillan.

Gerybadze, A. (1991), 'The implementation of industrial policy in an evolutionary perspective', in Witt (1991b).

Giddens, Anthony (1976), *New Rules of Sociological Method*, London: Hutchinson.

Giddens, Anthony (1984), *The Constitution of Society: Outline of the Theory of Structuration*, Cambridge: Polity Press.

Gleick, James (1988), *Chaos: Making a New Science*, London: Heinemann.

Gomulka, Stanislaw (1971), *Inventive Activity, Diffusion, and the Stages of Economic Growth*, Aarhus: Aarhus Institute of Economics.

Gomulka, Stanislaw (1979), 'Britain's slow industrial growth – increasing inefficiency versus low rate of technological change', in Wilfred Beckerman (ed.) (1979), *Slow Growth in Britain: Causes and Consequences*, Oxford: Oxford University Press.

Goodman, Edward, Bamford, Julia, and Saynor, Peter (eds) (1989), *Small Firms and Industrial Districts in Italy*, London: Routledge.

Goodwin, Richard M. (1986), 'The M–K–S system: the functioning and evolution of capitalism', in Hans-Jürgen Wagener and J. W. Drukker (eds) (1986), *The Economic Law of Motion of Modern Society*, Cambridge: Cambridge University Press, 14–21.

Gordon, Wendell, and Adams, John (1989), *Economics as a Social Science: An Evolutionary Approach*, Riverdale, Md: Riverdale.

Gould, Stephen Jay (1980), *The Panda's Thumb: More Reflections in Natural History*, New York: W. W. Norton.

Gould, Stephen Jay (1982), 'The meaning of punctuated equilibrium and its role in validating a hierarchical approach to macroevolution', in R. Milkman (ed.) (1982), *Perspectives on Evolution*, Sunderland, Mass.: Sinauer Associates, 83–104.

Gould, Stephen Jay (1987), 'The panda's thumb of technology', *Natural History*, 1, January, 14–23.

Gowdy, J. M. (1985), 'Evolutionary theory and economic theory: some methodological issues', *Review of Social Economy*, 43, 316–324.

Grandmont, Jean-Michel (ed.) (1987), *Nonlinear Economic Dynamics*, New York: Academic Press.

Granovetter, Mark, and Soong, Roland (1986), 'Threshold models of interpersonal effects in consumer demand', *Journal of Economic Behavior and Organization*, 7, 83–99.

Grant, Robert M. (1988), 'Diversification and firm performance in a changing economic environment', in Ergas *et al.* (1988, pp. 49–91).

Groenewegen, Peter D. (1985), 'Professor Arndt on political economy: a comment', *Economic Record*, 60(4), December, 744–51.

Grunert, K. G., and Ölander, F. (eds) (1989), *Understanding Economic Behavior*, Dordrecht: Kluwer.

Guckenheimer, John, and Holmes, Philip (1983), *Nonlinear Oscillations, Dynamical Systems, and Bifurcations of Vector Fields*, Berlin: Springer.

Hagen, E. E. (1964), *On the Theory of Social Change: How Economic Growth Begins*, London: Tavistock.

Haken, H. (1987), *Advanced Synergetics*, Berlin: Springer.

Hallagan, B., and Joerding, W. (1983), 'Polymorphic equilibrium in advertising', *Bell Journal of Economics*, **14**, Spring.

Hamilton, Walton H. (ed.) (1938), *Price and Price Policies*, New York: McGraw-Hill.

Hamilton, Walton H. (1957), *The Politics of Industry*, New York: Alfred A. Knopf.

Hamilton, Walton H. (1974), 'The price system and social policy', in W. H. Hamilton, *Industrial Policy and Institutionalism*, New York: Augustus M. Kelley.

Hamilton, Walton H. and May, Stacy (1968[1923]), *The Control of Wages*, New York: Augustus M. Kelley.

Hannan, Michael T., and Freeman, John (1989), *Organizational Ecology*, Cambridge, Mass.: Harvard University Press.

Hansson, Ingemar, and Stuart, Charles (1990), 'Malthusian selection of preferences', *American Economic Review*, **80**(2), June, 529–44.

Hanusch, Horst (ed.) (1988), *Evolutionary Economics: Applications of Schumpeter's Ideas*, Cambridge: Cambridge University Press.

Harcourt, Geoffrey C. (1972), *Some Cambridge Controversies in the Theory of Capital*, Cambridge: Cambridge University Press.

Harcourt, Geoffrey C. (1982), 'Post Keynesianism: quite wrong and/or nothing new?', *Thames Papers in Political Economy*, Summer; reprinted in Philip Arestis and Anthanos Skouras (eds) (1985), *Post Keynesian Economic Theory*, Brighton, Sussex: Wheatsheaf.

Harcourt, Geoffrey C., and Laing, N. F. (eds) (1971), *Capital and Growth*, Harmondsworth, Middx: Penguin.

Hay, Edward J. (1988), *The Just in Time*, New York: John Wiley.

Hayek, Friedrich A. (1945), 'The uses of knowledge in society', *American Economic Review*, **35**(4), 519–30; reprinted in Hayek (1949).

Hayek, Friedrich A. (1949), *Individualism and Economic Order*, London: Routledge & Kegan Paul.

Hayek, Friedrich A. (1964), 'The theory of complex phenomena', in M. A. Bunge (ed.) (1964), *The Critical Approach to Science and Philosophy*, New York: Free Press.

Hayek, Friedrich A. (1967), *Studies in Philosophy, Politics and Economics*, London: Routledge & Kegan Paul.

Hayek, Friedrich A. (1978), *New Studies in Philosophy, Politics, Economics, and the History of Ideas*, London: Routledge & Kegan Paul, and Chicago, Ill.: Chicago University Press.

Hayek, Friedrich A. (1979), 'The three sources of human values', 'Epilogue' to *Law, Legislation, and Liberty*, London: Routledge & Kegan Paul.

Hayek, Friedrich A. (1988), *The Fatal Conceit: The Errors of Socialism; Collected Works of F. A. Hayek*, vol. 1, London: Routledge.

Heiner, Ronald A. (1983), 'The origin of predictable behavior', *American Economic Review*, 73(4), December, 560–95.

Helmstädter, E. (1990), 'Ein makroökonomisches Rahmenmodell der Evolutorischen Ökonomik', in Witt (1990, pp. 163–82).

Hesse, G. (1991), 'A new theory of "modern economic growth"', in Witt (1991b).

Hirshleifer, Jack (1982), 'Evolutionary models in economics and law: cooperation versus conflict strategies', *Research in Law and Economics*, 4, 1–60.

Hobsbawm, Eric J. (1969), *Industry and Empire*, Harmondsworth, Middx: Penguin.

Hodgson, Geoffrey M. (1982), 'Theoretical and policy implications of variable productivity', *Cambridge Journal of Economics*, 6(3), September, 213–26; reprinted in Hodgson (1991b).

Hodgson, Geoffrey M. (1984), *The Democratic Economy: A New Look at Planning, Markets and Power*, Harmondsworth, Middx: Penguin.

Hodgson, Geoffrey M. (1988), *Economics and Institutions: A Manifesto for a Modern Institutional Economics*, Cambridge: Polity Press, and Philadelphia, Pa: University of Pennsylvania Press.

Hodgson, Geoffrey M. (1989), 'Institutional rigidities and economic growth', *Cambridge Journal of Economics*, 13(1), March, 79–101; reprinted in Antony Lawson, J. Gabriel Palma and John Sender (eds) (1989), *Kaldor's Political Economy*, London: Academic Press; and in Hodgson (1991b).

Hodgson, Geoffrey M. (1991a), 'Evolution and intention in economic theory', in J. S. Metcalfe and P. P. Saviotti (eds), *Evolutionary Theories of Economic and Technological Change*, Reading: Harwood Academic Publishers (forthcoming).

Hodgson, Geoffrey M. (1991b), *After Marx and Sraffa*, London: Macmillan.

Hollis, Martin, and Nell, Edward (1975), *Rational Economic Man: A Philosophical Critique of Neo-Classical Economics*, Cambridge: Cambridge University Press.

Hughes, Thomas (1985), 'Edison and electric light', in MacKenzie and Wajcman (1985, pp. 39–52).

Hunt, E. K., and Schwartz, Jesse G. (eds) (1972), *A Critique of Economic Theory*, Harmondsworth, Middx: Penguin.

Hyman, Richard (1988), 'Flexible specialization: miracle or myth?', in Richard Hyman and Wolfgang Streeck (eds) (1988), *New Technology and Industrial Relations*, Oxford: Basil Blackwell.

Ingrao, Bruno, and Israel, Giorgio (1985), 'General economic equilibrium: a history of ineffectual paradigmatic shifts', *Fundamenta Scientiae*, 6, 1–45, 89–125.

Iwai, Katsuhito (1984), 'Schumpeterian dynamics: an evolutionary model of innovation and imitation', *Journal of Economic Behavior and Organization*, 5, June, 159–90.

Jensen, Michael C., and Meckling, William H. (1976), 'Theory of the firm: managerial behavior, agency costs and financial structure', *Journal of Financial Economics*, 3, 305–60; reprinted in Putterman (1986).

Jevons, William Stanley (1879), *The Theory of Political Economy*, 2nd edn, London: Macmillan.

Johansson, Börje, Batten, David, and Casti, John L. (1987), 'Economic dynamics, evolution and structural adjustment', in Batten *et al.* (1987, pp. 1–23).

Johnson, Björn (forthcoming), 'Institutional learning', in Lundvall (forthcoming).

Jones, Robert A., and Ostroy, Joseph M. (1984), 'Flexibility and uncertainty', *Review of Economic Studies*, 51, 13–32.

Joskow, Paul L. (1975), 'Firm decision-making processes and oligopoly theory', *American Economic Review (Papers and Proceedings)*, 65(2), May, 270–9.

Kahn, Alfred E. (1975), 'Market power inflation; a conceptual overview', in Means *et al.* (1975b).

Kaldor, Nicholas (1934), 'A classificatory note on the determinateness of equilibrium', *Review of Economic Studies*, 1(1), February, 122–36; reprinted in Targetti and Thirlwall (1989).

Kaldor, Nicholas (1972), 'The irrelevance of equilibrium economics', *Economic Journal*, 82(4), December, 1237–55; reprinted in Targetti and Thirlwall (1989), and in N. Kaldor (1978), *Further Essays on Economic Theory:* (Collected Economic Essays, vol. 5), London: Duckworth.

Kaldor, Nicholas (1985), *Economics without Equilibrium*, Cardiff: University College Cardiff Press, and Armonk, N.Y.: M. E. Sharpe.

Kamien, M. I., and Schwartz, N. L. (1982), *Market Structure and Innovation*, Cambridge: Cambridge University Press.

Kaplan, A. D. H., Dirlam, Joel B., and Lanzillotti, Robert F. (1958), *Pricing in Big Business*, Washington, DC: Brookings Institution.

Kapp, K. William (1976), 'The nature and significance of institutional economics', *Kyklos*, 29, Fasc. 2, 209–32; reprinted in Warren J. Samuels (ed.) (1988), *Institutional Economics*, vol. 2, Aldershot: Edward Elgar.

Katzenstein, Peter J. (1985), *Small States in World Markets: Industrial Policy in Europe*, Ithaca, N.Y.: Cornell University Press.

Kefauver, Estes (1965), *In a Few Hands: Monopoly Power in America*, New York: Pantheon.

Keynes, John Maynard (1921), *The Treatise on Probability*, London: Macmillan; reprinted in (1973) *The Collected Writings*, ed. D. Moggridge, vol. 8, London: Macmillan.

Keynes, John Maynard (1936), *The General Theory of Employment, Interest and Money*, London: Macmillan; reprinted in (1971) *The Collected Writings*, ed. D. Moggridge, vol. 7, London: Macmillan.

Keynes, John Maynard (1937), 'The general theory of employment', *Quarterly Journal of Economics*, **51**, 209–23; reprinted in (1973) *The Collected Writings*, ed. D. Moggridge, vol. 14, London: Macmillan.

Kindleberger, Charles P. (1973), *The World in Depression, 1929–1939*, London: Allen Lane.

Kindleberger, Charles P. (1988), 'The 1930s and the 1980s: parallels and differences', *Banca Nazionale del Lavoro Quarterly Review*, no. 165, June, 135–45.

Kirman, Alan (1989), 'The intrinsic limits of modern economic theory: the emperor has no clothes', *Economic Journal (Conference Papers)*, **99**, 126–139.

Kirzner, Israel M. (1973), *Competition and Entrepreneurship*, Chicago, Ill.: Chicago University Press.

Kirzner, Israel M. (1979), *Perception, Opportunity, and Profit*, Chicago, Ill.: Chicago University Press.

Knight, Frank H. (1921), *Risk, Uncertainty and Profit*, Boston, Mass.: Houghton, Mifflin.

Koopmans, Tjalling C. (1964), 'On flexibility of future preference', in M. W. Shelley and G. L. Bryan (eds) (1964), *Human Judgements and Optimality*, New York: John Wiley, 469–80.

Kregel, Jan E. (1980), 'Markets and institutions as features of a capitalist production system', *Journal of Post Keynesian Economics*, **3**(2), Fall, 32–48.

Kuran, T. (1987), 'Preference falsification, policy continuity, and collective conservatism', *Economic Journal*, **97**(3), September, 642–65.

Lachmann, Ludwig M. (1976), 'From Mises to Shackle: an essay on Austrian economics and the kaleidic society', *Journal of Economic Literature*, **14**(1), 54–62.

Lachmann, Ludwig M. (1977), *Capital, Expectations, and the Market Process*, Kansas City: Sheed, Andrews & McMeel.

Lachmann, Ludwig M. (1978), *Capital and its Structure*, 2nd edn, Kansas City: Sheed, Andrews & McMeel.

Lachmann, Ludwig M. (1986), *The Market as an Economic Process*, Oxford: Basil Blackwell.

Landes, David S. (1987), 'Small is beautiful. Small is beautiful?', in D. Landes, *Piccola e grande impresa: un problema storico*, Milan: F. Angeli.

Landesmann, Michael A. (1986), 'Conceptions of technology and the production process', in Mauro Baranzini and Roberto Scazzieri (eds) (1986), *Foundations of Economics*, Oxford: Basil Blackwell.

Langlois, Richard N. (1986a), 'The new institutional economics', in Langlois (1986b, pp. 1–25)

Langlois, Richard N. (ed.) (1986b), *Economics as a Process: Essays in the New Institutional Economics*, Cambridge: Cambridge University Press.

Laszlo, Ervin (1987), *Evolution: The Grand Synthesis*, Boston, Mass.: New Science Library – Shambhala.

Lawson, Antony (1985), 'Uncertainty and economic analysis', *Economic Journal*, **95**(4), December, 909–27.

Lehmann-Waffenschmidt, M. (1990), *Economic Evolution: A General Equilibrium Analysis*, Heidelberg: Springer.

Leibenstein, Harvey (1979), 'A branch of economics is missing: micro-micro theory', *Journal of Economic Literature*, **27**, 477–502.

Leibenstein, Harvey (1980), 'Microeconomics and x-efficiency theory', *Public Interest*, special issue, 97–110; reprinted in Bell and Kristol (1981).

Leijonhufvud, Axel (1986), 'Capitalism and the factory system', in Langlois (1986b, pp. 203–23).

Leontief, Wassily, and Duchin, Faye (1986), *The Future Impact of Automation on Workers*, New York: Oxford University Press.

Lesourne, J. (1989), 'L'état des recherches sur l'ordre et le desordre en micro-economie', *Economie appliquée*, **42**, 11–39.

Lesourne, J. (1991), 'Self-organization as a process in evolution of economic systems', in Richard H. Day and P. Chen (eds) (1991), *Evolutionary Dynamics and Non-linear Economics: A Transdisciplinary Dialogue*, forthcoming.

Lippi, Marco (1979), *Value and Naturalism in Marx*, London: NLB.

Littlechild, Stephen C., and Owen, G. (1980), 'An Austrian model of the entrepreneurial market process', *Journal of Economic Theory*, **23**, 361–79.

Lloyd, Barbara B. (1972), *Perception and Cognition: A Cross-Cultural Perspective*, Harmondsworth, Middx: Penguin.

Loasby, Brian J. (1976), *Choice, Complexity, and Ignorance: An Enquiry into Economic Theory and Practice of Decision Making*, Cambridge: Cambridge University Press.

Lorenzoni, Gianni, and Ornati, Oscar A. (1988), 'Constellations of firms and new ventures', *Journal of Business Venturing*.

Lovelock, James E. (1979), *Gaia: A New Look at Life on Earth*, Oxford: Oxford University Press.

Lubben, Robert (1988), *Just-in-time Manufacturing*, New York: McGraw-Hill.

Lucas, Robert E. Jr (1988), 'On the mechanics of economic development', *Journal of Monetary Economics*, **22**, 3–42.

Lundvall, Bengt-Åke (1988), 'Innovation as an interactive process: from user–producer interaction to the national system of innovation', in Dosi *et al.* (1988, pp. 349–69).

Lundvall, Bengt-Åke (ed.) (forthcoming), *National Systems of Innovation*.

McCallum, J. and Blais, A. (1987), 'Government, special interest groups and economic growth', *Public Choice*, **54**(1), 3–18.

McKelvey, Maureen (1989), 'The European Economic Community: research policy, political ideology and the decision-making process', MA thesis, Research Policy Institute, University of Lund, Sweden.

McKelvey, W. (1982), *Organizational Systematics: Taxonomy, Evolution, Classification* (Berkeley, Cal.: University of California Press).

MacKenzie, Donald (1990), 'Economic and sociological explanation of technical change', paper presented at the conference on 'Firm Strategy and Technical Change: Microeconomics or Microsociology?', UMIST and University of Manchester, Manchester, 27–28 September.

MacKenzie, Donald, and Wajcman, Judy (1985), *The Social Shaping of Technology*, Milton Keynes, Bucks: Open University Press.

Maddison, Angus (1982), *Phases of Capitalist Development*, Oxford: Oxford University Press.

Maddison, Angus (1987), 'Growth and slowdown in advanced capitalist economies: techniques of quantitative assessment', *Journal of Economic Literature*, **25**(2), June, 649–98.

Mahajan, V., and Wind, Y. (1986), 'Innovation diffusion models of new product acceptance: a reexamination', in V. Mahajan and Y. Wind (eds), *Innovation Diffusion Models of New Product Acceptance*, Cambridge, Mass.: Ballinger, 3–25.

March, James G., and Simon, Herbert A. (1958), *Organizations*, New York: John Wiley.

Marglin, Stephen, and Schor, J. (eds) (1990), *The Golden Age of Capitalism: Reinterpreting the Postwar Experience*, Oxford: Clarendon Press.

Mariti, Paolo (1991), 'Constructive co-operation between smaller firms for efficiency, quality and product changes', in D. O'Doherty (ed.), *The Co-operation Phenomenon between Smaller Firms*, Boston, Mass.: Kluwer.

Mariti, Paolo, and Smiley, R. (1983), 'Cooperative agreements and the organization of industry', *Journal of Industrial Economics*, **4**, 437–51.

Marschak, Thomas, and Nelson, Richard R. (1962), 'Flexibility, uncertainty and economic theory', *Metroeconomica*, **13**, 42–58.

Marshall, Alfred (1920), *The Principles of Economics*, 8th edn, London: Macmillan.

See 39-52 in →

Marshall, Alfred, and Marshall, Mary P. (1879), *The Economics of Industry*, London: Macmillan.

Marx, Karl (1976), *Capital*, vol. 1, Harmondsworth, Middx: Penguin.

Massard, N. (1988), 'L'industrialisation des fibres optiques', *Revue d'economie industrielle*, **44**, 53–72.

Maturana, Humberto R. (1975), 'The organisation of the living: a theory of the living organisation', *International Journal of Man-Machine Studies*, **7**, 313–32.

Means, Gardiner C. (1959), *Administered Inflation and Public Policy*, Washington, DC: Anderson Kramer Associates.

Means, Gardiner C. (1963), 'Pricing power and the public interest', in Adams and Lanzillotti (1963, pp. 213–39).

Means, Gardiner C. (1975a), 'Simultaneous inflation and unemployment', in Means *et al.* (1975b).

Means, Gardiner C. *et al.* (1975b), *The Roots of Inflation*, New York: Burt Franklin.

Menger, Carl (1981[1871]), *Principles of Economics*, New York: New York University Press.

Merkhofer, M. W. (1975), 'Flexibility and decision analysis', PhD dissertation, Department of Engineering – Economic Systems, Stanford University.

Metcalfe, J. Stanley, and Gibbons, Michael (1986), 'Technological variety and the process of competition', *Economie appliquée*, **39**(3), 493–520.

Metcalfe, J. Stanley, and Gibbons, Michael (1989), 'Technology, variety and organisation: a systematic perspective on the diffusion process', in R. S. Rosenbloom and R. Burgelman (eds) (1989), *Research on Technological Innovation, Management and Policy*, vol. 4, Greenwich, Conn.: JAI Press, 153–93.

Metcalfe, J. Stanley, and Saviotti, Pier Paolo (1984), 'A theoretical approach to the construction of technological output indicators', *Research Policy*, **13**, 141–51.

Mills, David E. (1986), 'Flexibility and firm diversity with demand fluctuations', *International Journal of Industrial Organization*, **4**, 203–15.

Minsky, Hyman P. (1982), *Can 'It' Happen Again? Essays on Stability and Finance*, New York: M. E. Sharpe.

Minsky, Hyman P. (1985), 'Review of "The Second Industrial Divide"', *Challenge*, **28**(3), July-August, 60–4.

Mirowski, Philip (ed.) (1986), *The Reconstruction of Economic Theory*, Boston, Mass.: Kluwer-Nijhoff.

Mirowski, Philip (1988), *Against Mechanism: Protecting Economics from Science*, Totowa, N.J.: Rowman & Littlefield.

Mirowski, Philip (1989), *More Heat than Light: Economics as Social Physics, Physics as Nature's Economics*, Cambridge: Cambridge University

Press.

Mirowski, Philip (1990a), 'Learning the meaning of the dollar: conservation principles and the social theory of value in economic theory', *Social Research*, **57**(3), Fall, 689–717.

Mirowski, Philip (1990b), 'From Mandelbrot to chaos in economic theory', *Southern Economic Journal*, **57**(2), October, 289–307.

Mirowski, Philip (1991), 'Postmodernism and the social theory of value', *Journal of Post Keynesian Economics*, forthcoming.

Mises, Ludwig von (1949), *Human Action: A Treatise on Economics* (London: William Hodge).

Mokyr, Joel (1990), *The Lever of Riches: Technological Creativity and Economic Progress*, Oxford: Clarendon Press.

Mokyr, Joel (forthcoming), 'Evolutionary biology, technical change, and economic history', *Bulletin of Economic Research*.

Monden, Yasuhiro (1983), *Toyota Production System*, Atlanta, Ga: Institute of Industrial Engineering.

Morroni, Mario (forthcoming), *Production Process and Technical Change*, Cambridge: Cambridge University Press.

Moss, Scott J. (1981), *An Economic Theory of Business Strategy: An Essay in Dynamics without Equilibrium*, Oxford: Martin Robertson.

Moss, Scott J. (1984), *Markets and Macroeconomics: Macroeconomic Implications of Rational Economic Behaviour*, Oxford: Basil Blackwell.

Munkirs, John R. (1985), *The Transformation of American Capitalism*, Armonk, N.Y.: M. E. Sharpe.

Munkirs, John R., and Sturgeon, James I. (1985), 'Oligopolistic cooperation: conceptual and empirical evidence of market structure evolution', *Journal of Economic Issues*, **19**(4), December, 899–921.

Murray, James D. (1989), *Mathematical Biology*, Berlin: Springer.

Myrdal, Gunnar (1939), *Monetary Equilibrium*, London: Hodge.

Myrdal, Gunnar (1944), *An American Dilemma: The Negro Problem and Modern Democracy*, New York: Harper & Row.

Myrdal, Gunnar (1957), *Economic Theory and Underdeveloped Regions*, London: Duckworth.

Nardinelli, C., Wallace, M. S., and Warner, J. T. (1987), 'Explaining differences in state growth: catching up versus Olson', *Public Choice*, **52**(3), 201–13.

Nell, Edward J. (ed.) (1980), *Growth, Profits, and Property: Essays in the Revival of Political Economy*, Cambridge: Cambridge University Press.

Nelson, Richard R. (1981), 'Research on productivity growth and productivity differences: dead ends and new departures', *Journal of Economic Literature*, **29**, September, 1029–64.

Nelson, Richard R. (1987), *Understanding Technical Change as an Evolutionary Process*, Amsterdam: North-Holland.

Nelson, Richard R. (1988), 'Institutions supporting technical change in the United States', in Dosi *et al.* (1988, pp. 312–29).

Nelson, Richard R. (1990), 'Capitalism as an engine of progress', *Research Policy*, **19**.

Nelson, Richard R. (ed.) (forthcoming), *National Innovation Systems: A Comparative Study*.

Nelson, Richard R., and Rosenberg, Nathan (forthcoming), 'Technical advance and national systems', introductory chapter in Nelson (forthcoming).

Nelson, Richard R., and Winter, Sidney G. (1980), 'Firm and industry response to changed market conditions: an evolutionary approach', *Economic Inquiry*, **18**, 179–202.

Nelson, Richard R., and Winter, Sidney G. (1982), *An Evolutionary Theory of Economic Change*, Cambridge, Mass.: Harvard University Press.

Nichols, Theo (1986), *The British Worker Question: A New Look at Workers and Productivity in Manufacturing*, London: Routledge & Kegan Paul.

Nicolis, Gregoire, and Prigogine, Ilya (1977), *Self-Organization in Non-Equilibrium Systems: From Dissipative Structures to Order Through Fluctuations*, New York: John Wiley.

North, Douglass C. (1981), *Structure and Change in Economic History*, New York: W. W. Norton.

Northcott, James, and Walling, Annette (1988), T*he Impact of Microelectronics: Diffusion, Benefits and Problems in British Industry*, London: Policy Studies Institute.

Oakey, Raymond P. (1984), *High Technology Small Firms*, London: Frances Pinter.

Oakey, R., Rothwell, R., and Cooper, S. (1988), *The Management of Innovation in High-Technology Small Firms*, London: Frances Pinter.

O'Donnell, Rodney M. (1989), *Keynes: Philosophy, Economics and Politics*, London: Macmillan.

O'Driscoll, Gerald P. Jr, and Rizzo, Mario J. (1985), *The Economics of Time and Ignorance*, Oxford: Basil Blackwell.

OECD (Organization for Economic Co-operation and Development) (1988), *Employment Outlook*, Paris: OECD, ch. 6.

Ohmae, Kenichi (1985), *Triad Power: The Coming Shape of Global Competition*, New York: Free Press.

Okun, Arthur M. (1979), 'An efficient strategy to combat inflation', *Brookings Bulletin*, **15**(1), Spring, 1–5.

Okun, Arthur M. (1981), *Prices and Quantities*, Washington, DC: Brookings Institution.

Olson, Mancur, Jr (1982), *The Rise and Decline of Nations*, New Haven, Conn.: Yale University Press.

Panzar, John, and Willig, Robert D. (1981), 'Economies of scope', *American Economic Review (Papers and Proceedings)*, 71(2), 268–72.

Pavitt, Keith (1984), 'Patterns of technical change: towards a taxonomy and a theory', *Research Policy*, 13, 343–73.

Penrose, Edith T. (1959), *The Theory of the Growth of the Firm*, Oxford: Basil Blackwell.

Perez, Carlota (1985), 'Microelectronics, long waves and world structural change: new perspectives of developing countries', *World Development*, 13(3), 441–63.

Peterson, Wallace C. (1982), *Our Overloaded Economy*, Armonk, N.Y.: M. E. Sharpe.

Peterson, Wallace C. (1988), *Income, Employment and Economic Growth*, New York: W. W. Norton.

Phelps Brown, Sir Henry (1977), 'What is the British predicament?', *Three Banks Review*, no. 116, December, 3–29; extracted in David Coates and John Hillard (eds) (1986), *The Economic Decline of Modern Britain: The Debate Between Left and Right*, Brighton, Sussex: Harvester.

Phillimore, A. John (1989), 'Flexible specialisation, work organisation and skill: approaching the "second industrial divide"', *New Technology, Work and Employment*, 79–91.

Piacentini, Paolo (1987), 'Costi ed efficienza in un modello di produzione a flusso lineare', *Economia Politica*, 381–403.

Piacentini, Paolo (1989), 'Coordinazione temporale ed efficienza produttiva', in Zamagni (1989, pp. 163–79).

Piore, Michael J., and Sabel, Charles F. (1984), *The Second Industrial Divide*, New York: Basic Books.

Polanyi, Karl (1944), *The Great Transformation* (New York: Holt, Rinehart & Winston).

Polanyi, Michael (1957), *Personal Knowledge: Towards a Post-Critical Philosophy*, London: Routledge & Kegan Paul.

Polanyi, Michael (1967), *The Tacit Dimension*, London: Routledge & Kegan Paul.

Popper, Sir Karl R., and Eccles, Sir John C. (1977), *The Self and its Brain*, Berlin: Springer.

Porter, Michael (1990a), 'The competitive advantage of nations', *Harvard Business Review*, March–April, 73–93.

Porter, Michael (1990b), *The Competitive Advantage of Nations*, London: Macmillan.

Prais, S. J. (1981), *Productivity and Industrial Structure: A Statistical Study of Manufacturing Industry in Britain, Germany and the United States*, Cambridge: Cambridge University Press.

Pratten, C. F. (1976), *Labour Productivity Differences in International Companies*, Cambridge: Cambridge University Press.

Prigogine, Ilya (1976), 'Order through fluctuation: self-organization and social system', in Erich Jantsch and Conrad H. Waddington (eds) (1976), *Evolution and Consciousness: Human Systems in Transition*, Reading, Mass.: Addison-Wesley, 93–133).

Prigogine, Ilya, and Stengers, Isabelle (1984), *Order out of Chaos: Man's New Dialogue with Nature*, London: Heinemann.

Putterman, Louis (1986), *The Economic Nature of the Firm: A Reader* (Cambridge: Cambridge Univesity Press).

Radnitzky, G., and Bernholz, P. (1987), *Economic Imperialism*, New York: Paragon House.

Rahmeyer, Fritz (1989), 'The evolutionary approach to innovation activity', *Journal of Institutional and Theoretical Economics*, **145**(2), June, 275–97.

Reinganum, J. F. (1989), 'The timing of innovation: research, development, and diffusion', in R. Schmalensee and R. D. Willig (eds) (1989), *Handbook of Industrial Organization*, vol. I, Amsterdam: North-Holland, 849–908.

Riddell, Tom (1985), 'Concentration and inefficiency in the defense sector: policy options', *Journal of Economic Issues*, **19**(2), June, 451–62.

Robinson, Joan (1969[1933]), *The Economics of Imperfect Competition*, London: Macmillan.

Rogers, E. M. (1983), *Diffusion of Innovations*, 3rd edn, New York: Free Press.

Roland, Gérard (1990), 'Gorbachev and the Common European Home: the convergence debate revisited?', *Kyklos*, **43**, fasc. 3, 385–409.

Romer, P. M. (1989), 'Capital accumulation in the theory of long-run growth', in R. J. Barro (ed.) (1989), *Modern Business Cycle Theory*, Oxford: Clarendon Press, 51–127.

Röpke, J. (1977), *Die Strategie der Innovation*, Tübingen: Mohr.

Rosenberg, Nathan (1976), *Perspectives on Technology*, Cambridge: Cambridge University Press.

Rosenberg, Nathan (ed.) (1982), *Inside the Black Box: Technology and Economics*, Cambridge: Cambridge University Press.

Rosenberg, Nathan, and Birdzell, Luther E. Jr (1986), *How the West Grew Rich: The Economic Transformation of the Industrial World*, New York: Basic Books.

Rothwell, Roy, and Zegveld, Walter (1979), *Technical Change and Employment*, New York: St Martin's Press.

Rothwell, Roy, and Zegveld, Walter (1982), *Innovation and Small and Medium Sized Firms*, London: Frances Pinter.

Rullani, Enzo (1988), 'Flessibilità del lavoro e flessibilità di impresa: le nuove regole dello sviluppo industriale', in Mario Regini (ed.) (1988), *La sfida della flessibilità*, Milan: F. Angeli.

Russo, Margherita (1985), 'Technical change and the industrial district: the role of inter-firm relations in the growth and transformation of ceramic tile production in Italy', *Research Policy*, 329–43.

Samuels, Warren J., and Medema, Steven G. (1990), *Gardiner C. Means: Institutionalist and Post Keynesian*, Armonk, N.Y.: M. E. Sharpe.

Sawyer, Malcolm C. (1991), 'Market mechanisms and prices', *Social Concept*, June, forthcoming.

Scazzieri, Roberto (1983), 'The production process: general characteristics and taxonomy', *Rivista Internazionale di Scienze Economiche e Commerciali*, 7, 597–611.

Schelling, Thomas C. (1978), *Micromotives and Macrobehavior*, New York: W. W. Norton.

Schumpeter, Joseph A. (1934[1912]), *The Theory of Economic Development*, Cambridge, Mass.: Harvard University Press.

Schumpeter, Joseph A. (1942), *Capitalism, Socialism, and Democracy*, New York: Harper & Row.

Scitovsky, Tibor (1976), *The Joyless Economy*, Oxford: Oxford University Press.

Scott, Maurice Fitzgerald (1981), 'The contribution of investment to growth', *Scottish Journal of Political Economy*, 28(3), November, 211–26.

Scott, Maurice Fitzgerald (1989), *A New View of Economic Growth*, Oxford: Clarendon Press.

Screpanti, Ernesto, and Zamagni, Stefano (1992), *A History of Economic Thought*, London: Oxford University Press (in press).

Sen, Amartya K. (1976), 'Rational fools: a critique of the behavioural foundations of economic theory', *Philosophy and Public Affairs*, 6, 317–44.

Sen, Amartya K. (1981), *Poverty and Famines: An Essay on Entitlement and Deprivation*, Oxford: Oxford University Press.

Senghaas, Dieter (1985), *The European Experience: A Historical Critique of Development Theories*, Dover, N.H.: Berg.

Service, Elman R. (1960), 'The law of evolutionary potential', in Marshall D. Sahlins and Elman R. Service (eds) (1960), *Evolution and Culture*, Ann Arbor, Mich.: University of Michigan Press.

Shackle, George L. S. (1958), *Time in Economics*, Amsterdam: North-Holland.

Shackle, George L. S. (1972), *Epistemics and Economics: A Critique of Economic Doctrines*, Cambridge: Cambridge University Press.

Shackle, George L. S. (1983), 'The bounds of unknowledge', in Wiseman (1983, pp. 28–37).

Siegel, S. (1957), 'Level of aspiration and decision making', *Psychological Review*, **64**, 253–62.

Silverberg, Gerald (1988), 'Modelling economic dynamics and technical change: mathematical approaches to self-organization and evolution', in Dosi *et al.* (1988, pp. 531–59.

Simon, Herbert A. (1959), 'Theories of decision-making in economics and behavioral science', *American Economic Review*, **49**, 253–83.

Smith, Adam (1979[1776]), *An Inquiry into the Nature and Causes of the Wealth of Nations*, Oxford: Clarendon Press.

Solow, Robert M. (1957), 'Technical change and the aggregate production function', *Review of Economics and Statistics*, **39**, 312–20.

Solow, Robert M. (1985), 'Economic history and economics', *American Economic Review (Papers and Proceedings)*, **75**(2), May, 328–31.

Spulber, Daniel F. (1989), *Regulation and Markets*, Cambridge, Mass.: MIT Press.

Sraffa, Piero (1960), *Production of Commodities by Means of Commodities: Prelude to a Critique of Economic Theory*, Cambridge: Cambridge University Press.

Stanley, Steven M. (1975), 'A theory of evolution above the species level', *Proceedings of the National Academy of Sciences, USA*, **72**, 646–50.

Stanley, Steven M. (1980), *Macroevolution: Pattern and Process*, San Francisco, Cal.: W. H. Freeman.

Stewart, Ian (1989), *Does God Play Dice?: The Mathematics of Chaos*, Oxford: Basil Blackwell.

Stigler, George J. (1939), 'Production and distribution in the short run', *Journal of Political Economy*, **47**, 305–27.

Stigler, George J. (1963), 'Administered prices and oligopolistic inflation', in Adams and Lanzillotti (1963, pp. 262–76).

Stigler, George J., and Becker, Gary S. (1977), 'De gustibus non est disputandum', *American Economic Review*, **67**, 76–90.

Stiglitz, Joseph E. (1987), 'The causes and consequences of the dependence of quality on price', *Journal of Economic Literature*, **25**(1), March, 1–48.

Stinchcombe, Arthur L. (1965), 'Social structure and organizations', in J. G. March (ed.) (1965), *Handbook of Organizations*, Chicago, Ill.: Rand McNally, 142–93.

Stoneman, Paul (1987), *The Economic Analysis of Technology Policy*, Oxford: Oxford University Press.

Storey, David J. (ed.) (1983), *The Small Firm: An International Survey*, London: Croom Helm.

Storper, Michael (1989), 'The transition to flexible specialisation in US film industry: external economies, the division of labour, and the crossing of industrial divides', *Cambridge Journal of Economics*, **13**, 273–305.

Streissler, Erich (1972), 'To what extent was the Austrian School marginalist?', *History of Political Economy*, **4**, 426–41.

Streit, M. E., and Wegner, G. (1991), 'Information, transaction and catallaxy: reflections on some key-concepts of evolutionary market theory', in Witt (1991b).

Sugden, Robert (1990), 'Convention, creativity and conflict', in Yanis Varoufakis and David Young (eds) (1990), *Conflict in Economics*, Hemel Hempstead, Herts.: Harvester Wheatsheaf, 68–90.

Tani, Piero (1986), *Analisi microeconomica della produzione*, Rome: La Nuova Italia Scientifica.

Tani, Piero (1987), 'La decomponibilità del processo produttivo', in G. Becattini (ed.) (1987), *Mercato e forze locali: il distretto industriale*, Bologna: Mulino; revised version of (1976) 'La rappresentazione analitica del processo di produzione: alcune premesse teoriche al problema del decentramento', *Note Economiche*, no. 4/5, 124–41.

Tani, Piero (1988), 'Flows, funds, and sectoral interdependence in the theory of production', *Political Economy: Studies in the Surplus Approach*, **4**, 1–21.

Tani, Piero (1989), 'La rappresentazione della tecnologia produttiva nell'analisi microeconomica: problemi e recenti tendenze', in Zamagni (1989, pp. 19–49).

Targetti, Ferdinando, and Thirlwall, Anthony P. (eds) (1989), *The Essential Kaldor*, New York: Holmes & Meier.

Teece, David J. (1980), 'Economies of scope and the scope of enterprise', *Journal of Economic Behavior and Organization*, **1**, 223–47.

Teece, David J. (1982), 'Towards an economic theory of the multiproduct firm', *Journal of Economic Behavior and Organization*, **3**, 39–63.

Tellis, G. J., and Crawford, M. (1981), 'An evolutionary approach to product growth theory', *Journal of Marketing*, **45**, 125–32.

Therborn, Göran (1977), 'The rule of capital and the rise of democracy', *New Left Review*, no. 103, May–June, 3–41.

Tinacci Mossello, Maria (1989), 'Innovative capacities of industrial districts. Hypothesis and verification; the case-study of Prato in Tuscany', Dipartimento di Scienze Economiche, Università degli Studi di Firenze.

Tool, Marc R. (1986), *Essays in Social Value Theory: A Neoinstitutionalist Contribution*, Armonk, N.Y.: M. E. Sharpe.

Trotsky, Leon (1934), *The History of the Russian Revolution*, trans. by M. Eastman, London: Gollancz.

Ursprung, H. W. (1988), 'Evolution and the economic approach to human behaviour', *Journal of Social and Biological Structure*, **11**, 257–79.

Vanberg, Viktor (1986), 'Spontaneous market order and social rules: a critical reexamination of F. A. Hayek's theory of cultural evolution', *Economics and Philosophy*, **2**, June, 75–100.

Vanberg, Viktor (1988), 'Rules and choice in economics and sociology', in *Jahrbuch für Neue Politische Ökonomie*, vol. 7, Tübingen: Mohr, 1–22.

Varela, Francisco (1989), *Autonomie et connaissance*, Paris: Seuil.

Varela, Francisco, Maturana, Humberto R., and Uribe, R. (1974), 'Autopoiesis: the organization of living systems, its characterization and a model', *Bio-Systems*, **5**.

Veblen, Thorstein B. (1899), *The Theory of the Leisure Class: An Economic Study of Institutions*, New York: Macmillan.

Veblen, Thorstein B. (1904), *The Theory of Business Enterprise*, New York: Charles Scribner's Sons.

Veblen, Thorstein B. (1915), *Imperial Germany and the Industrial Revolution*, New York: Macmillan.

Veblen, Thorstein B. (1919), *The Place of Science in Modern Civilisation and Other Essays*, New York: Huebsch; reprinted 1990 with a new introduction by Warren J. Samuels, New Brunswick, N.J.: Transaction Publishers.

Veblen, Thorstein B. (1964), *The Instinct of Workmanship*, New York: Augustus Kelley.

Vercelli, Alessandro (1988), 'Technological flexibility, financial fragility and the recent revival of Schumpeterian entrepreneurship', *Recherches economique de Louvain*, **54**, 103–32.

Vercelli, Alessandro (1989), 'Uncertainty, technological flexibility and long term fluctuations', in M. Di Matteo, R. M. Goodwin and A. Vercelli (eds) (1989), *Technological and Social Factors in Long Term Fluctuations*, Berlin: Springer.

Vickery, Graham, and Campbell, Duncan (1989), 'Advanced manufacturing technology and the organisation of work', in *STI Review*, vol. 6, Paris: OECD.

Wallis, John J., and Oates, Wallace E. (1988), 'Does economic sclerosis set in with age? An empirical study of the Olsonian hypothesis', *Kyklos*, **41**, fasc. 3, 397–417.

Waltman, P. (1974), *Deterministic Threshold Models in the Theory of Epidemics*, Berlin: Springer.

Ward, Benjamin (1972), *What's Wrong with Economics?*, London: Macmillan.

Wärneryd, Karl (1989), 'Legal restrictions and the evolution of media of exchange', *Journal of Institutional and Theoretical Economics*, **145**(4), December, 613–26.

Watson, A. J., and Lovelock, James E. (1983), 'Biological homoeostasis of the global environment: the parable of Daisyworld, *Tellus*, **35**(B), 284–9.

Weise, P. (1991), 'Evolution of a field of socioeconomic forces', in Witt (1991b).

Weiss, Paul A. (1969), 'The living system: determinism stratified', in Arthur Koestler and J. R. Smythies (eds) (1969), *Beyond Reductionism: New Perspectives in the Life Sciences*, London: Hutchinson, 3–42.

Williams, Karel, Cutler, Anthony, Williams, John, and Haslam, Colin (1987), 'The end of mass production?', *Economy and Society*, **16**(3), August, 405–39.

Williamson, Oliver E. (1975), *Markets and Hierarchies: Analysis and Anti-Trust Implications; A Study in the Economics of Internal Organization*, New York: Free Press.

Wilson, Bryan R. (ed.) (1970), *Rationality*, Oxford: Basil Blackwell.

Winner, Langdon (1977), *Autonomous Technology: Technics-out-of-control as a Theme in Political Thought*, Cambridge, Mass.: MIT Press.

Winter, Sidney G. Jr (1964), 'Economic "natural selection" and the theory of the firm', *Yale Economic Essays*, **4**(1), 225–72.

Winter, Sidney C. Jr (1971), 'Satisfying, selection, and the innovating remnant', *Quarterly Journal of Economics*, **85**(2), May, 237–61.

Wiseman, Jack (ed.) (1983), *Beyond Positive Economics?*, London: Macmillan.

Witt, Ulrich (1985), 'Coordination of individual economic activities as an evolving process of self-organization', *Economie appliquée*, **37**, 569–95.

Witt, Ulrich (1986a), 'Evolution and stability of cooperation without enforceable contracts', *Kyklos*, **39**, 245–66.

Witt, Ulrich (1986b), 'Firms' market behavior under imperfect information and economic natural selection', *Journal of Economic Behavior and Organization*, **7**, 265–90.

Witt, Ulrich (1987), 'How transaction rights are shaped to channel innovativeness', *Journal of Institutional and Theoretical Economics*, **143**, 180–95.

Witt, Ulrich (1989a), 'Subjectivism in economics: a suggested reorientation', in Grunert and Ölander (1989, pp. 409–31).

Witt, Ulrich (1989b), 'The evolution of economic institutions as a propagation process', *Public Choice*, **62**, 155–72.

Witt, Ulrich (ed.) (1990), *Studien zur Evolutorischen Ökonomik*, Berlin: Duncker & Humblot.

Witt, Ulrich (1991a), *Individualistic Foundations of Evolutionary Economics*, Cambridge: Cambridge University Press.

Witt, Ulrich (ed.) (1991b), *Explaining Process and Change - Contributions to Evolutionary Economics*, Ann Arbor, Mich.: Michigan University Press.

Wolfson, M. (1987), 'Science and history: economics and thermodynamics', paper presented at the 14th History of Economics Society Meeting, Boston.

Young, Allyn A. (1928), 'Increasing Returns and Economic Progress', *Economic Journal*, **38**(4), December, 527–42.

Zamagni, Stefano (1987), *Microeconomic Theory: An Introduction*, Oxford: Basil Blackwell; trans. A. Fletcher from (1984) *Economia Politica: Teorie dei prezzi, dei mercati e della distribuzione*, Rome: La Nuova Italia Scientifica.

Zamagni, Stefano (ed.) (1989), *Le teorie economiche della produzione*, Bologna: Il Mulino.

Zeleny, Milan (ed.) (1981), *Autopoiesis: A Theory of Living Systems*, New York: North-Holland.

Zeleny, Milan (1987), 'Autopoiesis', in M. G. Singh (ed.) (1987), *Systems and Control Encyclopedia: Theory, Technology, Applications*, Oxford: Pergamon Press, pp. 393–400.

Zeleny, Milan (ed.) (1980), *Autopoiesis, Dissipative Structures and Spontaneous Social Orders*, Boulder, Col.: Westview Press.

Index